Guidance and Counselling

BESE-132

For

Bachelor of Education (B.Ed.)

Useful For

Magadh University (Bodhgaya), IGNOU, Bharathidasan University, Rai Technology University, KSOU (Karnataka), NIILM University, Bihar University (Muzaffarpur), Nalanda University, Jamia Millia Islamia, Vardhman Mahaveer Open University (Kota), Uttarakhand Open University, Kurukshetra University, Himachal Pradesh University, Seva Sadan's College of Education (Maharashtra), Lalit Narayan Mithila University, Andhra University, Pt. Sunderlal Sharma (Open) University (Bilaspur), Annamalai University, Bangalore University, Bharathiar University, Centre for Distance and Open Learning, Kakatiya University (Andhra Pradesh), KOU (Rajasthan), MPBOU (MP), MDU (Haryana), Punjab University, Tamilnadu Open University, Sri Padmavati Mahila Visvavidyalayam (Andhra Pradesh), Sri Venkateswara University (Andhra Pradesh), UCSDE (Kerala), University of Jammu, YCMOU, Rajasthan University, UPRTOU, Kalyani University, Banaras Hindu University (BHU) and all other Indian Universities.

Closer to Nature   We use Recycled Paper

GULLYBABA PUBLISHING HOUSE PVT. LTD.
ISO 9001 & ISO 14001 CERTIFIED CO.

Published by:

GullyBaba Publishing House Pvt. Ltd.

Regd. Office:
2525/193, 1st Floor, Onkar Nagar-A,
Tri Nagar, Delhi-110035
(From Kanhaiya Nagar Metro Station Towards
Old Bus Stand)
Ph. 011-27387998, 27384836, 27385249
  +919350849407

Branch Office:
1A/2A, 20, Hari Sadan,
Ansari Road, Daryaganj,
New Delhi-110002
Ph. 011-45794768

E-mail: hello@gullybaba.com, **Website:** GullyBaba.com
New Edition

Price:

ISBN: 978-93-88149-49-5
Author: Gullybaba.com Panel

Home Delivery of GPH Books

You can get GPH books by VPP/COD/Speed Post/Courier.
You can order books by Email/SMS/WhatsApp/Call.
For more details, visit gullybaba.com/faq-books.html
Our packaging department usually dispatches the books within 2 days after receiving your order and it takes nearly 5-6 days in postal/courier services to reach your destination.

Preface

Every human being comes across challenges and stress that must be faced. Sometimes, we feel the need for assistance and support to manage the problems and find solutions. Traditionally, in India, such support was readily and easily available through the family, particularly the joint or extended family, and the strong social network. Besides these, moral and emotional support was also available from teachers, friends and spiritual/ religious mentors. In the present, particularly urban, context there is an increasing speed in the pace of life, fragmentation of family and socioreligious support systems, and competitiveness. All such factors have led to a greater need for assistance to help individuals cope with their problems. Consequently, the field of guidance and counselling has evolved into a professional area.

Many times, we see or hear of people facing different types of challenging situations. A friend may be upset with her poor grades in examinations, a youth may be disturbed because his parents often quarrel with each other, another person may be having difficulty with friends, someone else may have financial problems. Many students on the threshold of college may be confused about choices to be made for further studies and such other issues. They are perhaps in situations which they are unable to deal with by themselves. Here they would benefit from professional guidance and counselling. These are processes that help people when they feel that they are in a challenging situation and cannot find a way to cope with it.

The present GPH book *"Guidance and Counselling (BESE-132)"* attempts to provide students with a broad overview of guidance and counselling services in school. Various techniques and procedures are also described. The book is written specially in question & answer format to provide students the instant gratification of a correct answer. In this book, we have tried to solve all possible questions from the exams' point of view. Solutions of previous years question papers have also been included to help students to understand the unique examination structure.

We hope that this book would not only be a favourite study material for the students but also can be a nice resource for teaching.

An attempt has been carefully made to present this book more useful and meet the requirements and challenges of the course prescribed by Indian Universities.

We wish you a successful and rewarding career ahead. Feedback in this regard is solicited.

– GPH Panel of Experts

Acknowledgement

Our compliments go to the **GullyBaba Publishing House Pvt. Ltd.,** and its meticulous team who have been enthusiastically working towards the perfection of the book.

Their teamwork, initiative and research have been very encouraging. Had it not been for their unflagging support, this work wouldn't have been possible. The creative freedom provided by them along with their aim of presenting the best to the reader has been a major source of inspiration in this work. Hope that this book would be successful.

– GPH Panel of Experts

Publisher's Note

The present book BESE-132 is targeted for examination purpose as well as enrichment. With the advent of technology and the Internet, there has been no dearth of information available to all; however, finding the relevant and qualitative information, which is focussed, is an uphill task.

We at **GullyBaba Publishing House Pvt. Ltd.,** have taken this step to provide quality material which can accentuate in-depth knowledge about the subject. GPH books are a pioneer in the effort of providing unique and quality material to its readers. With our books, you are sure to attain success by making use of this powerful study material. Provided book is just a reference book based on the syllabus of particular University/Board. For a profound information, see the textbooks recommended by the University/Board.

Our site **gullybaba.com** is a vital resource for your examination. The publisher wishes to acknowledge the significant contribution of the Team Members and our experts in bringing out this publication and highly thankful to Almighty God, without His blessings, this endeavor wouldn't have been successful.

– Publisher

Topics Covered

Contents

Question Papers

Introduction to Guidance and Counselling

INTRODUCTION

The most important person in the educational programme is the student. Every student requires guidance at some stage in his life; some need guidance and counselling constantly, while others need it rarely, in times of crisis. Generally we think, guidance and counselling are needed by students who have some psychological problems or difficulties. The purpose of the guidance and counselling service in schools is to bring all students to the ambit of a helping relationship. Thus, guidance is an indispensable part of our education system. It provides valuable input to teachers and parents in understanding their children so that their all-round development could be facilitated. Guidance and counselling serve as a supporting function in the educational process by directing and controlling activities to help each individual develop to his/her fullest potential. It also helps an individual to understand oneself and also cope up with his/her problems.

Q1. Define the term 'guidance'. Also, describe its need.

Ans. Guidance is a broad terms that is applied to a school's programme of activities and services that are aimed at assisting students to make and carry out adequate plans and to achieve satisfactory adjustment in life. Guidance can be defined as a process, developmental in nature, by which an individual is assisted to understand, accept and utilise his/her abilities aptitudes and interests and attitudinal patterns in relation to his/her aspirations. Guidance as an educational construct involves those experiences, which assist each learner to understand him/herself, accept him/herself and live effectively in his/her society.

Following are some definitions of guidance:

- **Jones:** "Guidance is the help given by one person to another in making choices and adjustments and in solving problems."
- **Crow and Crow:** "Guidance is assistance made available by personally qualified and adequately trained men or women to an individual of any age to help manage his own life activities, develop his points of view, make his own decisions and carry his own burdens."
- **Skinner:** "Guidance is process of helping young persons learn to adjust to self, to others and to circumstances."
- **Secondary Education Commission:** "Guidance involves the difficult act of helping boys and girls to plan their own future wisely in the full light of the factors that can be mastered about themselves and about the world in they are to live and work."

Need for Guidance

Life problems are becoming more and more complex. Traditional mores and personal convictions concerning rightness and wrongness of attitude and behaviour are breaking down. Many diverse factors inherent within our home, school and social and occupational activities and relationships pull us in different directions. We often find ourselves in such a state of confusion and bewilderment that it is difficult to steer ahead without the help of a proper guide.

According to **Mathewson (1954)**, educational personnel work is a professional process, which provides assistance to individuals in four areas:

- appraisal and understanding of the self;
- adjustment of the self to personal-social realities;
- orientation to current and future conditions; and
- development of individual potentialities.

The need for guidance arises from the following reasons:

- The bringing up of the human beings can be divided into the stages of infant, childhood, pre-adolescent, adolescence and manhood. One needs different types of help to adjust with every stage. The maximum problems are faced at the time of adolescence, when there are problems due to physical development, mental development, emotional development and social development.

- Guidance is needed for development of abilities and skills facilitating learning and achievement, and habits and skills for lifelong learning.
- Guidance is required for the development of healthy and positive attitudes, habits, values, etc. towards work through broadening aware of the world of work, planning and preparing for one's career.
- Guidance is required for assistance for understanding and developing a positive self-image and development of social skills for learning an effective and satisfying personal-social life.
- Gone are the days when a child was supposed to take up the profession of his father for earning his livelihood. Nowadays professions or occupations have become so varied and so complex that everyone has at first to get general education and then to undergo a long training for the profession to be adopted. He has also to get a special education pertaining to that profession.
- As the life pattern is changing fast and becoming complex, there are increased demands of society on parents, which has reduced the personal contact between the parents and children. Such developments have resulted in problems of maladjusted children that are becoming very common.
- Our country has certain problem areas where guidance is needed. These areas are caste problems, new economic policies and problems of retired persons.
- With the values changing and religious and moral exploitations by people with vested interests on the rise, need for guidance for students has become necessary to enable them to select a right path so that they develop independent understanding of religion and morality, rather than being misled by others.
- Guidance is also needed for an overall personality development of individuals.
- Due to the influx of women in almost all spheres including active defence services, more and more women are taking up jobs. Because of the double responsibility of home and office, women are facing all kinds of trauma, anxiety and stress. They need guidance to adjust to this changing scenario, especially in a male dominated society.

Q2. What is the purpose of guidance for students at elementary level and secondary level?

Ans. Guidance is to help one to adjust to abilities, interests and needs of the society. In other words, it means helping a person to develop in the desired direction and to orient him/her according to the needs and demands of changing times and society.

The purpose of guidance at **elementary school level** is focussed on assisting pupils to integrate such primary groups forces as the home, the school, religion and the peer-relationships. These are the forces which form the base for the students' adolescence, then blend those forces into a harmonious whole.

Guidance plays a vital role in preventing educational, personal, social, mental emotional and other similar problems among **secondary school students**. At this level, it is centrally focussed upon differentiating aspects of these forces as they effect the pupils knowledge, acceptance, and direction of him/herself. Secondary school guidance services focus on the assistance given to the students to develop themselves according to their potentialities and opportunities in the areas of educational planning, career choice, interpersonal relationships and interpersonal acceptance.

Thus, the purpose of guidance is to improve the capability of the individual to understand and deal with self-situational relation for greater personal satisfaction and social usefulness which includes students, teachers, parents, etc. Guidance offers opportunities to increase teachers understanding of their students through in service education programmes carried on by the guiding person.

Q3. How does guidance help students and teacher? Briefly discuss.

Ans. Following are the contributions of guidance to students:

- to get along better with other people and understand the world in which they live.
- to explore their own interests, abilities, learn about various aspects of the world of work and learn to make most of their abilities.
- to help them understand themselves by knowing more about their abilities, aptitudes, interests and limitations.
- in recognising gifted and slow learners and students having special needs and helping them to develop proper attitude and make maximum use of their potential ability.
- to get the most out of school by gaining information regarding career, subjects, etc.

Aid to the Teacher

- Guidance offers opportunities to increase teachers' understanding of their students through in service education programmes carried on by the guidance person. The school counsellor assists in administering tests and in familiarising teachers with the interpretation of the tests. These test results give information which assists teachers to better understand their students' classroom behaviour and performance.
- Data on students' special interests, capabilities and past experiences are provided on the cumulative record by the guidance faculty. Knowledge about students' physical condition, medical history, family background, scholastic record, scores on standardised tests, personal characteristics, etc. help the teacher to provide better instruction to the student.
- Beneficial to the parents: The teacher can provide a picture of the child's abilities, interests and potentialities to the parents so that they know, understand and accept the child as s/he is.

- Help the entire school in many ways, e.g. by aiding students in their choice of courses by counselling on the basis of their interests and aptitudes. Give administration information on those aspects of the school programme, which relate to the educational career and personality development of the students.

Q4. Describe the various scope of guidance.

Ans. The scope of guidance is all-pervading. Its scope is very vast in the light of modernisation and industrialisation and is ever increasing. As the life is getting complex day by day, the problems for which expert help is needed are rapidly increasing. The scope of guidance is extending horizontally to much of the social context, to matters of prestige in occupations, to the broad field of social trends and economic development. Crow and Crow have rightly quoted, "As now interpreted, guidance touches every aspect of an individual's personality-physical, mental, emotional and social. It is concerned with all aspects of an individual's attitudes and behaviour patterns. It seeks to help the individual to integrate all of his activities in terms of his basic potentialities and environmental opportunities."

Kothari Commission has stressed the need of guidance services in the schools. Regarding scope of guidance, commission was of the view. "Guidance services have a much wider scope and function than merely that of assisting students in making educational and vocational choices. The aims of guidance are both adjustive and developmental, it helps the student in making the best possible adjustments to the situations in the educational institutions and in the home. Guidance, therefore, should be regarded as an integral part of education."

The scope of guidance has been increasing with the advancement of science and technology, embracing all spheres of life and providing facilities for it. Therefore, it will be difficult to put a fence around it. While discussing the scope of guidance we may think of some specific or specialised areas of guidance. Even though the guidance programme is addressed to the whole individuals treated as an integral unit. It is possible to classify an individual's problems broadly into educational, vocational and personal.

This three-fold division of guidance illustrating its scope should not be taken to form watertight compartments, but it is more a matter of practical convenience for making the concept clearer. There is no real difference among the problems to which the different types of guidance services are addressed.

Mathewson while discussing the focus and scope of guidance programme has very aptly stated that the focus of guidance is improving the capability of the individuals to understand and deal with self-situational relations in the light of social and moral values. The scope of guidance operation in school is to deal with:

(1) personal and social relations of the individual in school,

    (i) Understanding of the self and personal characteristics.

    (ii) Understanding of others and relations with them.

    (2)   relation of the individual to the school curriculum, and

        (i)   Academic achievement and progress.

        (ii)   Personal development through curricular and co-curricular activities.

    (3)   relation of the individual to the educational and vocational requirements and opportunities.

        (i)   Preparing to meet future education and occupational requirements.

        (ii)   Utilisation of appropriate opportunities – educational and vocational areas.

Each one of the above mentioned areas of guidance to understand the scope of educational and vocational guidance.

    (1) (i) Academic Achievement and Progress: Sometimes it so happen that a student's scholastic achievement is low but shows high I.Q. In such a case guidance worker can find out with the help of certain psychological tests as to where the weakness lies and thus help the student to come up to the desired levels, or sometimes the student has certain problems relating to studies that s/he is not able to cope up with in his/her academics, guidance worker can be effective in such situations.

    (ii) Personal Development: Guidance programmes are so designed that personal development of students is nurtured optimally.

  (2) Personal-social Relations: Getting along well with others is an indicator that a person is well adjusted in the society. Guidance helps in understanding one's self to deal effectively with others.

  (3) Relation of the Individual to Educational and Vocational Requirements: Guidance helps the individual to make effective decisions at different stages of life such as choice of subjects, career selection, by providing necessary information related to different careers and their allied fields.

Q5. Elucidate the various principles of guidance.

Ans. Following are the various principles of guidance:

- **Principle of Continuity:** Guidance is a continuous process. Guidance is provided to every individual at any stage in the process of life cycle. It may start from childhood and continues till death. Guidance is not a service which begins and terminates at specified time or place. It is continuous process.

- **Principle of Individualisation:** Guidance lays emphasis on individualisation. It emphasises freedom to each individual to shape his/her personality and s/he should be guided whenever the need arises. Proper organisation of guidance services is very essential for individualising the education at different levels so that each individual develops his/her abilities, interests and aptitudes in unique ways.

- **Principle of Self-direction:** Guidance gives importance to self-direction. The main idea of guidance is to develop the individual so that s/he no longer finds it necessary to seek guidance. Guidance makes the individual better adjusted to his environment and leads him to self-direction.
- **Principle of Co-operation:** Guidance is based on co-operation. Guidance depends on mutual co-operation of individuals. No one can be forced to seek or offer guidance.
- **Principle of Universality:** Guidance is provided to everyone who needs it. The basic principle of guidance is that it should not be restricted to the privilege few.
- **Principle of Organised Activity:** Guidance is an organised activity. Guidance is not an incidental activity. It has a definite purpose to achieve. It is a systematic and well-organised activity.
- **Principle of Individual Differences:** Guidance gives respect to individual differences. No two individuals are alike. Guidance understands these individual differences among students and is concerned with the uniqueness of needs, problems and developmental characteristics of individuals.
- **Guidance Workers Need Special Preparation:** It is generally agreed that in addition to general survey course in guidance, which should certainly be regarded as a minimum essential in the preparation of all the teachers, the specialists need considerable background study in Psychology including child and adolescent development, mental hygiene and some course work with practical experience.
  The guidance worker should also know what agencies and resources are available in his/her community so that the individuals seeking help should be able to utilise these resources.
- **Individual Evaluation:** Programmes of individual evaluation are conducted and accurate cumulative records of progress and achievement are made available for the guidance of workers.
- **Guidance is Flexible:** Another principle of guidance is flexibility. An organised level guidance programme remains flexible according to individual and community needs.
- **Guidance Emphasises on Code of Ethics:** The ethical applications of guidance include respect for the personality of the individuals being counseled.
- **Interrelated Activity:** Guidance is an interrelated activity. Effective guidance needs complete information about the individual because it is difficult to see any problem in of g isolation without co-relating it with the total programme. For example, educational, vocational and personal and social, guidance are interrelated but could be distinguished as different aspects of the total guidance programme.

Q6. Discuss the types of guidance services, which are offered by schools.

Ans. Everyone needs assistance at some point in life. Some need it constantly throughout their lives while others need at a crisis point. Based on the necessity, there are different areas where guidance is given to manifold problems, viz. educational, vocational and personal.

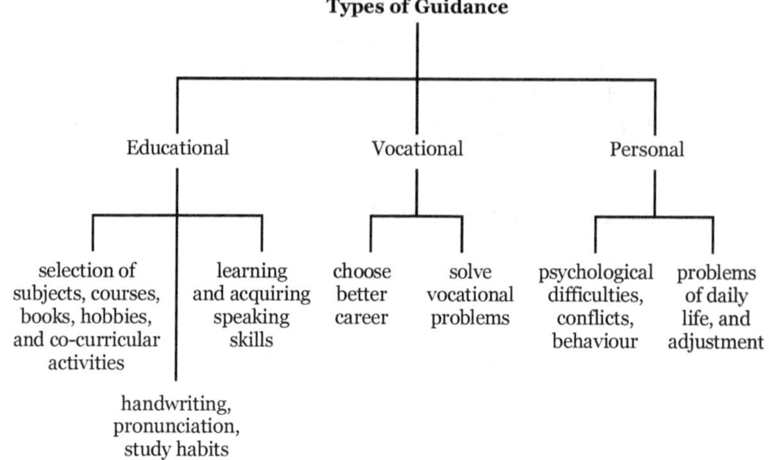

Fig. 1.1: Types of Guidance

(1) Educational Guidance: According to Ruth Strong, educational guidance is intended to aid the individual in choosing appropriate programme and in making progress in it. It is a positive developmental programme. It involves: (i) knowledge of the abilities and interests of the individual, (ii) awareness of a wide range of educational opportunities, and (iii) programmes and counselling which helps the individual to choose wisely on the basis of these two kinds of knowledge.

Brewer is of the opinion that the following is included in educational guidance: "How to study; using the common tools of learning; adjusting school life to other activities; regularly attending on school tasks; learning to speak, interview, compose in writing, take examination, and use libraries; and making the important educational decisions at each of the many forks in the roads."

Jones defines educational guidance as the assistance given to the pupils in their choices and adjustments with relation to schools, curriculums, courses and school life.

It deals with those problems related with the educational progress and learning experiences. Excellence in education is also brought about through such guidance. Other areas covered by educational guidance are improvement of study habits, adjustment problems in the class or school, language difficulties, excessive school workload, lack of co-curricular activities and other issues related in any way to the normal development to the students.

Educational guidance should be given to students right from the kindergarten stage moving on to the elementary stage and then proceeding to secondary and higher secondary stage in schools. "Wrong choice can make him a misfit and a right choice can lift him up."

(2) **Vocational Guidance:** Vocational guidance should empowers students beyond the narrow confines of academic grades. Schools need functional vocational departments to gather and disseminate up-to-date career information to students. Such information may include scholarships, careers in demand, different career options and profiles of personalities who have made it in different fields. Vocational guidance is not just about dishing out information. Schools need to empower students with decision-making skills, which will help them navigate their way through life.

Vocational guidance involves complete and comprehensive knowledge of each pupil, nature of jobs, psychological characteristics needed for success, achievement and job satisfaction, relevant data about vocational opportunities, type of training needed, opportunities of advancing in the field, etc. In this guidance, students are tested from different angles and then they are suggested to opt for a career on the basis of their potentialities and trends. Necessary information is also supplied to them to find a proper vocation. Vocational guidance cannot be separated from the other aspects of guidance such as educational, social, health, etc. It means that guidance is psychological as well as sociological in nature. Once such services are provided total development of the individual becomes a reality.

(3) **Personal Guidance:** Personal guidance is to help pupils to adjust to things and persons around them and to social situations. It is concerned with the problems of the self, viz. the problems that occurs within the individual. Anxiety, tension, aggressiveness, adjustment difficulties, lack of confidence, shyness etc are some examples of personal problems. If they are not tackled properly then the educational and vocational guidance progress will also be retarded. It is also concerned with the problems of their parents, family, friends, teachers and their own educational achievement and social adjustment.

From the above listed problems, personal guidance may be defined as helping students with psychological difficulties, conflicts, problems of daily life, behaviour and adjustment problems and so on.

Q7. What is meant by counselling? Enumerate its various definitions.

Ans. Counselling is usually viewed as one part of guidance services. Its main objective is to bring about a voluntary change in the individual or client. Counselling is often seen as assistance given to individuals to attain a clear sense of identity. Counselling as well as the total guidance programme, stresses rational planning problem-solving, and support in the face of situational pressures. The counselling relationship is usually characterised by much less intensity of emotional expression. Following are the various definitions of counselling:

"Counselling is a personal face-to-face relationship between two people, in which the counsellor by means of his relationship and his special competencies, provides a learning situation in which the counselee, a normal sort of a person, is helped to know about of himself and his present and possible future situations so that he can make use of his characteristics and potentialities in a way that is both satisfying himself and beneficial to society and further, can learn how to solve his future problems," (Tolbert).

- **Webster's Dictionary:** "Counselling" means "consultation, mutual interchange of opinions or deliberating together".
- **Popinsky and Popinsky:** "Counselling relationship refers to the interaction which (1) occurs between two individuals called 'counsellor' and 'client', (2) takes place within a professional setting, and (3) is initiated and maintained as a means of facilitating changes in the behaviour of the client. The counselling relationship develops from the interaction between the two individuals, one a professionally trained worker and the other a person who seeks his services."
- **Wren:** "Counselling is a dynamic and purposeful relationship between two people who approach a mutually defined problem with mutual consideration of each other to the end that the younger or less mature, or more troubled of the two is aided to a self-determined resolution of his problem."

Q8. Delineate the relationship of counselling with other fields.

Or

What is the relationship between instruction and counselling?

Ans. The relationship of counselling with other fields is discussed as follows:

- **Counselling and Psychotherapy:** The terms "counselling" and "psychotherapy" are often used interchangeably, but there is a slight distinction. Counselling generally refers to short-term consultation while psychotherapy typically refers to longer-term treatment. Counselling typically deals with present issues that are easily resolved on the conscious level whereas psychotherapy intensively and extensively examines a person's psychological history. In other words, counselling is more concerned with practical or immediate issues and outcomes while psychotherapy is more focussed on helping a person understand his/her life in a profound and reflective manner.

Counselling normally helps a client process powerful emotions such as grief or anger, deal with immediate causes of stress and anxiety, clarify values and identify options when making important personal or professional decisions, manage conflicts within relationships, develop better interpersonal and communication skills, or intentionally change unproductive thoughts and behaviours. Psychotherapy, on the other hand, is an evolutionary process that helps a person look at long-standing attitudes, thoughts, and behaviours that have resulted in the current quality of one's life and relationships.

Inspite of the distinctions mentioned above, it is very difficult to separate these two fields. There is more overlap than differences. In both the aim is to assist the person to lead a more adjusted and satisfying life. In both counselling and psychotherapy, the relationship between the client and the therapist/counsellor is of vital importance. Moreover, while handling emotional problem of a deep nature, counselling approaches psychotherapy very closely.

- **Guidance and Counselling:** As both guidance and counselling are psychological processes, and the main focus of psychology is human behaviour, another goal of both guidance and counselling would be to improve the behaviour of the client.

- **Instruction and Counselling:** Another term closely related to counselling is instruction. There are some differences between instruction and counselling. Instruction is usually obligatory to be followed by the person who receives it where as in the case of counselling the counselee is not obliged to act according to anything said by the counsellor. Actually, nothing is told to be done in counselling. Similarly, although the ultimate aim of instruction is the development of the individual. The immediate aim is the learning of a subject, skill, etc. But this is not so in the case of counselling. Moreover, the instructional programme is time bound and structured but counselling on the other hand is not structured and no time limit is also fixed in the case of counselling.

- **Advice and Counselling:** Advice and counsel have similar meanings, but counsel is used for a more formal situation, such as the advice given by a professional adviser. Counsel has some legal, academic, or mo ral weight. But anyone can advice; that may be just an opinion that someone offers. Advice may or may not be of any significance. All counsel is advice, but not all advice is counsel.

  Moreover, in advice giving the advisor is making decisions for the individual where as in counselling, decision-making is wholly the responsibility of the counselee. Therefore, the counsellor is fully responsible for his/her actions too. Advice giving may be an incident and will be over in a brief meeting. But counselling is a process.

Q9. Elucidate the principles of counselling.

Ans. The principles of counselling are discussed as follows:

(1)   Counselling is a process, as well as a relationship, between persons. Contrary to what some people believe, counselling is not concentrated advice-giving. The aim of the counselor is usually to assist the student/s to realise a change in behaviour or attitude, or to seek achievement of goals. Often there are varieties of problems for which the counselee may seek to find help.

(2)   Counsellor does not deprive the right of self-choice but simply facilitates choice. The counsellor should give due respect to the individual and accept him/her as s/he is.

(3)   Counselling is based on certain fundamental assumptions.

   (i)   every individual in this world is capable of taking responsibilities for him/herself.

   (ii)   every individual has a right to choose his/her own path, based on the principles of democracy.

(4)   Counselling is for all. Especially in the school situation, counselling is meant for all the students and not only for those who are facing problems or other exceptional students. As we have already discussed in the school situation counselling is more developmental and preventive than remedial in nature.

(5)   Counselling is not advice giving.

(6)   Counselling is not thinking for the client, but thinking with the client. Counselling is for enabling the client to do judicious thinking.

(7)   Counselling is not problem solving. The counsellor simply assist the person to find solution on his/her own.

(8)   Counselling is not interviewing but conversing with the client in order to help him/her develop self-understanding.

(9)   The counsellor should determine individual differences and provide for them.

(10)   The counsellor has to prepare the client to open to criticism including self-criticism.

(11)   The counsellor acts as a facilitator or catalyst only. S/he creates an atmosphere, which is permissive and non-threatening, through his/her warm and accepting relationship with the client which helps the client to explore himself/herself and understand himself/herself better.

Q10. What are the major goals/purposes of counselling? Explain.

Ans. Some of the major goals/purposes of counselling generally accepted by the counsellors are given below:

- **Achievement of Positive Mental Health:** It is identified as an important goal of counselling by some individuals who claim that when one reaches positive mental health one learns to adjust and response more positively to people and situations. Kell and Mueller (1962) hold that the "promotion and development of feelings of being liked, sharing with, and receiving and giving interaction rewards from other human beings is the legitimate goal of counselling."

- **Problem Resolution:** Another goal of counselling is the resolving of the problem brought to the counsellor. This, in essence, is an outcome of the former goal and implies positive mental health. In behavioural terms three categories of behavioural goals can be identified, namely, altering maladaptive behaviuor, learning the decision-making process and preventing problems (Krumboltz, 1966).

- **Counselling for Decision-making:** Some counsellors hold the view that counselling should enable the counselee to make decisions. It is through the process of making critical decisions that personal growth is fostered. Reaves and Reaves (1965) point out that "the primary objective of counselling is that of stimulating the individuals to evaluate, make, accept and act upon his choice".

  Sometimes the counselees have goals, which are vague and their implications are not fully appreciated. It is perhaps one of the primary functions of a counselor to help clarify a counselee's goal.

- **Improving Personal Effectiveness:** Yet another goal of counselling is that of improving personal effectiveness. This is closely related to the preservation of good mental health and securing desirable behavioural change(s).

- **Helping to Change:** Blocher (1966) adds two other goals. The first, according to him, is that counselling should maximise individual freedom to choose and act within the conditions imposed by the environment. The other goal is that counselling should increase the effectiveness of the individual responses evolved by the environment. Tiedeman (1964) holds that the goal of counselling is to focus on the mechanism of change and that the counselee should be helped in the process of 'becoming' – the change which pervades the period of adolescence through early adulthood during which the individual is assisted to actualise his potential. Shoben (1965) also views the goal of counselling as personal development.

- **Behaviour Modification:** Behaviourally-oriented counsellors stress the need for modification of behaviour, for example, removal of undesirable behaviour or action or reduction of an irritating symptom such that the individual attains satisfaction and effectiveness. Growth-oriented counselors stress on the development of potentialities within the individual. Existentially-oriented counselors stress self-enhancement and self-fulfilment. Obviously, the latter cannot be realise without first securing the former, namely, symptom removal or reduction as a necessary pre-condition for personal effectiveness.

Q11. Describe the directive approach of counselling with its six stages.

Ans. Counselling is possible only when the individual is able to accumulate adequate data to form the basis for an analytic diagnosis of the problem. The counsellor's role is to assist his student in getting such data to suggest suitable solutions.

The counsellor plays a prominent and leading role. The possible solutions are suggested by the counsellor himself. The counsellor gives direct advice, suggestions and explanations to the counsellee. The counsellor through repeated explanation convinces the counsellee regarding the suitability of the suggested solution. The initiative is taken by the counsellor. The responsibility of the counsellor is to analyse the problem, find out the causes, make decisions, and suggest appropriate solutions to the counsellee for his implementation, e.g. Williamson is the chief exponent of this viewpoint and it involves six essential steps:

(1) **Analysis:** It includes collection of information about the individual, which can be collected through structured interviews, psychological case history methods, Interaction with family members, friends, etc.

(2) **Synthesis:** After collection of lot data, the information is organised in the logical manner to analyse the individual in terms of his qualifications, assets, potentials, liability adjustment, cultural background, habits, etc.

(3) **Diagnosis:** The diagnosis consists of the interpretation of the data in relation to the nature and problem, the causes of problems. Drawing conclusions from the results of psychological testing, administration of questionnaires, etc. are done here.

(4) **Prognosis:** Under this step, a prediction is made about the future development of the problem.

(5) **Counselling:** The counselling here is to bring about adjustment and re-adjustment to the individual in relation to his problem. Attitudes and interest of the individual are considered during the counselling. It emphasis the individual to develop life cycle where an effort in the positive direction could lead to success and success in turn could lead to further efforts and motivations.

It may be direct teaching through explicit explanations, assistance in searching for relevant aptitudes, interests, etc. that illuminates the counselee's problems and so on. Sometimes the counsellor listens in a friendly encouraging way. It may also involve practice sessions where with the warm support of the counsellor the counselee acts out the way s/he should. Thus, s/he becomes his/her own teacher to the extent his/her capabilities and circumstances permits. Success thus achieved reinforces and retrains those successful behaviours, which in turn establishes an adjusted way of life.

Thus, counselling involves (i) assisting the student in self- appraisal, i.e. identifying his/her interests motives and capabilities (ii) helping him/her to plan a course of action, which utilises the capabilities and potentialities so identified and (iii) finally is establishing an adaptive life style.

(6) Follow-up: The sixth step in directive counselling is follow up which is extremely important. An individual may be able to solve immediate problems through counselling but new problems may occur or the original problem may re-occur. Follow-up with the client is extremely necessary. The role of counselor is important as he has to make the individual understand and accept his strength and also his weakness and faults.

Q12. Explain non-directive approach in counselling. Also, describe the central hypotheses of non-directive counselling.

Ans. Non-directive counselling is to listen, support, and advise, without directing a client's course of action. It has been influenced by humanistic theories in the tradition of Carl Rogers, but techniques used in non-directive counselling are common in many forms of psychological counselling and treatment today. In this type of counselling, the counsellor plays an active role and this type of counselling is a growing process. In this counselling, the goal is the independence and integration of the client rather than the solution of the problem. In this counselling process, the counsellee comes to the counsellor with a problem. The counsellor establishes rapport with the counsellee based on mutual trust, acceptance and understanding.

The counsellee provides all information about his problems. The counsellor assists him to analyse and synthesise, diagnose his difficulties, predict the future development of his problems, take a decision about the solution of his problems; and analyse the strengths and consequences of his solutions before taking a final decision. Since the counsellee is given full freedom to talk about his problems and work out a solution, this technique is also called the "permissive" counselling.

Central Hypothesis: Carl Rogers, the chief proponent of the client-centered approach has formulated a central hypothesis as follows:

- The individual has within him/herself capacity latent if not evident to understand those aspects of him/herself and of his/her life which are causing him/her dissatisfaction anxiety or pain and the capacity and the tendency to reorganise him/herself and his/her relationship to life in the direction of self-actualisation and maturity in such a way as to bring a greater degree of internal comfort.

- This capacity will be realised when the therapist can create a psychological climate characterised by genuine acceptance of the client as a person of unconditional worth, a continuing sensitive attempt to understand the existing feelings and communications of the client as a person of unconditional worth, a continuing sensitive attempt to understand the existing feelings and communications of the client and a continuing attempt to convey this empathetic understanding to the client.
- It is further hypothesised that in such an acceptant understanding and non-threatening atmosphere the client will reorganise him/herself.
- This adjusted way of life as achieved in the therapeutic relation with the counselor will be genrealised to real life situations as a whole.

Thus, the whole idea of the theory is that the clients are capable of correcting misperceptions or incongruencies between the self and experience, in the accepting environment of a counselling situation. The accepting counselling environment is when the counsellor possesses personal qualities like congruency (counsellor being a genuine and integrated person), unconditional positive regard (non evaluation attitude of the counsellor whereby client's thoughts, feelings or behaviour are accepted without judging them as good or bad) and empathy (consellor's ability to know the client's world as s/he does and to convey this understanding).

Q13. Explain the concept of Eclectic Counselling.

Ans. Eclectic counselling is defined as the synthesis and combination of directive and non-directive counselling. It represents a middle status between the two extremes represented by the 'non-directive' technique on one hand and the 'directive' technique on the other. In eclectic counselling, the counselor is neither too active as in the directive counselling nor too passive as in the non-directive counselling. He just follows the middle path between these two.

In eclectic counselling, the needs of a person and his personality are studied by the counselor. After this, the counselor selects those techniques, which will be useful for the person. The main techniques used are reassurance giving information, case history, testing, etc.

In eclectic counselling, the counselor first takes into consideration the personality and need of the counselee. He selects the directive or non-directive technique that seems to serve the purpose best. The counselor may start with the directive technique. When the situation demands, he may switch over to the non-directive counselling and vice-versa.

Characteristic of Eclectic Counselling: Various characteristics of eclectic counselling are as follows:

(1)   In this, objective and coordinating methods are used.

(2)   In the beginning of counselling, client-active methods are used and the counselor remains passive.

(3)   In this, more importance is assigned to the job efficiency and treatment.

(4)   In this, the principle of low expenditure is emphasised.

(5)   In such counselling, for the use of all the methods and techniques, the professional efficiency and skill of the counselor are must.

(6)   Keeping in mind the need of the client, it is decided whether directive method or non-directive methods should be used.

(7)   Making an opportunity available to the client is insisted so that he may find himself the solution of the problem.

According to F.C. Thorne, eclecticism is the most practicable and apt approach to counselling. Because no two people are able and as such no single theory of personality could explain the various behavioural pattern exhibited by individuals. So also, each problem is unique in its content and intensity and a technique or approach suitable in one case need not even be effective in the second case.

Thorne has coined the word 'Integrated psychology' to express his eclectic view. Its theoretical foundations are based on the following postulates:

(1)   All psychological conditions are examples of disorders of integrations and the goal of psychological counselling is to strengthen this integrative process, thus fostering high levels of self-actualisation. The focus is, therefore, the person in the present situation.

(2)   The therapist has to assess whether the client has the necessary resources to take on the responsibilities of life.

(3)   If the therapist is satisfied, he gives the client the responsibility of taking on some routine tasks to start with.

(4)   Therapy involves the training and reduction of the client in acquiring the controls necessary for self-regulation.

Thorne uses the term psychological case handling instead of psychotherapy. Steps involved in psychological case handling are:

(1)   Systematic diagnosis to obtain a complete picture of the clients problem.

(2)   Understanding the various counselling methods in terms of their strengths and limitations.

(3)   Concentrating on the underlying causes rather than symptoms.

(4)   Choosing a specific method suited to the needs of the client.

(5)   Evaluating the method on the basis of the results obtained.

(6)   Scientifically analysing the data and evaluating the result.

'Multimodal therapy' originated by Arnold Lazarus is yet another example of eclectic approach. He explains seven major areas of personality functions: (1) behaviour (observable action), (2) affective (emotional), (3) sensation (feelings), (4) images (imagination), (5) cognition (thought process), (6) interpersonal relationships (social) and (7) drugs/biological (physical). He uses the acronym BASIC ID to encompass all these modalities.

Q14. Enumerate and explain the processes of counselling.

Or

By which stages the process of counselling passes through.

Ans. Counselling is a process. It means that Counselling involves a sequence of identifiable events spread over a period. The time taken, the sequence of events, and dynamics, involved, the nature and extent of exploration, differ from individual to individual. However, there are certain basic stages, which form the essentials of counselling processes. The processes of counselling comprises of certain concepts, they are as follows:

(1) **Readiness:** The counselee is of two types, i.e. one who seeks assistance voluntarily and the other who are referred. The counselling presupposes a desire on the part of the counselee that makes him come for the assistance. This desire is referred to as readiness.

(2) **Counter Will:** People experience difficulty in asking for help and accepting it, because they are reluctant to face the consequences of change or an admission of inadequacy of failure. The negative feeling that holds back one from seeking help is referred to, as counter will.

(3) **Case History:** Case History is a systematic collection of facts about the counselee's past and present life. However, focus of attention varies from case to case.

(4) **Rapport:** It is a warm friendly and understanding atmosphere created by the counsellor, which is catalytical in the formation of an effective counselling relationship. Warmth of relationship and feeling of trust, which grows out of unconditional acceptance are important in contributing to the establishment of rapport.

(5) **Transference:** It refers to the counsellor transferring emotions originally felt towards someone early in life. The counselee is encouraged to express his/her feelings and emotions freely. The counsellor acknowledges these feelings and handles in a therapeutic way.

(6) **Counter Transference:** This occurs when counsellor project their unresolved conflicts upon the counselee. When counsellor feels uncomfortable and experience felling of anger, resentment or become overemotional. This is unhealthy.

(7) **Resistance:** It refers to counselee's move to oppose the counsellor's to work towards set goals. This influences counselling outcome positively. Resistance ranges from open hostility to passively resistant behaviour like being late for an appointment.

Stages of the Counselling Process: The process of counselling passes through certain stages, which are discussed as follows:

(1) **Initial Stage: Client Self-exploration:** In initial stage, the clients are encouraged in self-exploration and their concern are clarified. General counselling goals are set and the working alliance is established. Also by gathering information and observing the client, the counsellor arrives at some tentative hypothesis regarding the nature and complexity of the problem. To help in these decisions assessment devices like psychological tests, questionnaires, inventories, etc. are widely used.

The initial stage is sub-divided into (i) first interview and (ii) initial counselling sessions.

(i) **First Interview:** According to Hackney & Cormier, 1994, initial interview can fulfil two functions: It can be intake interview to collect needed information and it can signal the beginning of a relationship. This is the most challenging stage. Client approaches the counsellor with a feeling of uncertainty and ambivalence. Counselors through their words, facial expressions and overall behaviour conveys his understanding and acceptance of the client and his sincere interest in his problem. Simple courtesies like seating the clients comfortably, avoiding interrupting phone calls are very important in the development of rapport. During this interview the counsellor needs to make a tentative decision whether the task at hand is within his expertise. If not, it is necessary to refer the client to an appropriate professional agency. Clients should be made aware of what can be expected out of counselling and what they are hoping for. Confidentiality, rights of privacy, other ethical and legal considerations need to be clarified. Discussion about the length of sessions, payment of fees, arrangement of mutually appropriate meeting times, etc. are also done now.

(ii) **Initial Counselling Sessions:** Here, the counsellor mostly listen to the client's concerns and encourages the expression of feelings, without undue questioning. Thus, information is gathered by active listening, attending to client's self-talk, observing his body behaviour and other reactions, to be used later in deeper explorations. If clients have difficulty in expressing, non-threatening questions can help.

(2) **Middle Stage: Deeper Exploration and Analysis:**
People seek a counsellor to help resolve concerns or problems that are interfering with their daily life or causing them despair. The counsellor comes to the counselling situation

with the expectation to do something to ease or improve the client's situation. In the second stage of the counselling process, the counsellor attempts to assess the client. Assessment refers to anything counsellors do to gather information and draw conclusions about the concerns of clients. Assessment takes place at the beginning of the counselling process.

At this point, some counselors use more tests to further explore into the clients intellectual or personality functioning. Thus as the client moves to increased disclosure and awareness, the counsellor and client begins to develop emotional interactions like transference, counter transference, resistance, etc. Though rooted in psychoanalysis, experts are of the opinion that these are universal phenomena in all counselling relationships.

(3) Final Stage: Implementation of Goals Through Action: Sometimes, we hear both counsellor and client complain that the counselling session is going nowhere. This is where goals play an important role in giving direction. Goals are the results or outcomes that client wants to achieve at the end of counselling. Goals help the counsellor and client determine what can and what cannot be accomplished through counselling. In goal setting, the client indentifies with the help of the counsellor, specific ways in which they want to resolve the issues and what course of action should be taken to resolve the problem.

(4) Termination: The termination is primarily the counsellor's responsibility, although the client can terminate the sessions any time they like. The counsellor usually gives some sort of an indication that the next interview should just about wrap it up and may conclude by summarising the main points of the counselling process. Usually, the counsellor leaves the door open for the client's possible return in the event additional assistance is needed. Since counselling is a learning process, the counsellor hopes that the client has not only learned to deal with this particular problem, but has also learned problem-solving skills that will decrease the probability of the clients need for further counselling in the future.

Q15. Discuss guidance services in education.

Ans. Guidance is accepted as an integral part of education. No student has ever been able to manifest and maximise his potentialities on large extent, make appropriate career plans, get a suitable occupation and make satisfactory adjustment in the society without assistance of guidance programme organised in school.

To say that guidance services are central and integral part of the total educational effort is not to say that these services are identical with or substitutes for either teaching or administration. Guidance services have an identity of their own yet the boundaries between guidance and some aspects of teaching and administration are zones of interrelationships rather than sharp lines of delineation. The good teacher of course performs a number of guidance functions. Among other things, s/he contributes valuable information and helpful insights towards understanding students motivation and difficulties not only in achievement but also in adjustment, s/he creates the kind of classroom atmosphere which makes for mental health, s/he may discuss with the student and her/his parents about educational and vocational plans; or s/he may do a number of other things.

Education and guidance are closely related. In short, education involves guidance. All guidance is education, but some aspects of education are not guidance. The objectives of both may be the same, viz., the development of the individual, but the methods used are different. The latest stress in the field of education is vocationalisation of secondary level. Hence, vocational education is essential.

Vocational Education is a skill based training which is imparted through various courses and classes available in many career fields – healthcare, computer technology, office management and skilled trades. Vocational Education is offered through public and private education institutions. The duration of the course and classes depends upon the time required to finish the course. Vocational education is training that is provided to the students with skills that would help them in their work. The method used to teach the students is by providing them hands on experience so that they get more practical exposure.

Q16. Delineate about curriculum from education and guidance point of view. Also, explain how curriculum of the school must meet the needs of the students.

Ans. In the context of education, a curriculum means, the total situation (all situations) selected and organised by the institution and made available to the teacher to operate and to translate the ultimate aim of education into reality.

From the guidance point of view, the curriculum is viewed as the "planned" learning experiences provided by the school. Certainly, it must be recognised that students learn from all their experiences and not just from those in the classroom, e.g. extra-curricular activities provide learning experiences different from those available in regular classes of the school.

Meeting Individual's Needs: The curriculum of the school must meet the needs of the students. In a sense, they set the boundaries of school activities. This is an important contribution, because in every community the services from which students could profit are of such a wide variety that it is impossible for the school to provide all of them. Thus, the school must select those for which it takes the primary responsibility to provide.

Therefore, a curriculum must provide certain opportunities for the students for (1) discovering a place in life and clarifying a philosophy of living, (2) establishing satisfying peer relations, (3) achieving independence from family, and (4) adjusting to physical growth and changes.

Q17. Elucidate the criteria for a relevant and meaningful curriculum.

Ans. The criteria for a relevant and meaningful curriculum are given below:

(1) Needs of Youth: The first criterion is concerned with students' common/general needs and special/individual needs which are as follows:

(i) Common Needs: Generally, all students have some basic needs in common; they are all citizens; nearly all of them will marry and raise families; they will earn a living; they must meet and try to get along with other people, etc.

(ii) Special Needs: Besides the above basic needs, there are particular or individual needs and interests. For example, some students will like to go to a college for their further studies; some will like to join certain vocational courses; some of them would join their parents' business still there would be some who would wish to join any professional course/college such as medical, engineering or architecture. The common needs are easily identifiable and can be met by planning different "courses of study".

(2) Meeting Demands of Our Social Order: Identifying many of these demands is difficult, and yet some of these are extremely obvious. Our society demands that all citizens should have functional literacy skills. Some societal pressures are more complicated. For example, physicians are expected to continue their study independently in order to keep in touch with latest advances in medical research.

(3) Learning Process and Curriculum: The third criterion can be understood in a better way by going through the following table:

Table 1.1

A Necessary Consideration Providing a Good Learning Experience	How to Accomplish	Contribution of Guidance Programme
(1) Instruction must be geared to the readiness of students	Review of previous work	Group discussion and career talks
(2) The mental ability of students must be taken into account	Testing	Psychological testing and interviews

(3) Students must be Motivated	Needs Identification	Occupational information and motivational talks
(4) When students make an adequate response it must be reinforced	Rewards	Career fairs and career exhibitions
(5) Students must have some means of evaluating the adequacy of their responses	Questionnaires and Counselling	Self-appraisal and career courses

Q18. Identify the similarities between guidance and curriculum.

Ans. Following are the similarities between guidance and curriculum:

    (1) Similarity of Goals: The main similarity between guidance and counselling would be that they are designed to help the students. The focal functioning center in both fields is the students. Curriculum has moved from a "subject-matter-centred" approach to a "student-centered" approach. Since the student is with the teacher most of the time in school, an important goal for both fields becomes "helping the teacher" to help the student to learn, to adjust and to be competent.

    (2) Similarity of Function: Some of the important similarities in function are:

        (i) Needs of the Whole Person: This function is to see that the needs of the "whole person" – physical, emotional, social as well as mental – are met. The ongoing, active behaviour of students in such action settings as the playgrounds, the extra-curricular activities, and the halls/corridors between classes is important to observe. Both, the teacher and the guidance counsellor should not be content with merely knowing the student's background data and his/her classroom performance.

        (ii) Identification of Student Needs and Problems: If guidance counsellor, curriculum specialists and teachers combine their work, using their own particular skills, insights and specialisation, a more successful result will be accomplished in identifying the needs of the young people.

        For the most part, guidance staffs have chosen counselling as the way to identify student problems but too often they keep their knowledge (of what problems students have) within themselves. Outstanding common problems stated by counsellors are: failure to achieve according to ability, school course failure in general, broken homes, social adjustment, whereas teachers have mentioned delinquency, absenteeism and lack of orientation. All of these problems have implications for guidance, for curriculum, for work with home and community, and for general good group morale in the school.

(iii) Work with Same People: Guidance and curriculum staffs have complementary function and work with same people – students, parents, teachers and the community. The help of a counsellor with curriculum staffs and teachers would be invaluable, e.g. s/he could inform them of all the records that are available for their use in the guidance office. S/he could help the teacher and the students find curricular and work experiences that would give them the necessary background for solving their problems and meeting their needs.

(3) Similarity in Content and Educational Resource Materials: Practically, the whole content of the guidance programme has potential as curricular experiences for students. The topics such as Vocational and Occupational Guidance, Home and Family, Health and Physical Development, getting along with others, could be made curricular experiences.

Also, the guidance unit usually has a well-established corner in the library and in the guidance office, which provides books and other reading materials that could be used advantageously for curricular purposes in the classroom.

(4) Similarity in Approaches: The diagnostic and remedial approaches have been used in both guidance and curriculum fields, e.g. via tests and examinations. The developmental and therapeutic aspects have not been realised to the fullest extent, e.g. when a student fails, very few teachers would look for reasons of his/her failure, especially when the reason is not obvious. No item-by-item diagnosis is done usually. Both fields have also neglected the full potential of the preventive approach.

(5) Similar Methodology and Techniques of Working with Students: Guidance techniques like the case study, the interview, anecdotal records, socio-metrics, socio-drama and simple projective techniques such as autobiography, picture projection, story making, etc. are practiced in many classrooms at the present time. Teachers have always carried out interviews and have given various kinds of educational and occupational information to students. However, it has been observed that sometimes teachers use these techniques without realising their full potentialities. The guidance staff can give them a thorough understanding of how to administer, use and interpret their methods more effectively.

Q19. How do students get guidance through school curriculum? Discuss.

Or

Briefly explain guidance through the study of literature.

Ans. Learning is an important outcome of both curriculum and guidance. Thus, guidance and curriculum become indispensable elements of the total process of education. In school, almost every subject offers unique opportunities for guidance. Mathematics should develop capacities for precise and logical thinking. Social studies–history, geography and civics should help students make a better adjustment to the changes that are occurring in the world and show them what they can do to resist demoralising trends. Language should make a definite contribution to the development of the student's communication skills and to his/her understanding of himself/herself and others. Physical education offers fine opportunities for guidance in the areas of recreation and health. Home economics or home science should include guidance in health and in present and future family living. Business education or business studies, art and the various work experience subjects have personal as well as vocational values if the teachers are guidance-minded. Following subjects are given in detail by which students can get guidance:

- **Mathematics:** We may notice that a number of great philosophers, e.g. Plato and Aristotle, were also mathematicians. One may more easily transfer the logic and discipline involved in solving math problems to the wonders of a universe which seems to be orderly, predictable, and logical.

  In algebra, the teacher can help students see that mathematics is a "sign language" which humans have learned to use, over the centuries, to facilitate both abstract and practical thinking. Students will also be interested in the role of mathematics today in attempts to conquer outer space.

- **Literature:** In literature classes, it is most obvious to develop values. Short stories, plays, novels essays and poems present situations in which motives are revealed, problems solved, decisions made. In literature, an important part of guidance while teaching is the study of characters - why did they behave as they did, what were the consequences of their acts, what similar conflicts may arise in our lives today? Many situations in true-to-life literature can be used to illuminate the perplexities of today's adolescents and help them develop sound values. Guidance-minded teachers believe that this is their most important objective in teaching literature. Literature lives because, through its discipline and art, it reflects life.

- **Social Studies:** The way in which social studies is taught in many schools seems to have aroused considerable student resistance. To deal with this problem, the teacher may first encourage the students to express their negative feelings about the course. This shows them that s/he understands their point of view and wants their ideas about how to make the course more worthwhile and interesting to them. S/he may then discuss the reasons why the subject is required and why s/he thinks it has value for students.

In social studies, students learn how the present grew out of the past and influences the future. It should teach young citizens how to avoid some of the mistakes of the past.

- **Personal and Social Values of all Subjects:** Any subject whether an academic subject like art, music, business studies, education or home-science, is a means to an end. It should contribute to a better life for the individual and for mankind. Students should see each subject in relation to their social and personal development and to the long-range goals of mankind.

Q20. Interpret the nature of the learning process in a guidance-based curriculum.

Ans. The process of learning has great value for enriching human life in all spheres of life. All activities and behaviours that make personal, social and economic life peaceful and pleasurable are learned. The nature of the learning process in a guidance-based curriculum is as follows:

- **Goals in Learning:** Effective learning is an organised (or ordered) process, proceeding from simple to complex. Thus, there exists direction set 'beforehand'. Hence, the teacher decides, before starting the class, what s/he is going to teach that day: after the class, s/he tells the students what kinds of questions can come from that topic and discusses with them.

- **Learning as a Unified Process:** Guidance, involved as it is with growth and development, has also to consider the problem of mind and body dualism. Research has shown that the child responds using both aspects of his/her personality, intellectual and physical, e.g. throwing a ball requires logical thinking (which other player is more likely to catch it) and motor co-ordination (moving his hand and arm in a particular direction). In a similar manner mastering arithmetic table requires rote memory (learning it again and again and use of special ability to speak and write).

- **Experience and Learning:** The term experience has very different meanings. Usually it refers to immediate experience or experiencing, i.e. to the kind of experience that every moment of life is full of, i.e. immediate, engaged beingness or life as lived through. Each student brings his/her own experience to the classroom, which in turn leads to new experiences. It is the sum total of these experiences which makes up the pattern of learning. Thus if a teacher can accept each child for what s/he is and go on from there s/he is following in the best tradition of guidance.

- **The Physiological Basis of Learning:** The mechanisms of learning and remembering seem to depend on relatively enduring changes in the nervous system. Apparently the effects of learning are first retained in the brain by some reversible process, after which a more permanent neural change takes place. Two types of neurological processes have therefore been suggested. The short-term function of memory, temporary and reversible, may be achieved through a physiological mechanism (e.g., synaptic electrical or chemical change) that keeps the memory trace alive over a limited period of time. The ensuing, more permanent (long-term) storage may depend on changes in the physical or chemical structure of neurons; synaptic changes seem to be particularly important. Many learning disabilities such as dyslexia, underachievement, poor achievement, slow learning, etc. can be accounted for by some kind of developmental difference in the brain.

- **Emotion in Learning:** Periods of tension, pleasure/disturbance tend to inhibit/reinforce learning. The teacher creates much of the emotional climate in the classroom. Effective learning depends on the well-adjusted teacher and students.

- **Learning and the Self-concept:** As most behaviour is directed towards the attainment of those goals which seem important to the person in the satisfaction of his needs, how the individual interprets his goals and the acceptable methods of attaining them are significant in the learning process.

Q21. What is the importance of learning material and teacher in guidance programmes of schools?

Ans. Learners are oriented towards the instruction and learning. Any syllabus or curriculum has the goals of learning, the methods of learning, etc. and teachers help the learners to learn. Teachers are required to follow the curriculum and provide a better platform to understand the curriculum with the help of materials. Teachers may adapt, supplement, and elaborate the materials to disseminate the content to the students and they need to monitor the progress of the students and finally evaluate the students. Teachers and students rely on materials to comprehend the content, and the materials become the centre of education.

Therefore, it is important for the teachers to know the correct methods, to choose the best material for instruction and they should also know how to make supplementary materials for the class, and how to adapt materials.

Guidance programmes in the past have tended to neglect the role of the teacher. However, it has now become evident that specialists alone cannot operate the guidance programme in the school. It is the teacher who arranges the subject matter, directs the course of learning and interprets the goals, which have been set up for him/her.

(1) **Need for Organised Procedures:** An "ordered" arrangement of classroom procedure is necessary if the desired learning is to take place. Therefore, the teacher has to select those kinds of experiences, which are designed to educate the student, e.g. after deciding which topic to teach, the teacher can first present an overview of the entire chapter in a summarised form and then begin with the introduction part.

(2) **Learning and Effective Work Habits:** What happens to the student after s/he has departed from the classroom? That is outside the classroom also, the students have a real need related to learning; the establishment of effective work habits.

The well-adjusted human being is our goal but students need also to be taught that learning is not just a game. It needs concentrated effort, mastery of subject-matter through hard work, interest and a definite schedule for studying at home.

(3) **Suggestions for Classroom Discipline:** The most effective means of evaluating the discipline, which is maintained in the classroom, comes through the students themselves.

Waller has suggested certain rules for maintaining good discipline in the classroom. The teachers should:

(i) plan the day's work in advance.

(ii) be sure that the students know the assignment.

(iii) place time-limit on all written work.

(iv) be firm in dealing with students: "I mean business" firmness.

(v) be in room/classroom ahead of the students.

(vi) develop an interest in every student in classroom.

(vii) be sure to grade and return all written work submitted by students.

(viii) be sure that s/he does not allow favours to jeopardise class morale.

(ix) plan to control his/her own classroom. Send offenders to Vice-principal, or Principal, only as a last resort.

(x) not make a lot of rigid statement. S/he should be sure that s/he could defend a statement when s/he makes it.

Q22. Enumerate and explain the guidelines for teachers and counsellors for helping the students.

Ans. The guidelines for teachers and counsellors for helping the students are discussed as follows:

(1) **Expect the Best of Each Student:** Most students can do more than adults expect of them. Teachers should not do things for the students that s/he can do for himself/herself, e.g. if the teacher had taught the formula for solving the sums of an exercise with examples, then s/he should not do the exercise on the blackboard.

(2) Encourage Each Student: Encouragement is not the same as reward and praise. The latter can be overdone, e.g. if a teacher writes 'good' on every notebook that has all the sums of homework correct, this praise will lose its value. On the other-hand, if s/he writes 'good' on only a few selected notebooks with a comment on what was good about it (say "very organised work" or "neatly done"), such praise would be more encouraging.

(3) Listen More: Many teachers talk too much. That is why some children become "teacher-deaf". How much time teachers waste to explain things the students already know. How much time they waste scolding the class! One youngster said, "My Hindi teacher spends so much time scolding us, s/he doesn't have time to teach us".

(4) Try to Understand what a Child's Behaviour Means to Him/Her: What is s/he trying to gain by his/her behaviour? What satisfaction is it giving him? If s/he wants to be accepted by the group, s/he may make silly remarks, defy the teacher or insist on talking; this is his/her way of getting attention, being recognised, feeling that s/he is playing a part in the group, however unhelpful or even negative it may be.

(5) Try to Gain Knowledge of the following Three Things:
   (i)   The child himself/herself-his/her aptitudes, values, goals, personality, previous education, general experience and physical condition.
   (ii) The task itself-its interest, difficulty and usefulness.
   (iii) The situation-the child's interaction with his classmates and his relation to the teacher; the attitudes and morale of the group; the motivation, anxiety or stress inherent in the situation; the immediate work environment – lighting, ventilation, distractions.

Q23. What are the principles, which have proved helpful in providing the setting in actual classroom situations to facilitate classroom learning?

Ans. Following are certain principles, which have proved helpful in providing the setting in actual classroom situations to facilitate classroom learning:

- **Motivation:** The concept of motivation helps to understand and explain facts about behaviour and learning. Motivation is often tied to other factors that influence the energy and direction of behaviour, such as interest, need, value, attention, attitude, aspiration, and incentive.

  Learning is found to be more effective and permanent when the learner is made to feel part of the activity. Children learn motives from their own experiences. 'The child knows that he wants things and learns that he can do something to get them, that his wanting is the motive for his behaviour' (Huddings, 1983). Motivation serves as a spark for achievement.

- **Adjustment to Level of Maturation:** Another process that produces change in the behaviour, for reasons other than learning, is maturation. A certain level of maturity is prerequisite to learning when a pupil is to learn a new skill, he must be sufficiently mature for the task. The guidance programme should be prepared to demonstrate the relationships between the individual's interest in lesson or skill and the chances of his achieving any proficiency.

  The use of this principle involves that the teacher should be careful not to tax the student too beyond his capability.

- **Pattern Learning:** Learning tends to proceed more rapidly and become permanent when the learner is provided with the opportunity for perceiving meaningful relationships among the essential elements of the goal towards which he is striving. The more clearly the pattern of an objective is understood the more permanent the learning tends to become.

- **Evaluation of Progress:** Evaluation and Measurement are applied in the classroom for objective assessment of the student's progress, and effectiveness of teacher's methods and school programmes and policies.

  There are several ways, which teachers can use to arrive at judgements of their student's abilities and academic achievements. Teachers ought to know the different kind of evaluations; pre teaching, during teaching, and post teaching. Evaluation may be may be used as a positive form of guidance to help the students to make accurate judgements about their own knowledge and skills.

- **Broad Based Integrated Development:** It is an accepted principle that a pupil learns most adequately when provided with those opportunities that satisfy his personal needs, e.g. personality adjustments and social growth. Learning is best promoted when the pattern of learning experiences is integrated with the pupil's fundamental organismic, personal and social needs. Development of an integrated personality is one of the main concerns of guidance.

Q24. Discuss classroom discipline and guidance methods for handling discipline problems in schools.

Ans. Guidance of pupil activities in terms of interest, motivation, and achievement serve as the key to well adjusted classrooms. Without some kind of order in the classroom, nothing much of educational value can be done. Guidance functions in all sorts of problems and situations, it is the help received by all personnel in the school system. Guidance is the help given whenever there are problems to be solved in teaching, in supervision, in discipline. In fact we can say that discipline offer us one of the most useful and challenging areas for guidance.

The class teacher in particular is most concerned about what is best for the student. This means that s/he has to play a judgement role in deciding what is good or bad for her students. To maintain a good learning climate, s/he must enforce the rules of the school and limit the activities of those who cannot discipline themselves.

The best working atmosphere exists in a classroom when the teacher helps his/her students become acquainted with school rules and regulations, tells them why such rules are made, and helps them learn how to assume personal responsibility for enforcing them.

Guidance Methods for Handling Discipline Problems

In working with discipline problems, guidance method can be used effectively. Perhaps the most important contribution of guidance to discipline is the use of child study techniques. All who work with a discipline problem should become acquainted with the child's needs and interests, his/her home background and the information on various aspects of his/her school performance, which can be obtained from the cumulative record and from case conferences. Knowing those factors, which have shaped the child's attitudes towards life and those around him, makes the teacher's task easier and more useful.

A Guide for Handling Discipline Problems

As in other social settings, every classroom will have a few students who will choose not to involve themselves in classroom activities and, instead, be disruptive forces. The teacher/counsellor is responsible for what is happening in the classroom, including not only the learning process taking place but also behaviour. As the teacher/the counsellor answers the following questions, s/he becomes better acquainted with himself/herself as well as the child and is able to identify the causes of the child's unacceptable behaviour:

- What did the child do the last time that s/he misbehaved in teacher/counsellor presence?
- How does teacher/counsellor feel about this child, outside of the incidents in which discipline problems arise?
- What did teacher/counsellor do when s/he misbehaved in teacher/counsellor presence the last time?
- Does teacher/counsellor have any information about his/her general health, his/her diet and his/her living conditions?
- Does teacher/counsellor know of anything which is worrying him/her?
- How do the members of his/her family feel about one another?
- What is most important in the life of the family as a group?
- How is the child disciplined at home? How does s/he feel about the restraints in the home and the methods of enforcing them?
- Did the child know what teacher/counsellor expected from him/her and his/her peers? Does s/he know what s/he should expect from his/her peers and teacher/counsellor?

- How does the pupil "rate" with his classmates? Who are his/her friends?
- What are the working conditions in classroom?
- What is the quality of the child's school work?

The child learns very early in life that there is some behaviour even his/her parents cannot tolerate. There are certain limits on his/her behaviour. But parents and teachers sometimes forget that it makes a difference how they enforce these limits. Teachers in particular need to remember that the child must understand the limits before s/he is expected to live within them.

In enforcing limits on the behaviour of individual student for the good of the whole class, the teacher should recognise that merely suppressing the child would not solve the problems, which account for his/her unacceptable behaviour. The child whom the teacher faces as a problem has taken months or years in learning to be what s/he is. Somewhere in his/her personal history, there is an explanation for his/her unacceptable behaviour.

Q25. What makes children misbehave in the class or outside the classroom?

Ans. Following are the possible contributors to classroom or outside misbehaviour:

(1) **Ignorance:** Ignorance of the rules is certainly one of the reasons for a student becoming a deviant. Even if a student is presented with a neatly organised set of rules, s/he never really knows which rules are operational and which are just on paper. So, they have a very practical way of solving this problem. They simply proceed to "try out" the teacher to see what they can "get away with".

(2) **Conflicting Rules:** When the behaviours that brought results at home (made parents happy) are deemed improper or immoral at school a student faces a conflicting situation, e.g. a neighbourhood kid knocked him/her down and s/he hit back for revenge. When s/he came home bleeding, the parents treated his/her injuries and never said a negative word or reprimanded him/her. The child repeated the same behaviour at school and was in for a great surprise when the teacher punished him/her.

It is obvious that a number of students break discipline, merely because they have failed to discriminate between the rules of the home and school situations.

(3) **Frustration:** Problems in maintaining classroom discipline have often shown that aggression in students increases significantly after they have experienced failure. There are at least three sources of frustration in a classroom that may influence any student:

(i) The teacher

(ii) His/her classmates

(iii) The activities

(4) Displacement: Inappropriate feelings are often displaced upon the people and objects in the school. For example, Ritu was quite open about the fact that she could not stand Miss Pooja or her Physics class. She never answered to any of the teacher's question. Miss Pooja had rarely heard her voice in the class. During practical periods also, she would ask fellow students to explain an experiment rather than ask the teacher. Miss Pooja never thought of this as unusual, but one day she happened to be passing the corridor where Ritu's classroom was and was surprised to hear her loud voice reciting a poem in the class. Next day Miss Pooja deliberately passed that corridor several times in the day and found to her surprise that Ritu was actively participating in all the subject classes except Physics. After talking with Ritu's parents, it came out Pooja was also the name of Ritu's step-sister with whom she did not get along and so the unusual behaviour in Miss Pooja's class.

Q26. Which factors influence the ripple effect in a classroom? Also, enlist example of teacher's use of focus-control techniques.

Ans. The "ripple effect" occurs when the teacher corrects a misbehaviour in one student, and this positively influences the behaviour of other nearby students. The ripple effect is influenced by the clarity, firmness and focus of the correction. The effect is greater when the teacher clearly names the unacceptable behaviour and gives the reasons for the desist. Firmness, that is, conveying an "I mean it" attitude, enhances the ripple effect. The following factors influence the ripple effect:

(1) Clarity: A 'clear control' technique is one that specifies the deviant, the deviancy and the preferred alternative behaviour. The teacher who hears a disturbance in the back of the room and yells, "Hey, you boys, stop talking", has used a control technique with no clarity at all. In addition to interrupting every other student within earshot, not even the deviants are sure that the reprimand was meant for them.

The same teacher might have walked towards the noisy group and said, "Raghav, Ali and Suresh, stop talking and get those algebra problems finished!" The clarity of this command is very high and can be expected to have two beneficial effects on the audience students:

(i)   They will be less likely to become deviant themselves.

(ii) Their learning behaviour is less likely to become disruptive than would be true for an unclear technique like the first one.

(2) Firmness: A 'firm control' technique has an "I mean business" quality about it. This may be accomplished by the teacher's tone of voice, facial expression, or gestures. It may also be accomplished by "follow-through", meaning some way of seeing to it that your disciplinary prescription is carried out, e.g. Rakesh was playing with a pen by hitting it on his desk again and again.

His action had got the attention of most of his classmates and the teacher's working on the blackboard was going unnoticed. She stopped abruptly and commanded in a stern voice, "Rakesh, put that pen in your bag and pay attention".

Focussing her whole attention upon Rakesh, the teacher followed his action of opening his bag-pocket, putting his pen inside and closing the bag and only after he looked at the teacher again did she resume her work.

(3) **Focus:** Two 'focus control' techniques are 'approval-focussed' and 'task focussed' control techniques. An **approval-focussed** technique depends for its effect upon the relationship between the teacher and the deviant while a **task-focussed** techniques "make connections" between the teacher's demand and the work to be accomplished.

Example of teacher's use of focus-control techniques:

(i) **Task-focussed:** "You must be quite during my class or else you will not be able to answer my questions afterward. I won't repeat this class".

Evidence has shown that task-focussed control techniques have a more desirable ripple effect than do approval-focussed methods.

(ii) **Physical Proximity:** While managing a class, the principle of proximity is also very useful. That is by making the offenders sit nearer to the teacher's chair, she is able to put a control over their mischiefs.

(iii) **Approval-focussed:** "I am very disappointed that you talked when I asked you not to. I thought you had more respect for me than that".

(iv) **Signal Interference:** Without using any words, angry or otherwise the teacher conveys to the indisciplined students that she knows about them and their misbehaviour. For instance, using an angry stare at them standing near their seats, etc.

(v) **Post-mortem Session:** When teacher finds a student misbehaving in the class, she does not say anything at that time other than saying in general "Behave yourselves". But after the class, she takes that student out of the classroom to have a discussion regarding his misbehaviour in the class.

(vi) **Motivational Recharging:** Sometimes, students misbehave in the class for the simple reason that they are bored with the routine. Some change in the teaching methods is preferable at this stage. For example, the teacher, in the beginning or at the end of the period, may play some short game with them to recharge their motivation., e.g. quiz, role-play, etc.

(vii) Comic Relief: This is another method to control students when they misbehave out of boredom. Here, the teacher makes some witty remarks and encourages the students to do the same.

Q27. Interpret the importance of art, health and physical education school curriculum.

Ans. The National Curriculum Framework provides the framework for making syllabii, textbooks and teaching practices within the school education programmes in India. The National Curriculum Framework (2005) emphasised the importance of art, health and physical education in the school curriculum. Mostly, schools do not consider these as curricular areas and do not pay much attention to them. These are usually considered as leisure activities and sometimes celebrated as cultural/sports day. The guidance workers and teachers should consider arts, health and physical education as curricular areas that have the potential to contribute to the overall well-being of the children.

Art Education

There are innumerable reasons for the arts to be included in an educational system, and just as many ways that involvement in the arts has been shown to help students in their personal, social, and academic development. All art forms (music, dance, theatre and craft) contribute to the development of the self, both cognitive and social. However, schools do not give any importance to art education. Schools focus on cognitive development of the children through the subject based curriculum. Children, who do not perform well in the school achievement tests are considered as under-achievers. Poor performances in the achievement tests slowly start eroding the confidence of the children in their abilities. School practices regarding subject-based curriculum do not encourage multiple ways of expressions by children. The singularity of expression expected by the schools through achievement tests, make some children poor performers. Using the art forms, the guidance workers and teachers can demonstrate to such children that they can explore and express knowledge in multiple ways, thus instilling confidence in their cognitive abilities.

Role-play is a powerful tool for exploring the self and its relation to others. Some children may need help in social and emotional adjustment with the self and others. Through role-play, guidance workers and teachers can help such children to explore and express their self and the self-other relationship. Thus enabling the children to discover the blocks in their social-emotional adjustment behaviour and learning to modify them for a healthy life.

Health and Physical Education

Health and Physical Education is the curriculum area that engages students in worthwhile learning experiences to develop skills, knowledge, self-efficacy and dispositions that will enable young people to live healthy and active lifestyles. Under nourishment and communicable diseases put many children at health risk. "Health is a critical input for the overall development of the child and it influences enrollment, retention and school completion rates significantly" (NCF 2005, p.56). Guidance workers and teachers, therefore, need to provide health and physical education to the children for their physical, social, emotional and mental development. Another concern is related to the reproductive and sexual health of the adolescents. Matters related to sex and sexuality are seldom discussed in the family environment. Therefore, guidance workers and teachers should be concerned about the reproductive and sexual health needs of the adolescents. The absence of proper guidance may prove risky to the physical and mental well being of the adolescents and their future life.

Q28. Describe about role of virtual world in guidance.

Or

How media is helpful in guidance? Discuss.

Ans. Social media are interactive computer-mediated technologies that facilitate the creation and sharing of information, ideas, career interests and other forms of expression via virtual communities and networks. Social media is all-pervasive in our life today. Children spend a lot of time browsing the internet and are active on social media – facebook, Instagram or any such platforms.

(1) **Guidance and the Virtual Media**: Advances in the information communication technology (ICT) have made it possible for the human beings to interact with each other in a virtual world without being physically present in the same location. We can access information from across the world at the click of a mouse. Similarly, information can be disseminated across the world at the click of a mouse.

(2) **Social Media:** Many children are users of one or the other social media websites and they spend a lot of their time online connected with the virtual communities. On social media, people create, share and receive unfiltered content. Therefore, guidance workers, teachers and parents need to be alert and guide children about the content they create, share and receive. Guidance workers and teachers should help the children to test the trustworthiness and reliability of the information they receive on their social media platforms.

(3) **Cyber Bullying:** Cyber bullying is the use of technology to harass, threaten, embarrass, or target another person. By definition, it occurs among young people. Often cyber bullying has serious consequences to the victim as the content used for bullying may be shared further among other people and remain accessible to many others for a long time. Victims may find it difficult to deal with prolonged cyber bullying. This may lower satisfaction, lead to emotional unstability, or

depression and in extreme case the victim ending life. Children should be, therefore, told about the possible online behaviour of the virtual community members and how to tackle it. Guidance workers and teachers should develop in children the confidence to seek help and deal with cyber bullying in the first instance itself.

(4) Cyber Ethics: The guidance workers, teachers and parents should develop awareness about ethical online behaviour in children. Children should be monitored for their online behaviour because the social media are free and unchecked. Everyone is free to express anything in any form. Such unbridled freedom in some cases may lead to irresponsible behaviour and children may come in conflict with the legal, moral systems of the society. Therefore, children should be told that certain online behaviours are unethical and unacceptable and they should refrain from indulging in such behaviours. For example, online behaviours such as the following are unethical and unacceptable:

(i) Cyber bullying which means creating, posting or sharing contents in any electronic form with the intention to cause hurt and harm to other people.

(ii) Accessing unauthorised resources of the internet.

(iii) Snooping into other people's computer files.

(iv) Destroying or damaging other people's computer files.

(v) Disregard for other people's privacy.

(vi) Stealing other people's intellectual property using any electronic device.

(vii) Appropriating other people's personal data and creating fake identity.

Q29. Discuss the need for guidance programme and personnel in schools.

Ans. The need for guidance programme and personnel in schools are discussed as follows:

Need for Guidance Programme

Life-problems are becoming more and more complex. Traditional morals and personal convictions concerning rightness and wrongness of attitude and behaviour are breaking down. Guidance is something that is no longer added to the educational programme but is an indispensable part of the programme itself. Today, the world has grown complex. In little more than one generation, our whole pattern of life has been radically changed. These changes make guidance services an invaluable and indispensable part of the education. Guidance should not be treated as a special psychological or social service, which is peripheral to education. Some hold the view that guidance is not possible without professional training. One can't deny the need for professional service to help the child to solve some of the more intricate personal-social problems peculiar to the child. However, one can visualise the role of guidance oriented teachers can play in furthering growth and development of children in areas such as academic, vocational maturity, personal and social development of the student.

Need for Guidance Personnel

The success of the implementation of guidance work in a school depends on the joint effort of all the school personnel. Every staff in a school has an important role to play in helping to achieve the objectives of school guidance work. All of them should recognise their own roles and contribute their effort in school guidance through their day-to-day contact with students.

The school students need guidance since they are still in the formative years in all the aspects of their personality. S/he is developing physically, intellectually and emotionally into what our culture intends, a well-adjusted member of society. Thus, one of the deep underlying reasons for adequate and well-trained personnel in guidance is basically the dependence of the young upon the adult. Another reason for maintaining guidance personnel in the schools arises out of the growth and development of a high degree of complexity in almost all aspects of social, professional, vocational and educational life. Nowadays our schools are not concerned with only the three R's. The home takes care of certain things like personal and social problems. However, as the times have changed, more and more responsibility has been with the trained personnel for guiding children and youth. The student must have help from trained personnel to know his/her own potentialities and limitations, to live satisfactorily. To meet the need for guidance, the school must secure an adequate number of well trained guidance workers. The concept of guidance was originally limited to vocational planning. Now it has been in use in a much broader sense.

Guidance is not the function of the school alone, but rather it is the joint function of persons within the school, the home, the community and the country. The guidance personnel assists the individual to develop and become more able to solve his/her problems and to live with satisfaction and benefit to himself/herself and to society.

Q30. Elucidate the role of guidance personnel.

Or

Describe the roles of counsellor, career master and teacher in the context of guidance services in schools.

Ans. The roles of three important personnel are given below:

(1) **Counsellor:** The counsellor is the nerve centre of the guidance programme. S/he should be a qualified guidance leader in a position to stimulate, initiate and organise the guidance programme in the school.

The Counsellor should collect information about the pupils through testing and non-testing techniques and school examinations. Blanks, checklists, interest inventories, sociograms and autobiographies are some of the non-testing techniques, which the counsellor can use for collecting information about pupils.

The counsellor should be able to administer various psychological and intelligence tests, interest inventories, and aptitude tests.

The following is a list of duties and responsibilities of the counsellor:

(i) To explain the guidance point of view to all members of the school faculty and parents and to introduce guidance programmes in the school with their active co-operation.

(ii) Organise the school guidance committee.

(iii) Set up an educational and occupational information centre/corner in the school.

(iv) Give orientation talks to pupils regarding guidance services available in the school.

(v) Orientate pupils and their parents regarding the curricular offerings, work experience programme, co-curricular activities programme available in the school.

(vi) Orientate pupils of X class regarding the courses—educational and vocational—available to them.

(vii) Orientate pupils regarding scholarships, stipends, grants, loans, freeships and concessions available and the eligibility requirements for them.

(viii) Collect, classify and file educational and occupational information.

(ix) Display educational and occupational information in an attractive way.

(x) Disseminate educational and occupational information through educational and career talks, group discussions or film shows.

(xi) Arrange career talks by experts from different fields.

(xii) Organise career days, career weeks and career conferences.

(xiii) Organise parents' day.

(xiv) Prepare news albums.

(xv) Organise a 'Guidance News' section in the school magazine.

(xvi) Acquaint pupils with proper study habits and assist them in their development.

(xvii) Introduce cumulative record cards and get them maintained with the co-operation of other members of the faculty and use them in guiding the pupils.

(xviii) Arrange individual discussions with pupils and parents for giving them educational and occupational information.

(xix) Arrange visits to places of work like industries, business establishments, offices, higher educational institutions.

(xx) Help in the placement of pupils.

(xxi) Maintain an active relationship with the state bureau and the district offices in the State.

(xxii) Administer psychological tests.

(xxiii) Provide counselling service to the pupils, and also cater similar needs of other local high/higher secondary schools, if so requested.

(xxiv) Conduct research projects relating to the field of educational, vocational and personal guidance in the high/higher secondary schools and convey the findings to all concerned.

(2) Career Master: The career master is not supposed to operate counselling service. If a pupil expresses his desire for counselling or appears to be in need of counselling, the career master should refer such a pupil to the visiting counsellor/district counsellor, if there is one.

The Career Master's responsibilities are restricted in scope as compared to counsellor's but they form a part of the essential service. The major responsibilities of the Career Master are educational and occupational information service and the related work. S/he has to discharge these duties even in the absence of a counsellor in the school, which is the case with many of our schools.

Formal training to in-service teachers comprising information services should be a prerequisite for one to work as a Career Master. This type of training is imparted to school teachers by the State Bureau of Educational and Vocational Guidance and the duration of such courses varies from 2 to 4 weeks.

The career master should introduce the cumulative record cards and get them maintained with the help of other members of the faculty. He should use them when he discusses with pupils their educational and occupational needs and future plans. Consideration of height, weight or vision, for instance, may rule out certain occupations for certain pupils. The information can also be helpful in referring problem pupils to the proper agencies for further guidance. Besides, on the basis of the information provided in the record cards, the career master can assist the pupil in making more appropriate choice of elections, improve his study habits and plan his future vocation better.

(3) Teacher: The teachers occupy the pivotal position in a guidance programme. It is they who have the closest; the most frequent, and extended contacts with the pupils in a natural situation. A guidance service can never become an integral part of an educational programme without their co-operation.

The teacher's role in school guidance programme is as follows:

(i) The first line of contact between the student and the school guidance programme.

(ii) Identification of needs and problems of students.

(iii) Setting up and maintenance of Career Information Centre in the school – for educational and career planning.

(iv) Creating a harmonious and sound classroom environment for the student.

(v) Support and create a motivating environment for school guidance programme.

(vi) Creating a positive attitude among the students, parents and all others concerned towards school guidance programme.

The teachers observe the student in the classroom, in the library, on the sports field, and during the short intervals between classes. And, in such daily contacts they are in an enviable position to detect early symptoms of any abnormality in their make-up and draw the counsellor's attention.

The teacher employs a number of techniques to affect pupil guidance. S/he gains knowledge of the pupil and his/her environmental opportunities. The teacher gains deeper understanding by testing, by observing, by keeping anecdotal records and by talking with pupils, with parents and with other individuals. Many facts of the life of the student are made clear to the teacher. Knowing the pupil is an indispensable basis for guidance. As the teacher becomes aware of the more difficult problems, s/he may be able to offer guidance him/herself or refer such cases to specialists.

The Teacher as Guidance Worker: The teachers can contribute to the guidance programme by introducing the pupils to careers in their particular field. It is often difficult for pupils of high school age to understand why some courses of study are included in the curriculum. A survey of the careers to which the study of a particular subject will contribute and acquaintance with the accomplishments of others in the field, should give young people a deeper understanding of opportunities open to them and aid them in planning their careers. Vocational motivation also increases the students' interest in the subject.

Good guidance is not a duty in excess of teaching load but it is part of that load, and should not be made an additional burden.

The teacher can prevent maladjustments. The teacher who teaches academic subjects and teachers of Physical Education, Yoga, etc. courses have opportunity to gain close rapport with students. The teacher has two main functions in guiding their students; classroom counselling and vocational guidance.

As a classroom counsellor, the teacher should endeavour to develop the best personal, social and educational qualities in each student. As vocational guide, the teachers have opportunities to assist students with their occupational plans.

Teachers' Co-operation: Teachers cooperate with specialists along three lines.

(i) recognise individual students who need the help of a specialist.

(ii) supplying information about the student referred, and

(iii) helping to carry out the specialist's recommendations for an individual or a group.

The teachers' opportunities for guidance while teaching may be summarised as comprising following seven kinds of action:

(i) Sharing educational goals with students;

(ii) Individualising instruction;

(iii) Building self-esteem and competence;

(iv) Using personal relationships;

(v) Following up student needs;

(vi) Guiding daily learning; and

(vii) Discussing common problems.

Q31. Discuss the comparative roles of counsellor, career master and the teacher.

Ans. The comparative role of each of the personal, viz., counsellor, career master and teacher are as given in below table:

Table 1.2

S.No.	Counsellor	Career Master/Teacher
(1)	Conducts classroom session, "careers for future".	Plans activities with counsellor.
(2)	Conducts session on "skills for living and working".	Plans activities showing importance of discipline to living and working.
(3)	Administers interest inventory.	Assists counsellor.
(4)	Conducts group sessions on, "personal needs and wants".	Develops activities that challenge students to evaluate personal needs and wants.
(5)	Conducts classroom session on "Entrepreneurship".	Plans classroom sessions and activities.
(6)	Conducts classroom session on, "Planning a high school curriculum based on a career goal".	Relates course of study to various careers. Plans activities which give students the opportunities to explore their career goals.

(7)	Plans group and individual sessions on "Preparation for Employment".	Discusses emotional and physical development and how they can affect employment opportunities.
(8)	Plans role playing sessions and other activities.	Plans activities with counsellor.
(9)	Conducts classroom session on, "Career clusters and occupations".	Coordinates with counsellor.
(10)	Plans activities showing various career avenues (apprenticeship, college, preparatory school, technical, on the job, etc.).	Supports activity with assignments (written, oral). Media specialist, provide information and materials.
(11)	Conducts classroom sessions on how business/industry in community affects lives.	Coordinates with counsellor.
(12)	Explores resources available for career information.	Coordinates with counsellor.
(13)	Conducts individual counselling and classroom sessions on, "What the employer expects from employees".	Co-ordinates with counsellor.
(14)	Conducts classroom session on "Financial Aid".	Coordinates with counsellor.
(15)	Arranges for student experiential assignments at a worksite.	Plans oral and written assignments based on assigned work experience.
(16)	Conducts group and individual sessions "The work ethic".	Coordinates with counsellor.
(17)	Provides and assists students with career information resources.	Plans activity using information.
(18)	Conducts classroom session; "Symptoms of stress and anxiety and how to cope".	Coordinates with counsellor
(19)	Coordinates and supervises group activities related to job seeking skills.	Plans activities involving job seeking skills.
(20)	Conducts classroom session; "Resumes, applications and interviews".	Coordinates with counsellor to develop skills in writing resumes, applications and attending interviews.

(21)	Conducts group session; "The economy and employment".	Plans with counsellor.
(22)	Conducts classroom session "How society's needs influence business and industry".	Coordinates with counsellor.
(23)	Provides individual and group sessions discussing life styles as they relate to careers.	Coordinates with counsellor.
(24)	Conducts individual and group discussions on "Career decisions".	Plans activities for developing decision-making skills.
(25)	Conducts classroom session on "Your health and your career".	Coordinates with counsellor.
(26)	Conducts classroom sessions to organise a job fair.	Coordinates with counsellor.
(27)	Conducts classroom individual and group sessions, "Careers and life-long learning".	Coordinates with counsellor.

Q32. What steps are involved in the organisation of need based minimum guidance activities in schools? Briefly discuss the role of personnel in this regard.

Ans. The steps involved in the organisation of need-based minimum guidance activities in schools are as follows:

   (1)   Formation of guidance committee
   (2)   Chalking out the annual programme of work
   (3)   Meeting of the guidance committee
   (4)   Orientation to new entrants
   (5)   Group guidance activities of the different types like:
      (i)   Class talks
      (ii)   Career talks
      (iii)   Career conferences
      (iv)   Career exhibition
      (v)   Career visits
      (vi)   Career fair
      (vii)   Career corner and its maintenance

Formation of a Guidance Committee

The school Guidance Committee is part of the selection of the programme structure, and the established leadership is responsible for the design of the programme.

While forming the guidance committee, the constituency of the committee should be as follows:

(1)	Head Master/Principal	– President
(2)	Counsellor/Career Master/Teacher	– Secretary
(3)	All the subject teachers	– Member
(4)	Chairman of the village panchayat/municipality	– Member
(5)	Representative of the School Management Committee	– Member
(6)	Representative of the Parents Teacher Association	– Member
(7)	Local/secondary school Head Master	– Member
(8)	Local Doctor	– Member
(9)	Representative of Agriculture Department	– Member
(10)	Representative of Industries and Commerce Department (Extension worker)	– Member
(11)	Representative of Police Department	– Member
(12)	Representatives of Voluntary Agencies like Rotary, Lions, Jaycees, etc.	– Member

This committee will be the policy-making as well as the progress reviewing body. The guidance committee should meet once in a month or two depending upon the nature and discussions to be carried out on the agenda.

With the help of the guidance committee, the Teacher or Career Master develops the annual programme of guidance work and gets it approved in the meeting. The annual work plan should be need based one and it should not dislocate the regular work of all the concerned.

Orientation to New Entrants

Orientation activity helps students to be familiar with the school, courses, activities, facilities, staff, etc. and adjust to the school environment and develop positive attitudes.

Orientation could be done through group and individual activities, like organising assemblies, class talks, discussions on school regulations and programmes and also by providing individual assistance in adjustment.

Community Resources in Terms of Personnel

The local community members can be treated as a resource. Organisations concerned with human resource development such as the YMCA, YWCA, Scouts and Guides, Lions, Jaycees, Rotary and others serve in various ways. Parents have the earliest and strongest influence in guiding the child. They guide individually and as organised groups such as the PTA and through evening classes in family life education. Technically and professionally trained personnel in such organisations or departments as health office, psychiatric clinics, welfare agencies, police departments, fire departments, industrial and business organisations, and almost all of the community organisations can at times play a role as guidance personnel in schools.

The students get influenced by many people, such people can be considered as optional or unofficial guidance personnel. The responsibility for directing the programme rests with the career master/teacher and the other are supplementary resources.

Q33. Define individual counselling. Also, enumerate the various benefits and issues of individual counselling given by Dryden.

Or

What are the advantages of individual counselling? Also discuss various issues involved in individual counselling.

Ans. Individual counselling is a one to one interactive situation involving a counsellor and a client. The use of interactive skills helps to build a relationship and provides a communication base to facilitate positive outcomes. Individual counselling can help to deal with many personal topics in life such as anger, depression, anxiety, substance abuse, marriage and relationship challenges, parenting problems, school difficulties, career changes, etc.

With the trusting relationship of an individual counselling session, the counsellee, can focus on personal problems, conflict areas, affective confusions. The counsellor's skill and knowledge provide the framework and direction that maximise the client's potential for positive outcomes. Untrained and unskilled helpers, in spite of their best intentions, cannot duplicate the functions of the professional counsellor.

Following are the benefits of individual counselling given by Dryden (1984):

- Individual counselling provides an opportunity to develop closer relationship between counsellor and client. Group counselling situation may be threatening to some people initially.
- Individual counselling is therapeutic when clients' major problems involve their relationship with themselves rather than their relationship with other people.
- Individual counselling is helpful for clients who want to explore whether or not they should differentiate themselves from others. For example, those who are unhappy in their relationship but are not sure whether to work to improve the relationship or to leave it.
- Individual counselling provides complete confidentiality. People who are not comfortable with disclosure before others would prefer individual counselling.
- Individual counselling is beneficial for clients who have profound difficulties sharing therapeutic time with other clients.
- Individual counselling is helpful for clients who wish to differentiate themselves from others. For example, those who

have decided to leave a relationship and wish to deal with individual problems that this may involve.

- Individual counselling offers counselors an opportunity to vary their interactive style with clients free from the concern that such variation may adversely affect other clients present.
- Individual counselling can be conducted to match the client's pace of learning.

Dryden (1984) has also pointed out some issues involved in individual counselling, which are given below:

- Close proximity/interaction may be threatening to some clients.
- Clients who are shy, retiring and afraid to take risks may benefit more from group counselling.
- In individual counselling the client may become over dependent on the counsellor and hinder the healing process. In group counselling intense dependency is less likely as the counsellor has to relate to many others.
- Individual counselling situation may not provide enough challenge for change to clients.

Q34. What is the meaning of group counselling? Describe the assumptions of groups counselling.

Ans. A group counselling is usually comprised of six to eight students who meet face to face with one or two trained group therapists and talk about what most concerns them. Members listen to each other and openly express thoughts and feelings about what other members do or say. These interactions give members an opportunity to increase understanding of self and others, try out new ways of being with others, and learn more effective ways to interact. The content of the group sessions is absolutely confidential; members must commit to confidentiality: that is they may talk about their own experience with whom they choose, but may not identify other members or what they say outside of group.

The Assumptions of Group Counselling

There are some certain assumptions of group counselling. The first assumption is that individuals possess the necessary talent and capacity to trust and to be trusted by other group members. They should exhibit a basic concern for others in the group. This encourages group cohesion and provides an atmosphere of support and security for each member of the group to experience and share individual problems.

The second assumption is that each individual has the potential to take responsibility for self-change. On the other hand, if the individual feels that his life is controlled by others, he will not be left with any alternative but take recourse to disruptive behaviour.

The third assumption is that group members can learn and understand from the objectives and methodology of group process. The objective is to reform the members and not to make them conform.

Q35. How do you structure the groups for group counselling?

Or

Delineate structuring of groups for group counselling.

Ans. We structure the groups for group counselling in the following manner:

(1) Selection and Induction of Members: Prior to assignments to group, a personal interview is the most frequently used procedure for selection and induction of members for group counselling. The initial interview gives the counsellor an opportunity to establish identification with the members so that feelings of respect, acceptance and assurance is experienced from the beginning. To help the individual decide whether s/he wishes to join the counselling group the counsellor briefs him of the nature of the work, how it can benefit him, what can be expected and the rules concerning confidentiality, etc. This interview helps the counsellor to decide whether an individual will be helped by group counselling and also whether a particular group will benefit or lose by one being a member.

(2) Size of the Group: The size of the group should be relatively small for group counselling. Although it is difficult to recommend a specific number, as a rule of thumb, about six to ten members could be there in a group. Big groups become unmanageable. But too small groups are also not desirable because the group resources will be too limited and the tension too gets great due to the pressure to participate. Moreover, in too small a group, where one or more members are absent by chance, the functioning becomes almost impossible.

(3) Composition of the Group: There is controversy regarding the composition of groups for counselling. Opinions differ as to whether the group should be homogeneous or heterogeneous with respect to problems, education, intelligence, age, sex and so on. Homogeneous groups are composed of individuals who are similar, such as adolescent boys, single parents or individuals working with grief and loss issues. Heterogeneous groups are made up of people who differ in background, such as adults of various ages with varied careers. While homogeneous groups can concentrate on resolving one issue, their members may be limited experientially. In contrast, heterogeneous groups offer diverse but multi-focussed membership.

A group composition can be done in the following ways:

(i) heterogeneous groups made up of members with 'various' complaints and symptoms

(ii) grouping clients with similar concerns and similar purposes for group counselling because, the similarity facilitates a working bond and a more cohesive group relationship in the session

  (iii) grouping in a similar age range permits the group to focus on developmental concerns appropriate for all members.

(4) Frequency and Duration of Meetings: Various recommendations have been made regarding the frequency of meetings. The population and the sittings in which group counselling occurs determine the frequency and duration of meetings. Weekly and twice weekly meetings are recommended most often. In a community agency, college or in private practice two-hour weekly sessions are optional. But in the school settings shorter durations, twice a week may be more suitable because of the shorter attention span of younger students. Moreover, they will miss less class period. In schools, groups usually run from 11 to 15 weeks. It is more convenient and at the same time, it ensures a reasonable amount of time for the group to attain its goals.

(5) Physical Setting: Physical setting is less important in comparison with emotional atmosphere and the skill of the counsellor. A skillful counsellor and the group obviously will function more effectively on a poor physical setting than an inept one and his group in an ideal setting. However, privacy and freedom from interruptions are of course important. The room should be small rather than large. Seating should be flexible and varied. A circular seating arrangement with each member sitting where he pleases is to be preferred to a formal arrangements and permanent seat assignments.

Q36. Elucidate the process of group counselling.

Or

Which stages are involved in the process of group counselling?

Ans. There are four main stages of group counselling process. Once the group is formed there is generally a pre-group meeting. Each group member is screened to make sure they will be an asset to the group rather than a setback. These stages are given below:

(1) Initial Exploratory Stage: The first stage of a group is the initial stage. The purpose of the initial stage of a group is to establish expectations of what the group is going to be like. These expectations include trust, roles, and goals. Confidentiality and conflict need to be addressed immediately. Also, any culture concerns must be dealt with. The counselors are there to explain the process and to support each member when dealing with confrontation. The group members must be participatory and involved. This can be tricky with court appointed group members but if the expectations of involvement are explained thoroughly they will learn that it is either participate in the group or face legal consequences.

(2) Transition Stage: The transition stage is a very difficult stage to get through. This stage comes after the initial stage and is when most of the group members feel anxious about sharing their feelings with strangers. Some members become defensive and resistant while others may be shy and fearful. It is the role of the counselor to keep the transition period on track and as pleasant as possible. This stage can be extremely uncomfortable for the counsellor as they may be confronted, belittled, or attacked. If the counsellor is good at leading groups the group will learn to trust and respect the counselor during this stage by leaving the negativity out. For the members to get the most out of the group they must participate cordially and this includes listening and giving advice.

(3) Working Stage: Once the transitional stage has settled, group members will start to feel comfortable enough to really get into the deeper issues that the group was designed for. This is called the working stage. This stage comes after all the kinks get worked out during the transition stage and is when each member is able to explore their thoughts and emotions which may be triggered by someone else's words. The counsellor in this stage will guide the group through this process using techniques and challenges that bring out emotions.

A good counsellor will know how to guide by using minimal words themselves. Counsellors should be able to read each group members verbal and non-verbal language. Group members in this stage need to be honest about their feelings and not be afraid to speak their mind. They should not feel as though they are being judged or criticised and if they are, it is the counsellor's job to address these issues.

(4) Consolidation and Termination: Termination may be determined by the counselor or by the group members and the counselor together'. Termination, like all other stages of the group counselling experience, requires skill and planning by the counselor. It is most appropriate when the group goals and the goals of the individual members have been achieved and new behaviours or leanings have been put into practice in everyday life outside the group.

At times, the group members resist termination of a counselling group and continue indefinitely as the counselling group provides a base for interpersonal relationships, open communication, trust, and support. Therefore it becomes important that from the very beginning the group counselor keeps on emphasising the temporary nature of the group and establish, if appropriate, specific time limitations and reminds the group, of the impending termination as the time approaches.

Under less favourable circumstances, groups may be terminated when their continuation promises to be nonproductive or harmful, or when group progress is slow and long-term continuation might create over dependency on the group by its members.

The point of termination is a time for review and summary by both counselor and clients. Some groups will need time to allow members to work through their feelings about termination. Even though strong ties may have developed along with pressures from the group to extend the termination time, those pressures must be resisted, and the group must be firmly, though gently, moved towards the inevitable termination.

Q37. Enlist the advantages and limitations of group counselling.

Ans. Advantages and limitations of group counselling are as follows:

Advantages

- Groups provide support and make one realise that other students experience similar challenges. S/he is not as different or alone as s/he thinks.
- Groups provide a sounding board. Groups can offer a different perspective. The student can receive support and share his/her wisdom.
- Groups can propel the student forward. Hearing from others on how they've overcome can be encouraging. During the group experience, s/he will likely meet people representing a wide variety of backgrounds and experiences. Listening and learning from every member's perspective provides members with greater insight into his/her personal growth and development.
- Groups promote social skills. While it is common for students to feel anxious prior to attending their first group, most students feel relieved and more comfortable as the session's progress. We should remember, it takes time to feel comfortable speaking up in a group, adjust to group norms, and experience the benefits of group. It is important that that students share at their own pace.
- Groups are not limited. There are no session limits on groups and the student fees have already paid for the service, so it's a way to receive more counselling than is possible individually.
- Groups teach students about themselves. Groups can be a way of uncovering the areas that may be blocking their ability to overcome their issues.
- Group helps individuals to socialise their attitudes, habits and judgements.

Limitations

Group counselling is not suitable for all individuals. Some individuals find the group situation too threatening. Moreover, some individuals have a very low level of tolerance and will not be able to adopt their behaviour to the demands of the group. Similarly, very personal and private problems cannot be discussed in the group situation. Apart from these, the counsellor has less control over the situation in group counselling. As a result, the counsellor may sometimes find himself seriously impeded in establishing good working relationship with members.

Therefore, the counselor has to take into consideration all these factors and decide whether group counselling is suitable for particular individuals and type of problem.

Q38. What are the similarities and differences between individual and group counselling?

Ans. Following are the similarities and differences between individual and group counselling:

Similarities

- The objectives of both techniques are similar, i.e. helping the counselee achieve self-integration, self-direction and responsibility.
- In both the techniques, the counsellor presents an accepting, permissive climate for the clients to participate freely such that their defences are reduced.
- Both techniques aim at clarifying feelings, restatement of content, and the like. The counsellor helps the client to become aware of their feelings and attitudes and also to examine them.
- Both approaches provide for privacy and confidentiality of relationship.

Differences

- Individualised counselling is a one to one, face-to-face relationship marked by intimacy, warmth and rapport between the counsellor and counsellee. In group counselling, there is the physical proximity of other members with perhaps similar problems. The client may obtain solace from the knowledge that he is not only one with problems and that there are others who have similar problems.
- In group counselling unlike in individualised counselling, the counsellees not only receive help but also give help to others. The more cohesive the group, the more are the members able to help one another. This cooperative feeling brings the members closer, which in turn helps in facilitating the mutual expression of feelings.
- The counsellor's task is somewhat more complex in group counselling. He has not only to follow sense and appreciate what a member says but also how this affects other members and their reactions. The counselor in a group-counselling situation has more demands to meet and satisfy.

Q39. What do you understand by peer counselling? Enumerate some of the benefits of peer counselling.

Ans. Peer counselling refers to people who stutter helping each other by listening, sharing common experiences, exploring options and giving support. Peer counselling is based on communication, empathy and understanding. People who stutter can provide peer counselling in a variety of settings including one to one or in a self-help group.

In school settings, peer counselling means one student counselling another student or a group of students. Peer counselling gains importance, as many schools do not have a regular full-time trained professional counsellor. Even if the school has a regular counsellor, it is difficult for a counsellor to deal with the varied needs of so many students in a school. Then, there are many students who may not find it easy to open up to the teachers or counselors if they are in distress or trouble. Naturally, we may be thinking now if the peer counselors may be able to handle complex situations/issues. Our concern is well placed. The idea is to use peer counselors in appropriate situations.

Peer counselling or peer mentoring is not a new concept although it is gaining momentum these days. Certain boarding schools have been practicing a type of peer mentoring for a long time. Often a senior student plays the role of a mentor/buddy to two or more new entrants in the school. This senior student provides mentoring to the new entrants by familiarising them with the school routine, helping them to adjust socially and emotionally in the new environment away from home, guiding them in different academic tasks, etc. In day scholar schools too, some teachers have always encouraged peer mentoring. Teachers often would ask a peer to 'tutor' other students who experience difficulty in any particular academic learning activity. Teachers used peer counselling in the school because they found it beneficial to their students welfare. Some of the benefits of peer counselling are:

- It is economical as the peer counselors are drawn from the student population.
- Peer counselling enhances the school counselling programme.
- Peer counselling benefits both the peer counsellor (mentor) and the counselee (mentee).
- Peer counselors bridge the gap between the students and the professional counsellor.
- Peer counselling is informal, therefore, the client can approach the counsellor without any inhibition.
- Peer cousnelling brings more students to the fold of the counselling programmes.
- Peer counselling is easily available.

Q40. Identify the various functions of peer counsellor in the school settings.

Or

Which functions can be performed by the peer counsellor in the school settings? Discuss.

Ans. Some of the functions that the peer counsellors can perform in the school settings are given below:

(1) Supporting in Academic Activities: Students who experience difficulties in certain areas of learning can be tutored by peer counsellors. The peer counsellor is paired with a student or group of students who may need additional help in different learning activities. For example:

    (i) providing help in understanding a difficult learning content.

    (ii) helping student to develop better study skills.

    (iii) helping a student who returned to the class after a long leave of illness.

    (iv) helping students to manage their time better.

    (v) helping a student to improve his/her reading/writing skills.

(2) Helping in Resolving Conflict: In a school, students come from different social, cultural and economic background. They also come with different types of abilities. During secondary school stage, students go through one of the most crucial stages of their life, adolescence. All these factors cited here, can contribute to conflicting situations very often in a school. Peer counselors can mediate between students and help them in resolving their conflict.

(3) Inducting New Comers: Initially, children experience difficulties in adjusting with the new settings when they join school. When children enter school the first time, senior students can act as peer counsellors (also known as cross-age counsellors/mentors) to acquaint them with the school functioning and help them in adjusting socially and emotionally in the new settings. The peer counsellor can do the same for a peer who has come from another school. The new entrant can be helped by the peer counselors to get familiar with the school routine, ethos and socio-cultural environment. Such a helping relationship makes the new entrant feel accepted in the new settings.

(4) Helping in Preventing Absenteeism and Dropout: Some students keep away from school without informing or taking leave. In certain cases, truancy may also lead to dropping out of the school. Peer counselors can interact with such students and motivate them to attend the school.

Q41. Mention the guidelines/steps one can follow when setting up a peer counselling programme.

Ans. Following are some guidelines we can follow when setting up a peer counselling programme:

(1) Conducting Need Assessment Survey: Before designing the peer counselling programme, teacher should conduct a survey to identify the areas of development (academic, social and emotional adjustment, interpersonal skills, etc.) that need intervention. Then s/he should assess if peer counselling is a desirable option for developing these areas.

(2) Defining the Goals: The students population a teacher to want to serve and areas of development s/he have identified for the programme are important factors which affect the peer counselling programme. The design of the programme whether same-age group (peer counselling) or cross-age group (senior-junior) may also determine the goals of the programme. Defining the expected outcome brings clarity to the specific activities to be undertaken, the resources needed for the activities, the partnership involved in the activities, etc.

(3) Selecting the Peer Counsellors: The most important partners in the peer counsellling programme are the peer counsellors. Therefore, we should be very careful when selecting the peer counselors. Peer counsellors should exhibit characteristics that are found in good counsellors. Therefore, we may select those students who have demonstrated:

(i) empathy;

(ii) self-confidence;

(iii) the ability to listen to others;

(iv) non-judgemental behaviour;

(v) an innate need to help others;

(vi) pluralistic orientation;

(vii) good communication skills; and

(viii) trustworthiness.

(4) Training the Peer Counsellors: After identifying the peer counsellors, the next task is to train and prepare them to play the role of peer counsellors. Such a training programme should be conducted by a professional counsellor.

(5) Defining the Roles of the Partners: There are different players in a peer counselling programme. Hence, it is important to define the role of each player. A coordinator is needed to coordinate the activities of the different players in the programme. For the success of the programme, first we should identify the different partners and then define the role of each of them.

(6) Enlisting Support of the School Administration: Without the support of the administration, we cannot conduct any activity in the school. Support from the principal, teachers and staff is crucial for the success of the programme.

Q42.Explain the concept of multicultural counselling in the functioning of the schools.

Ans. Cultures have a significant influence on our life. We are surrounded by our culture everywhere and culture influences each and everything we do and think. Culture influences our perceptions, thoughts, feelings and actions. Therefore, we need to be aware of the influence of our culture on our behaviour.

According to Gertz 1973; Maruyama 1992; Seeley 2000, multicultural counselling can be defined as "Becoming a multicultural counselor does not only mean gaining more knowledge of other cultures, but even more it means understanding the complex processes through which people become members of communities and societies and construct their worldviews, basic attitudes, values, norms, etc."

Multicultural counselling evolved as an effort to understand what happens when a professional counsellor works with clients from a different socio-cultural background and how the differences affect the quality of the interaction and healing process. Indian population is constituted of multiple identity, i.e. diverse culture groups, castes, tribes, socioeconomic class, religion, language, minority, gender, age, sexual orientation, geographical location, etc. This reality is reflected in the school population also. Teachers and students may not come from the same background. There exist differences in the student community too. Therefore, multicultural counselling gains importance in the school counselling programme. In multicultural counselling a counsellor needs to acquire and demonstrate additional multicultural competencies. Multicultural counselling involves gaining knowledge about the culture of the clients, understanding the process of socialisation in their culture and understanding the complex process through which they construct gender-role identity, values, attitudes and world views. Multicultural counselling requires that as a counsellor we reflect on the 'self' and identify our beliefs, values, attitudes, biases, prejudices and world views about those who are different from us. Being self-aware and learning about the clients' culture help us to develop appropriate intervention strategies and techniques for addressing the clients' realities.

Q43.Discuss about crisis counselling. Identify a few crisis situations that may occur in the life of a student.

Ans. Crisis involves a threat and an opportunity. Crisis is also a turning point. Crisis intervention is a short-term counselling aimed at reducing the impact of the crisis situation that the individual faces and helping the individual to take the necessary steps in making the best use of the crisis.

In this kind of counselling, the counsellor has a supportive role. The main goal of this counselling is to help the client to identify the unhealthy coping mechanisms and replace them with more healthy ones.

Giving proper insight, helping the person to make use of all his/her physical, psychological and spiritual potentials are important aspects of crisis counselling. The individual in a crisis condition is often out of touch with reality. His/her thinking is unrealistic and irrational. The concern of the crisis intervention counsel is to help the client to overcome his/her irrational thinking and accept reality and its consequences.

Crisis is a turning point. A person in crisis is like a stranger at a junction, unable to make a decision as to which way s/he should turn.

The counsellor can effectively support him to see where he wants to go and how s/he can go there.

Following are some crisis situations that school children may face in their life:

- **Child Abuse:** Children who have been physically or sexually abused exhibit many mental disturbances such as anxiety, aggressive behaviour, suicidal behaviour, poor self-esteem, depression, substance abuse, etc. School counsellors have to often deal with the resulting impact of child abuse in the form of disruption of classroom teaching, abuse and bullying on playgrounds, anti-social behaviour in classes. These need to be handled by teachers and in more severe cases, the school counsellor. Awareness about the issue needs to be created among all, more specifically parents need to be helped to develop strong bridges of communication with their children.

- **Severe Illness:** Prolonged or severe illness may be a reason for crisis in a child's life. The child herself or a family member may be suffering from serious illness. There is stigma attached to illness such as HIV/AIDS. Statistics show an increasing incidence of HIV/AIDS in Asian countries which is a cause of great concern. Awareness especially needs to be created in the youngsters as they stand more vulnerable to such problems due to lack of information and facilities. School teachers and counsellors should be made well aware of the factors causing it. The teachers/counsellors need to collect the relevant information and communicate the same for creating awareness. Anyone has a risk of getting infected, therefore it is essential for everyone to be aware.

- **Suicide Prevention:** The phenomenon is on the increase in recent years. Schools serve as the building blocks in an individual's life, therefore, teachers and counsellors can play a vital role in preventing suicide. Through the coordinated actions of teachers, counsellors, peers, parents, children can be helped to build value systems, explore self-identities, establish meaningful goals, build coping mechanisms to face adversities of life. Counsellors and teachers need to be aware of the causes and the characteristics to identify those who may be prone to suicide.

Q44.Elucidate specialised areas in counselling as family counselling, career counselling and counselling for prevention of substance abuse.

Ans. Family counselling, career counselling and counselling for prevention of substance abuse are given as follows:

- **Family Counselling:** Family counselling, like the name suggests, is a type of therapy that involves the whole family. The idea behind is it is that families having difficulties or that have one person who is going through a tough time go to see a counsellor/therapist and try to sort out the issues together.

Family counselling passes through four specific stages. Initial stage consists of developing a relationship and assessing the problems. In the middle stage family members develop an emotional understanding of the reasons behind their problem. Ending stage is helping the family learn alternative ways of behaving thus transforming the family system. Termination stage is the weaning period where the family helped to function productively without the help of the counsellor.

In the initial sessions, counselors try to establish rapport, confidence and trust. Each member is treated as important and insist that members should speak for themselves. Members are promoted to speak out what they think as their problem and also to discuss their expectations of the family.

In the middle stage, members are helped to arrive at an emotional understanding of the problem. Counsellor becomes more confrontative leading to emotionally charged disclosures. Expression of unresolved grief like death of loved one, divorce, loss of childhood, etc. is encouraged at this stage. Here members begin to realise that relationships can be changed for the better. With this, roles become less rigid and communications become direct and constructive.

In the ending stage, members are encouraged to generalise these changes to interactions at home and in the termination stage the family is weaned and helped to function productively without therapists help. Review of what happened, discussion of potential problems ahead and how they intend to handle the matter, etc. are helpful here.

- **Career Counselling:** Career counselling is a global approach to individuals under all aspects of their personal, professional and social life. It consists in providing information, counselling and guidance services with a view to supporting each and every person – in any stage of their life – in the development of their own career through decision-making as regards to education, work, and community life. Clients are helped to select, prepare to enter and function effectively in an occupation in career counselling.

  According to E.G. Williamson (1939), client problems could be classified into four categories, viz. no choice, uncertain choice, unwise choice and discrepancy between interests and aptitudes. Process of counselling in these context is very much similar to that in general counselling because the development choice and establishment of a career are closely related to social and environmental influences and personality development.

  Client problems are identified and clarified through establishment of rapport and on the basis of information so gathered, the counsellor forms a tentative hypothesis. Client problem resolution is then accomplished with the help of the counsellor followed by evaluation. The major difference being that in career counselling additional information is gathered in occupational areas. Occupational history is reviewed, resort to occupational testing if need be and exploration of occupation and training possibilities are made. Finally decisions about career choice or development are taken.

- **Counselling for Prevention of Substance Abuse:** Substance abuse counsellors provide a necessary support system for individuals recovering from eating disorders, drug and alcohol issues, gambling addictions, and other behavioural issues. By forming a relationship built on trust with their patients, counsellors provide the support, resources, and judgement-free guidance that patients can utilise on their road to addiction recovery.

  Counsellors in this field help addicts with both crisis and long-term addiction management issues, which can range from immediate medical intervention, to supporting them manage their recovery long-term.

  Counsellors after ruling out the need for hospitalisation inducts the client into the counselling programme. They insist that the client abstain from taking drugs, as the first step. Because without that, proper rapport or communication is impossible. Family members are also counseled and made aware of their faulty roles, dysfunctional communication, etc. which have caused or precipitated the problem. Both the client and family members receive help to develop feelings of self worth and responsibility for their behaviours. They learn to express their needs more directly. Through exploration of childhood experience they become aware of repressed negative emotions that are affecting their present behaviour. They also learn new ways of dealing with stress. Drug addicts should receive group counselling because they often lack social skills.

Q45. Enlist and explain the problems in evaluation of effectiveness of counselling.

Ans. Counselling outcomes are not so easily amenable to evaluation. The question of suitable criteria poses serious difficulties. It would be of help to list briefly some of the problems inherent in the evaluation of counselling outcomes.

- One of the major objectives of counselling concerns personality growth. The concept of personality growth cannot be defined easily in operational terms. It is so broad and vague that no two psychologists would define it in identical terms. Naturally, this creates problems in setting up appropriate criteria for evaluation.

- The goal of counselling is sometimes defined as helping the client to secure self-direction and self-dependence. With such a goal evaluation is not going to be a simple process.

- The most important aspect of counselling is giving the client a feeling of well-being. This is a subjective experience and evaluation, in this sense, has to be on the basis of the subjective criterion of the client's experience, which often suffers from serious shortcomings.
- The outcomes of counselling for each counsellee will be unique, complex and dynamic. No single tool can adequately assess changes in all the outcomes. Evaluation, therefore, becomes a very challenging task.
- One of the important requisites of evaluation is that the pre-counselling status of the client be available for comparison with his post counselling status. Quite often the pre-counselling data are not available, thus making meaningful evaluation impracticable.
- It is sometimes pointed out that evaluation should be independent, which means that a third agency other than the client or counsellor should evaluate the outcome so that the evaluation is more objective, reliable and dependable. The very nature of counselling is such that it precludes the third party approach in any meaningful way. However, this does not mean that such an evaluation is impossible or that it cannot be done.
- Evaluation is a time consuming process and involves not only monetary but also personnel resources. While it may be feasible to find funds it is comparatively difficult to find trained personnel who are well versed with the techniques of evaluation.

Q46. What are the different ways of evaluation in effectiveness of counselling?

Ans. Following are the different ways in which evaluation is done for effectiveness of counselling:

(1) **Survey Approach:** The counselling outcomes can be evaluated by employing the survey approach. The survey approach is simple and is commonly employed in several disciplines. It consists of identifying the population and obtaining a representative sample from it, collecting information or evidence from the subjects in the sample, employing a suitable evaluative schedule and making judgements in terms of the pre-determined criteria. In this approach, the clients could be asked questions, such as how they feel about the effectiveness or usefulness of counselling, whether they have specifically profited from it, what flaws they have observed, what suggestions they could offer for improvement and so on. Information on such items from a number of clients could be useful to assess, in broad terms, he effectiveness or usefulness of counselling. One of the practical problems of the survey approach is the non availability of subjects for questioning. The other common criticisms relate to issues, such as the unreliability of subjects' answers, the

tendency on the part of the subjects to give socially desirable responses and the like. Still other serious drawbacks of this approach are the lack of experimental validation, sampling errors leading to biased conclusions and difficulties in inferring causal relationships.

(2) Case Study Approach: The case study approach is designed to study the individual and assess the changes that take place in him as a result of his exposure to counselling. The advantage of this approach lies in its emphasis on the individual and his growth. It is considered to be a more reliable approach. The drawback of this approach is that, by its very nature, it is a time-consuming method. Also, since each individual is unique, generalisations from individual data are open to serious limitations. The massing of data pertaining to different individuals may obliterate the unique features of the individual approach.

The obvious advantage of this approach lies in the in-depth nature of the studies. However, from the methodological point of view, it is an idiographic approach (which is an individual approach) as contrasted with the homothetic approach (which is generally considered the scientific approach).

(3) Experimental Approach: The experimental approach in the counselling situation is fraught with serious problems, for an experiment involves controls. In the counselling situation, control is very difficult. However, in a limited sense the experimental approach could be employed to evaluate the counselling outcomes. The basic requirements of this approach are: (i) determining the objectives, (ii) choosing appropriate methods, (iii) selecting two or more groups of subjects who are comparable with one another, (iv) applying counselling techniques, which could be measured or scaled, and (v) measuring or assessing the final outcomes. The vital step in this approach is the study of two or more comparable groups. This is a tall order, for with all the, ingenuity at our disposal it would not be possible for us to assemble groups of subjects who are comparable with one another to control several variables such that the independent variable of the counselling process could be related to the outcome of it (dependent variable).

✍ ✍ ✍

Techniques and Procedures

Chapter 2

INTRODUCTION

The fundamental purpose of guidance is to develop in each individual up to the limit of his/her capacity the ability to solve his/her own problems and to make his/her own adjustments. The techniques which are generally employed by guidance worker for collecting basic data about the individual are either standardised or non-standardised. The non-standardised techniques include interview, ratings, questionnaire, observation, sociometry, biography, cumulative record, anecdotal records. The standardised techniques are tools of measuring interests, intelligence, aptitudes and personality traits. To organise a school guidance programme, some of the preliminary steps to be undertaken are formation of guidance committee, arrangement of required facilities, budget and orienting the students, parents and community. Evaluation of the guidance programme also forms an essential component in a school guidance programme.

Q1. Explain the term 'techniques of guidance'.

Or

Describe the major techniques of guidance.

Ans. The aim of all guidance is to assist the learner to acquire sufficient understanding of himself/herself of his/her environment to be able to utilise most intelligently the educational trained opportunity afforded by the school and community. Children come into world genetically endowed with all their human potential for growing, developing and learning. Guidance is one of the means employed by educationist to develop the human potential. The child learns from a teacher, not only mastery over a particular subject but also develops social proper values, attitudes and habits.

Guidance is providing help to one person in making choices and adjustment and solving problem. It aims at aiding the recipient to grow in who, independence and ability to be responsible for one. The techniques which are generally employed by guidance workers for collecting basic data about a person are either standardised or non-standardised ones. The standardised techniques are tools of measuring interests, intelligences, aptitudes and personality traits. Both the categories of techniques are used in getting primary data either it be standardised or non-standardised. All the techniques are useful. The only consideration, which the guidance worker should keep in mind, is that the techniques employed should give reliable and objective information. Standardised tests of intelligence, interests and aptitudes provide reliable and valid information. Non-standardised techniques used in the study of human being are also useful and helpful. These techniques are commonly employed for individual analysis by counsellors in various settings. These techniques provide a broader variable and more subjective approach to data gathering and interpretation for human being is also useful and helpful.

Q2. Describe 'questionnaire' and 'observation' as non-standardised techniques of guidance.

Ans. Questionnaire

A questionnaire is a device consisting of a series of questions dealing with some psychological, social, educational, etc; topic(s) sent or given to an individual or a group of individuals, with the object of obtaining data with regard to some problems under investigation. Goode and Hatt (1952, p. 33) state that in general the word 'questionnaire' refers to a device for securing answers to a series of questions by using a form which the respondent fills in himself. The questions in a questionnaire are basically of two types:

> **(1) Close-ended Questions:** This type of questionnaire includes questions with 'yes' or 'no' type answers, short answers or checking of alternate responses to some test items.
> *For example*:
> (i) Gender ☐ Male/Female

(ii)   How often do you watch Discovery Channel on TV?
Every day/once in a week/Occasionally/Never

(2)   Open-ended Questions: There is provision of a student's free responses in his/her own words in such questionnaires. It makes a student's picture more clear regarding his/her experience about something, some event or some process.

For example:

(i)   Which types of programmes do you like to watch on TV?

(ii)   What steps would you like to take to improve science teaching in your school?

Observation

Observation is one of the most frequently used ways to gather information and get a picture of what's happening in the school or classroom. We can use it to assess students' performance in various co-curricular activities. Systematic classroom observation is a quantitative method of measuring classroom behaviours. Information about a child (his/her behaviour) can be collected in and outside the class through observation. Observation can be used as a tool of assessment in a variety of situations like debates, elocution, group work, practical and laboratory activities, projects, play fields and school prayers, clubs and festivals. Observation can be biased and subjective. However, such errors and risks can be substantially reduced by using an observation schedule. Observation schedule is used to collect information systematically and with objectivity.

Q3. Delineate 'sociometry' and 'autobiography' as non-standardised techniques of guidance.

Or

Explain sociometry as a technique of guidance.

[June-2018, Q.No.-3 (c)]

Ans. Sociometry

Sociometry is developed by Jacob Moreno for the purpose of facilitating group task effectiveness and satisfaction of participants by bringing about greater degrees of mutuality amongst people and greater authenticity in teacher-student relationship. Teachers know that the groups of children they work with are more than an aggregation of individuals. They know that the groups have form and structure that there are patterns of sub-groups, cliques and specific friendships.

Sociometric techniques measure the inter-personal preferences among the members of a group in reference to a criterion. The purpose of this technique is to measure each individual's social worth or personal value as viewed by his peers. According to Barclay (1966), sociometry is a method of discovering and analysing patterns of friendship within a group setting.

There are usually three types of sociometric techniques, i.e. (1) the nomination, (2) the social acceptance and (3) the 'who's who' or 'guess who'. In the nomination techniques, the student is asked to select and name his/her peers in terms of some criterion suggested by the teacher. For example, the teacher may ask students to name three best friends in the class. In the social acceptance technique, levels of social relationship are stated and the student is asked to express his/her sociometric choice. In the 'Guess who' technique, brief descriptions of various types of students are provided and they are asked to guess who in the class matches with the description. For example, one of the statements may be 'The boy is always in trouble with his parents', who?

In order to determine the internal social structure in a class, a teacher may construct a sociogram. A sociogram is simple to construct and may provide valuable information on the social structure of a class.

Autobiography

Autobiography means life-sketch written by a person himself. In autobiography, descriptions regarding a person's past and present moments are given. If psychologists want, they can give different titles to the autobiography. A person describes his own aims of life, achievements, interests, desires, events, reactions, etc. with a touch of reality in the autobiography.

As a guidance technique for studying the individual, it gives valuable information about the individual's interests, abilities, personal history, hopes, ambitions, likes, dislikes, etc. In guidance, structured autobiographic items are given to the individual and s/he is asked to write them out.

Q4. Identify 'rating scales' as a non-standardised technique of guidance. Also, explain the characteristic situations and limitations of rating scales.

Ans. In guidance programme, use of rating scale is becoming more popular. Rating is a technique in which we systematise the expression of opinion concerning a particular trait.

According to **Ruth Strang**, "Rating is, in essence, directed observation."

According to **A.S. Barr and others**, "Rating is a term applied to expression of opinion or judgement regarding some situation, object or character. Opinions are usually expressed on a scale of values. Rating techniques are devices by which such judgements may be quantified."

A rating scale is a selected list of 'words, phrases, sentences, paragraphs, following which an observer records a value or rating based on some objective scale of values'.

In a rating scale, the characteristics are rated according to given number of points. The points are in terms of grades or numbers. For example, meeting strangers may present a serious problem to one individual and no problem at all to another. Between these two extremes, the seriousness of the problem may differ from one individual to another. The ratings may be qualitative or quantitative. For example, seriousness of the problem may be rated as below:

Table 2.1

Qualitative Rating	Quantitative Rating	Grading
Never a problem	0	E
Seldom a problem	1	D
Occasionally a problem	2	C
Fairly serious problem	3	B
Serious problem	4	A

Characteristic situations in which rating scales are used given below. These are the situations when no other technique gives reliable and valid measurements of the individual's characteristics seeking educational or vocational guidance.

- Rating scales are used to supplement the information collected by standardised psychological tests. For example, a test of achievement is administered to a class of students. The test results can be verified with the help of ratings the class teacher has given to them.
- In situations when the construction of standardised tools for studying the individual require special expertise, money and time, information can be obtained through rating scales which are relatively easy to prepare.
- Areas, which cannot be objectively measured.
- In guidance and counselling when self-analysis and self-evaluation by the client is needed. Self-rating scale provides useful information for self-analysis, which leads to better self-understanding.
- In situations when the guidance worker wants to collect information about many things and many students in a short-time, teacher's ratings could be obtained.

Limitations of Rating Scales

- These scales are subjective.
- They lack reliability.
- In making decision with the help of rating scales, no one works hard.
- It is very difficult to assess the inferiority complexes, self-dependence, etc. by these rating scales.
- Sometimes, a person's own feelings and sympathy makes him more generous while rating something and he will try to hide the defects of other persons or his fellows.
- Halo error is possible, i.e. rating on the basis of previous experiences.
- Some raters like to give average rating.

Q5. Enlist and explain different types of rating scales.

Ans. Following are the different types of rating scales:

    (1) Descriptive Rating Scale: In such a scale, the trait described in words is to be tick marked as in the blank space left before the statements concerning that trait.

> *For Example:*   - Is this pupil physically active?
>   - Lazy
>   - Smart
>   - Over Smart
>   - Lazy and Passive

In such scales, words like seldom, all and never are used. Such as, does this pupil obey his teachers? While responding this question, take care of the fact whether the pupil obeys all the time or seldom or never. Only one alternate is to be tick marked out of these.

(2) Numerical Scales: In such scales, scores are assigned to each trait. Also, such scales can be of various types. This classification is on the basis of scores, such as 3-point scale, 5-point scale and 7-point scale.

If it is 3-point scale, each statement carries three options of responses. The pupil is asked to tick mark that response with which he agrees. In this 3-point scale, score of '3' means that maximum occurrence of that trait of which the score of '3' is assigned. Similarly, in 7-point scale, the score of '7' indicates the occurrence of maximum quantity of that trait to which the score of T is assigned.

(3) Rank Order Scales: In this type of scale, descending ranks are given to the pupils. In this rank order, the pupil is placed at some specific rank. In this method, the pupil is placed at the rank according to his talent. This is to be done by those teachers who teach him. Then all the ranks given by all the teachers are subjected to the calculation of an average rank. In this method, statistics is used.

(4) Graphic Scales: Graphic scale is also known as 'Behavioural Statement Scale'. It is similar to descriptive scale. The difference lies in writing only. This scale is used frequently. In this scale, line is divided into many parts and the traits are written on these parts. The pupils are asked to tick mark anyone of these traits. Guilford as advocated some principles for the construction of such rating scales, which are as follows:

(i)   The line should be of 5" length.

(ii)   The line should not be interrupted by the gaps.

(iii)   3 or 5 adjectives should be used.

(iv)   Neutral or average words should be placed in the centre.

(v)   Distance between marked symbols may not be equal.

(5) Paired Comparison Scales: In this, no scale is used. According to this method, a person is examined by pairing him with the other members of the group in rotation. Then, a decision is taken whether he is better than the other or not. Such comparison are then treated with statistics and analysed.

The persons subjected to the comparison are placed in an order.

(6) Forced Choice Scales: Sometimes, in the process of determining the rank, the person doing this job fails to express his decision regarding the ranking of the person. It usually occurs in the descriptive and graphic scales. In order to remove this defect, forced choice methods are used. In this method, a person is forced to choose one pair of two alternates. Hence, this method is helpful to know a person's exact idea. To make the choice out of the following alternates is an example of this method.

(i) He is an effective teacher.

(ii) He has developed rapport with pupils.

(iii) He studies regularly.

(iv) He comes to the level of the pupils.

Q6. Elucidate 'anecdotal record' as a non-standardised technique of guidance. What are its basic considerations and uses?

Or

Write down few basic considerations to keep in mind while maintaining anecdotal records of students.

Ans. Anecdotal records are systematically kept notes of specific observations of student behaviours, skills and attitudes in the classroom. Anecdotal records provide cumulative information regarding progress, skills acquired and directions for further instruction. Anecdotal notes are often written as the result of ongoing observations during the lessons but may also be written in response to a product or performance the student has completed. Systematic collection of anecdotal records on a particular student provides excellent information for evaluation of learning patterns and consistency of student progress. Well-kept anecdotal records provide a valuable, practical and specific reference about a student.

An anecdote may be compared to a snapshot of an isolated incident of the behaviour of the student, which suggests some special significance. Just as a camera catches the pose of an individual at a given time, similarly the anecdote should report exactly the behaviour observed. If we accept the uniqueness of the individual as a basic principle of guidance, this word snapshot is of immense significance to us for guidance purposes. An individual's behaviour is always in response to some felt need.

(1) Maintaining Anecdotal Records: An anecdotal record is the result of observation by a teacher about the specific behaviour of the student in a situation. It is written down to get a better understanding of the student because the teacher may forget the incident if it is not written down. The teacher writes down what s/he observes and does not give any remarks. S/he may describe the behaviour and say something by way of comment or s/he may describe the behaviour and suggest possible remedial measures.

(2) **Areas to be Noted Down:** Haphazardly noting down bits of information serves no purpose. Hence, in the proforma supplied, areas are clearly marked, on which observations are to be made. An anecdotal record is a record with a purpose. For instance, a boy's interest in industrial work may be exhibited by his article on the visit to a local factory. A girl's interest in a literary magazine may be indicative of her literary taste. A teacher can find many such occurrences in the life of his/her students, of which s/he has to make a note. For example, a boy's comment on a radio newscast is a good item for an anecdotal record if he is interested in studying the text for current history. A girl's comment on some recent scientific invention may show her interest in science. An anecdotal record is of special interest in understanding social and emotional behaviours. If a boy is found sitting alone when all are rejoicing and making merry in a holiday excursion, shows that he has some emotional problems.

(3) **Longitudinal Approach:** Only those anecdotal records are of any help to the guidance worker, in which behaviours of an individual are described over a long period of time. Longitudinal anecdotal records maintained from the nursery school to the high school are very useful. The anecdotal record file should not contain irrelevant material. The file should be scrutinised from time-to-time and irrelevant material may be removed. Anecdotal records pertaining to all aspects of life should be maintained.

A few basic considerations to be kept in mind are given below:

(i) Reports should be of some significant episodes. The episode described should show a marked tendency from the norm of the individual or the group.

(ii) The anecdotes should be the reports of the actual observations and written just after the events.

(iii) The form should be short and informal.

(iv) Both positive and negative incidents of behaviour should be noted down.

(v) The anecdotes should be written about all students and not just about the high achiever or the problematic ones, i.e. stereotypes.

(vi) We should know what to look for, where to look for and how to record.

(vii) A single incident is of no value.

(4) **Uses of Anecdotal Records**

(i) Anecdotal records are of special value in indicating social and emotional situations.

    (ii)   A healthy teacher-pupil relationship is established when teachers are asked by the school organisation to write down anecdotal reports.

    (iii)   Anecdotal records supply useful information about the individual's personality characteristics, reactions to different situations, interests in studies/vocation and interpersonal relationships. They give a realistic picture of students' personality.

    (iv)   Systematically kept anecdotal records provide an exceedingly valuable information to the counsellor.

    (v)   Anecdotal records are very useful in fields where formal measurements are very difficult. For example, in judging sociability, social alertness, social behaviour, attitudes, acceptance of personal responsibility and work habits.

**Q7.	Interpret 'case study' as a non-standardised technique of guidance. Also, enlist facts to be collected in a case study.**

Ans. A case study is an analysis and documentation of data collected in a case history. It comprises the information gathered about a client, including the family history, physical development, etc. Educational, social and vocational history is also covered in the case study.

Shertzer and Stone (1981) defined the case study as "the collection and report of all available evidence social, psychological, environmental, vocational, that explains the individual, including an analysis of the interrelationships among the various data" (p. 294).

A case study is initiated when a teacher, counsellor, administrator or parent believes that a student may need to be placed in an exceptional class, is not achieving as s/he should, or is constantly fighting with other students. In such instances, the student may be referred to the counsellor. The teacher may indicate the reason for referral either in writing or orally to the counsellor. If the counsellor believes that the student needs additional help, s/he may refer the student to the school psychologist.

The purpose for writing a case study is to organise, summarise and analyse this enormous amount of data. Once this is completed, the school psychologist can determine whether placement in a special education class or referral to another professional such as psychologist or psychiatrist is needed. Whatever course of action is decided upon, everyone involved must place the welfare of the student as top priority.

Facts to be Collected in a Case Study: A case study about a person presents basic information on the following topics:

    **(1)	The Physical, Socio-economic and Cultural Environment:** The physical environment includes the neighbourhood in which the individual has grown up and now lives, rural/urban, working/middle class surroundings, living in own/rented/makeshift home, small/large house, etc. The socio-economic environment refers to the society in which the individual is brought up and its condition regarding material prosperity.

(2) Family: Numerous diverse information about the family has to be collected to understand the characteristics of the individual being studied.

What is the status of health and physique of the family members – father, mother, brothers and sisters? Are most of these members active, lethargic, strong or frail?

What is the educational or occupational status of the family members? What are their special abilities or disabilities?

Is there harmony in the family or is it a broken family? Does the individual get proper care and security? What has been the attitude of the parents towards the individual – affectionate, indifferent, dominating or interfering?

(3) Personal History of the Individual Under Study: The study of the individual is to be made in a similar way as done under family history.

(i) Individual's Physical Health: Has the physical growth been normal as shown by height, weight measurements or by age, of walking, talking and reaching puberty? Has there been some illness or physical defects, for example, those of hearing and vision? Is the individual by appearance active, vigourous or ailing? What are the findings of the medical check-ups?

(ii) Individual's Abilities: Has the individual been given tests of intelligence? What is his ability? Has his mental development been normal or has he developed certain faculties earlier than normal? Has he done well or poorly at school?

(iii) Emotional Development: Is he emotionally mature or unstable? Does he show strong antagonism, jealousy or affection? Is he timid, anxious, worried, nervous or withdrawing? Is he bad-tempered or hard to control? Is he good-natured and overconfident?

(iv) Social Development: What is his position in the family? Is he the only child, a favoured child or the eldest child? How does s/he get along with siblings? How does s/he get along with his classmates? Is s/he shy or retiring? Is s/he a leader, follower or isolate? Is s/he a bully who uses his/her strength or power to hurt others? Does s/he show manners which are disliked by his/her companions? Is s/he in the habit of antagonising others?

(v) Ideals and Attitudes: Is s/he a person who believes in ideals? Has s/he sophisticated tastes? Has s/he ever been a delinquent? Has s/he ever created troubles at home, in the school and in the community?

Q8. Discuss 'cumulative records' as a non-standardised technique of guidance. Also explain the need and importance of cumulative record.

Ans. For providing suitable guidance and counselling to youngsters, it is essential to procure full particulars about them. The form in which this information is stored is called the 'cumulative record'. This cumulative record is the prime requisite for the study of a student or an individual. Without this documentation, no guide or teacher will have adequate information about a student or an individual's personality, his behavioural pattern, his aptitudes and abilities.

In order to provide counselling and guidance to the pupils, various types of information related to the pupils are collected. After their collection, the style in which these are maintained is known as cumulative card.

Cumulative records usually contain a section on personal and family background, where a teacher may find the student's address, date and place of birth, and telephone number. Also included are the names of the student's parents with information about whether they are living or deceased, married, divorced or separated. Additionally, the record of enrollment, race and primary language spoken at home may be included.

Need and Importance of Cumulative Records

Cumulative records usually provide useful information about students to teachers, counsellors and administrators. The need and importance of cumulative records are given below:

Importance in Guidance

- The basic principle and assumptions of guidance take into consideration the individual differences. Every individual differs from the other in some psychological character, quality or trait.
- The cumulative record is a permanent history of the educational development of the individual student. It indicates his/her attendance, health, achievement and various other aspects of school life. Hence, it is useful in analysing the future needs of the individual student and proper educational and occupational guidance can be offered on the basis of his/her needs.

Importance in Teaching

- The cumulative records of different students help the teacher in classifying students in accordance with scholastic aptitudes and mental abilities.
- Cumulative records indicate to teachers about students who need individual attention.
- The cumulative record of an individual student indicates if the achievements cunts are in proportion to his/her mental abilities. If the student is under achieving, s/he can be guided as to what steps s/he should take to remedy the defect.
- Teachers can locate children needing special help and adjust the teaching accordingly.

- They are diagnostic tools to analyse a behaviour problem or an educational one. For example, why is a student backward in academic performance? What steps can be taken to remove his/her backwardness?
- For making case studies, the cumulative record is very useful to teachers, because there is some similarity of items collected.
- The cumulative records of different students of a class help the new teacher in understanding the needs of students.
- Cumulative records help the teachers in writing reports about individual students, and the principal in writing a character certificate most objectively.

Importance to Administrators

Cumulative records give enough information to the juvenile courts, probation officers for understanding the delinquent behaviour of a student.

The cumulative record is needed by teachers/counsellors for the same reason as that a cumulative record is maintained by a physician. Records maintained over a long period of time tell the story of growth and deterioration of the client.

Q9. What are the characteristics of a good cumulative record?
Ans. Guidance is provided to students on the basis of accumulated information only. In other words, these cumulative records are extremely useful in providing significant information about students. Hence, it is necessary that they should have the following characteristics:

- **Simple and Complete Information:** A good cumulative record should contain complete information about a student's progress, as incomplete information does not give a clear picture for proper guidance. Hence, to present a clear picture about a student, there should be a brief account of all the various situations of his/her student life written in simple language.
- **Factual Information:** To ensure the validity of a cumulative record, it is essential that it should contain factual information only. Hence, only the observed facts should be recorded.
- **Secrecy:** It is essential to maintain secrecy of information contained in the cumulative records. New information should not be influenced by previous information.
- **Re-evaluation:** It is essential to carry out timely evaluation of the cumulative record. On the basis of re-evaluations, necessary changes can be made and new information can be incorporated in the records.
- **Continuity:** Continuity is of prime importance in an ideal cumulative record, so that it is easy for anybody to peruse it. Continuity means updating information regularly.
- **Group-based Evaluation:** In order to make cumulative record more reliable and valid, facts should be entered after evaluation or verification by a number of different teachers.

- **Usefulness:** Information contained in the cumulative record should lend itself to easy retrieval and interpretation for more meaningful and extensive use.

Q10. Define interviews. Enumerate different types of interviews.

Ans. Students' answers on tests don't always show their true level of understanding. Sometimes they understand more than their answers indicate, and sometimes, despite their regurgitating the correct words, they don't understand what they write. The interview discusses a method to probe what they actually understand.

An interview is a conversation with a purpose. According to Bingham and Moore, it is a serious conversation directed towards a definite purpose other than satisfaction in the interview itself. The purposes for which interviews are arranged are introductory, fact finding, evaluative, informative and therapeutic in nature. Other characteristic is the relationship between the interviewer and the interviewee. The occasion should be used for a friendly informal talk. The interviewee should be allowed to talk in a permissive atmosphere with confidence and freedom.

Following are the different types of interviews:

- **An Employment Interview:** Its purpose is to assess the fitness of a person for the job. The interviewer talks too much and the interviewee too little. S/he simply answers the questions asked.

- **A Fact Finding Interview:** The purpose of this interview is the verification of facts and data collection from other sources.

- **Diagnostic Interview:** The purpose of a diagnostic interview is remediation. An effort is made by the interviewer to diagnose the problem of the interviewee and find out symptoms.

- **Counselling Interview:** The purpose of a counselling interview is to provide an insight, a suggestion, or a piece of advice to the interviewer. The counselling begins with the work of collecting information and proceeds with guidance and finally ends with psychological treatment of the problem.

- **Group vs. Individual Interviews:** When several persons are interviewed in group such an interview is called group interview, but basically all group interviews are individual interviews because it is not the group that is interviewee. The purpose behind group interview is collecting information and the knowledge of common problems facing the wound up. In the individual interview, the emphasis lies on the problem faced by the individual.

- **Authoritarian vs. Non-authoritarian Interview:** In the authoritarian type of interview, the client and his problems are submerged and the interviewer dominates the interview because of the elevated position that he holds. The non-authoritarian rejects the authoritarian role. The interview may still regard the interviewer as a man of authority, but the interviewer does not act as an authoritarian. S/he accepts the feelings of the clients and does not reject them. S/he uses a variety of techniques during the interview such as suggestion, persuasion, advice, reassurance, interpretation and giving information.

- **Directive vs. Non-directive Interview:** In the directive interview, the interviewer directs, shows the path through advice, suggestion, persuasion or threat. But in a non-directive interview, it is assumed that the interviewee has the capacity to grow and develop. S/he has complete freedom to express his/her feelings and emotions. The interviewer does not try to probe into the past of the clients makes no suggestion. S/he does not try to re-educate or change the climate.

- **Structured vs. Unstructured Interviews:** In the structured interview, a definite set of questions is predetermined. The interviewer confines himself/herself to only those points, which he decides to discuss in the interview. In a structured interview, definite questions are asked.

Q11. Enlist the guidelines to make an interview successful.

Ans. The guidelines to make an interview successful are given below:

- The counselee should feel the need of interview and counselling.
- Interview should start with cordial and pleasant greetings and should not indicate that one has authority over the other.
- Interview situation should offer a good listening by one who has greater experience and training.
- When the counselee expresses himself/herself, s/he should be accepted. The counsellor will gain nothing by antagonising or embarrassing the counselee.
- A rapport should be established between the counsellor and the counselee. It is a sort of personal relationship of mutual trust and respect based on the feelings of confidence and security.
- The counselee should be allowed to take the lead in making decisions.
- Discussion should be restricted to issues at hand.
- The interview should end with a constructive note.
- Interview should aim at helping the counselee gain insight into the problem and reach conclusions.
- The counsellor should have all relevant data about the client before he starts counselling.

Q12. What are the advantages and disadvantages of interview as a technique of guidance and counselling?

Ans. Following are the advantages and disadvantages of interview as a technique of guidance and counselling:

Advantages

- It is very flexible. It is useful in almost all situations and with all people having different backgrounds.

- It has a great therapeutic value. An interview establishes a face-to-face relationship between the interviewer and the interviewee. The direct relationship gives a great insight into the problem faced by the client. The interviewer gets about the client knowledge, which has a great therapeutic importance.
- The face-to-face contact gives very useful clues about the client's personality. The facial expressions, gestures, postures convey meaning and reveal feelings and attitudes indirectly.
- Interview is useful to the client also because it enables him to think about the problem. It is the most useful situation in which the client gets a better understanding of his 'self; his abilities, skills, interests and also of the world of work, its opening and their requirements.
- It is a widely used technique in guidance because personal data can be more easily collected in much shorter time by using this technique.
- Interview provides a choice to the client and the counselor to exchange ideas and attitudes through conversation.
- It serves a variety of purposes.
- Interview is helpful in diagnosing a problem. It is very helpful in revealing the causes of a problem faced by the client. Hence, some psychologists regard interview a very useful technique for diagnoses and remediation.

Limitations

- The personal bias makes the interview less reliable and valid.
- The usefulness of an interview is limited. The success of an interview depends on the personality qualities of the interviewer, his preparation for the interview and the way in which he interviews. If the interview monopolises talking or does not listen patiently to what the client says. The interview loses value.
- An interview is a subjective technique. It lacks objectivity in the collection of data about the client. The bias and the prejudices of the interviewer enter into his interpretation of the data collected through an interview.
- The results of an interview are very difficult to interpret.

Q13. **Describe aptitude tests as a standardised technique of guidance. Also, explain different types of aptitude tests.**

Or

Discuss the concept of 'aptitude tests'.

Ans. An aptitude test is an exam used to determine an individual's propensity to succeed in a given activity. Aptitude tests assume that individuals have inherent strengths and weaknesses, and have a natural inclination towards success or failure in specific areas based on their innate characteristics. An aptitude test does not test knowledge; it is not a test for which a person can study. The aptitude tests are also used for guidance, as well as prediction of success in some occupation. Training or academic courses are possible on the basis of scores on standardised aptitude tests.

Aptitude tests may potentially be used by counsellors and others because:

- they may identify potential abilities of which the individual is not aware;
- they may encourage the development of special or potential abilities of a given individual;
- they may provide information to assist on individual in making educational and career decisions or other choices between competing alternatives;
- they may serve as an aid in predicting the level of academic or vocational success on individual might anticipate; and
- they may be useful in grouping individuals with similar aptitudes for development and other educational purposes.

There are different types of aptitude tests. Some of them are single aptitude tests like tests of mechanical aptitude, clerical aptitude, teaching aptitude, musical aptitude and so on. Such tests covering a group of related abilities are necessary for performing in an occupation like becoming a mechanic, clerk, teacher, musician, etc. Another type of aptitude test is work sample aptitude test. It requires the individual to perform all or part of a given job under the conditions that exist on the job. An example of a work sample test for the job of automobile mechanic is to repair a faulty carburetor. Besides this, there are differential test batteries as well. A commonly known is Differential Aptitude Tests (DAT). Bennett, Seashore and Wesman (1984) battery consists of eight subtests of verbal reasoning, numerical reasoning, abstract reasoning, spatial reasoning, clerical speed and accuracy, mechanical reasoning, language usage, spelling and grammar occupations. Such test batteries can provide comprehensive information about the relative picture of the student's specific abilities. Administration of total battery can prove to be costly in terms of time but one can make selective use of certain sub tests. For example, a student trying to explore whether s/he will have the required aptitude to go to engineering, may not be required to take tests like clerical speed, language usage, grammatical or verbal reasoning tests but may be required to take numerical abstract and spatial reasoning tests. Most of the batteries of tests available for assessment of aptitude at school stage are in the form of test batteries consisting of the underlying abilities required for success in different occupations rather than direct assessment of job aptitudes.

Q14. Explain in brief about achievement tests.

Ans. Achievement is what one successfully accomplishes in an area of study/activity/domain. In the case of students, it may be conceptualised as successful learning of the assigned educational material. Such learning is usually demonstrated to teachers and others either through a verbal presentation or a written examination.

An achievement test measures knowledge and skills attained by the student in a particular area, usually acquired after classroom teaching or training. In an educational system, achievement test scores are often used to determine the level of instruction for which a student is prepared, to indicate academic strengths and weaknesses, and to indicate the relative standing of the student in a group/class. Achievement test data, in combination with other data, is used to help guidance counselors plan student's future educational programmes.

Q15. Define 'interest inventory' as a standardised technique of guidance. Enlist its purposes.

Ans. An inventory is a kind of self-report instrument that measures tendencies or traits with the help of responses to certain questions or statements. An interest inventory is one such inventory. In 1907, Hall, a psychologist, created standardised Recreational Interest Inventory and in 1934, Kuder, another psychologist came up with standardised Occupational Interest Inventory.

Interests are related to general ability, special aptitudes and values in various ways. Linguistic and scientific interests are positively correlated with intelligence, technical interests are related to mechanical aptitude and business interests are related to the tendency to stress material as opposed to theoretical, social or aesthetic values and so on.

Interest testing is done to achieve some purposes, i.e.

- to help the students to identify and clarify their interests in terms of the demands of varied courses and careers and choose work and experiences consistent with their interests.
- to help channelise the energies of the youth in appropriate directions.
- to provide teachers and counsellors with information regarding the students preference and aversions which will help them acquire better understanding of students and their problems.
- to help in the selection of the right person for the right work, and thus, save frustration, unhappiness and disappointment in the lives of the individuals and increase productive capacity of individuals.
- to enable teachers, counsellors and parents to know the kinds and intensity of the student's interests and assist him/her to prepare his/her educational and vocational plans consistent with his/her interests.

Q16. What are the methods of measuring interests?

Ans. By the following methods, we can measure the interests of individuals:

(1) **Observation:** We may observe manifest interests. What an individual actually does is a good indication of what his interests are.

(2) **Claims of the Counselee:** We can know the interests by knowing the expressed interests of the individual, in a subject,

activity, object or vocation. Verbal claim can be an indicator of his/her interests.

(3) Use of Instruments: We may assess interests using an instrument like Michigan Vocabulary Test on the grounds that if the individual is really interested in something, s/he will know the vocabulary involved in that area.

(4) Use of Inventories: We may determine the pattern of an individual's interest from his/her responses to lists of occupations and activities. Interest inventories provide information about the student's preferences, which are more stable than the verbally claimed interests. The latter are too often influenced by his/her limited and faulty knowledge of occupations. This technique is by far the most common means of assessing interests and is commonly used.

Q17. Enumerate the advantages and limitations of interest inventories.

Ans. The advantages and limitations of interest inventories are as follows:

Advantages of Interest Inventories

- They are useful for the counsellor too as they are less fraught with emotional significance. The subject can discuss the interest scores with the counselor freely.

- They are economic – They can be given to a group; interpretation of profiles can be carried out in group discussion.

- They are well-adapted to vocational counselling – The student expects his/her interests to be considered. The interpretation, when given, carries considerable force because the student can see that s/he is looking at himself in a mirror, that s/he is only receiving an analysis of what s/he himself/herself has said.

- They provide excellent preliminary information either to further group study of careers or to individual counselling.

- They assist counsellor in dealing with many other student problems.

- They are helpful devices for the counselee too – Students do not mind revealing their interests and are eager to have a report of their scores. A promise to interpret scores is an excellent, non-threatening gambit to entice the student into the counsellor's office.

Limitations of Interest Inventories

- The inventories can have validity only with persons whose likes have been long and varied enough to have provided them with experiences of the kind, which will enable them to choose between alternatives presented by each item in the inventories. These inventories are, thus, more useful with mature than immature students.

- Vocational choice or success cannot be predicted on the basis of even clearly defined patterns shown by the inventories alone. Ability, training and opportunity for training – all need to be considered. Interest test results cannot be overemphasised.
- Many students fail to show through their responses to interest inventories strong likes and dislikes or clearly defined preferences.

Q18. How do you estimate interests?

Or

Describe the ways of assessing interests.

Ans. One can know the interests by asking the individuals what they like and dislike. The other way is to analyse the activities that a person performs. The third method of assessing interests is by the use of interest tests and inventories. There are many instruments now in use and majority of them deal with occupational interest:

(1) **Kuder Interest Inventories:** There are various forms, versions and editions of the Kuder Interest Inventories. They help in the measurement of interests from different angles and are designed for different purposes. The items in the Kuder inventories are of the forced-choice triad type. For each of three activities listed, the respondent indicates which s/he would like the most and which s/he would like the least.

The following forms of Kuder Interest Inventories are quite common:

(i) **The Kuder Vocational Preference Record:** It provides 10 interest scales plus a verification scale for detecting carelessness, misunderstanding and the choice of socially-desirable but unlikely answers. The interest scales include Outdoor, Mechanical, Computational, Scientific, Persuasive, Artistic, Literary, Musical, Social Service and Clerical. Forced-choice triad items are used. The respondents indicate which of the three activities they would like the most and which the least. The scores are obtained not for specific vocations but for 10 broad interest areas.

(ii) **Kuder General Interest Survey (KGIS):** It has been developed as a revision and downward extension of the Kuder Vocational Preference Record. It is designed for grades 6 to 12. It employs simpler language and easier vocabulary. It is a revision of the Strong Vocational Interest Blank (SVIB).

(iii) **Kuder Occupational Interest Inventory (KOII):** The occupations covered by this inventory vary widely in level, ranging from baker and truck driver to chemist and lawyer.

(2) **Strong Vocational Interest Blanks (SVIB):** It is based on the assumption that a person who has the interest patterns

typical of successful people in a given occupation will enjoy and find satisfaction in that occupation.

Q19. Define personality. Write down the purposes of personality testing.

Ans. Often by persons use the term personality to indicate the physical make up of an individual. The term "Personality", however, signifies much more than simply the physical looks of a person and has a very broad meaning. It includes the emotional, motivational, inter-personal, attitudinal and even moral aspects of a person. Some researchers have included intelligence also as part of personality. Personality refers to a unique combination of characteristics of an individual, which pre-disposes the person to behave in a particular and consistent way.

Purposes of Personality Testing: Following are the various purposes of personality testing:

- It helps the individual in resolving emotional conflicts. Personality diagnosis becomes essential when the difficulty the individual encounters in making proper adjustment with the educational and occupational choices, lies in emotional conflict about which the client has no knowledge. When the cause of the individual's mental conflict is diagnosed, it may be possible for him/her to solve his/her problem in his/her own way.

- It helps the clinical psychologist. A clinical psychologist can use personality assessments to help choose the best therapy for his/her clients.

- It helps the teacher and the counsellor. Personality testing through various techniques will help the teacher and counsellor to get this information and help the individual on the basis of this information.

- It helps the students in proper educational and vocational choice. Personality plays an important role in individual, personal, educational and vocational adjustment and success. It is, therefore, important to diagnose the individual's personality pattern to see whether s/he possesses the traits, which are likely to contribute significantly to his/her adjustment to the course or career s/he is choosing.

- It helps the employer in proper selection of the personnel.

Q20. Enlist the limitations of paper and pencil personality tests.

Ans. Following are the limitations of paper and pencil personality tests:

- Subject's unconscious resistance also affects individual's responses to a great extent. According to Philip E. Vernon, "People literally do not know themselves well enough to answer many of the questions correctly: their responses are only too likely to be rationalisations or un-willing self-deceptions." These questions are just like psychoanalytic techniques. Just as in psychoanalytic techniques, the psychoanalyst can never expect to get valid information from direct questions or introspections;

similarly, here it is very difficult to get valid and correct information.

- Majority of the questions in these inventories deal with personal matters. The subject may hesitate to commit anything in writing. The subject may make his/her own guesses as to the object of the test and answer each question not so much at its face value as in accordance with his/her own interpretation of the object and with how much s/he is willing to reveal.
- Suggestion is another important factor, which tampers with validity. Our recollections of emotionally toned experiences are liable to be false. Moreover, it is quite easy that suggestive questioning may lead us to accept experiences as our own, which never really occurred. Thus, while most subjects may be expected wittingly or unwittingly to disguise their emotional weaknesses in answering personality questionnaires, others of a more suggestible type may greatly exaggerate.
- The influence of temporary mood, optimism, worry, etc. might also affect test responses.

Q21. Describe about situational or behavioural test and daily diary.

Ans. Situational or Behavioural Test

Situational judgement tests are a type of psychological aptitude test that assesses judgement required for solving problems in work-related situations. It is a test in which the behaviour of the individual is evaluated in action by judges or by his/her peers or s/he is confronted with the situations related to his/her own life, in response to which s/he gives expression to his/her feelings for other persons. The subject reveals some of his/her personality traits through his/her preference for or against certain contacts with others and through his/her spontaneous methods of dealing with life-situations that confront him/her. Psycho-drama and socio-drama are the two techniques of this type.

As the word psycho-drama implies, the individual has to play a role spontaneously in a specified situation. His/her behaviour is observed by trained observers. It is assumed that individuals project their inner feelings and conflicts in the role they play.

The Daily Diary

A diary is a daily written account of what someone does, thinks or feels. The daily diary maintained by students can also serve as a device for the measurement of personality. The diary, being of a very personal nature, can contain the record of such events, thoughts and feelings as are of great importance to the student. The diary, if properly maintained and made, can serve as a useful medium of throwing light upon many aspects of the personality of the individual. It, being an hour by hour record of the individual, is valuable for showing the general pattern of a student's life, the activities in which s/he is currently engaged regularly, and some of his/her special interests.

Q22. What is orientation service? Describe the objectives and activities of orientation service.

Ans. Entering in a junior or senior college is a critical factor in a students' life, as it involves the process of initiation in to a larger world in a new environment. A feeling of loneliness as well as insecurity accompanies the student when s/he enters a school for the first time. S/he cannot be presumed to know what to do, where, how to study, or how, or how to act in a new educational environment. As s/he moves from a familiar school environment to unfamiliar college campus, s/he needs assistance in the form of information about the institution and an assurance that s/he would make the transition and the adjustment to the new environment successfully. To help students minimise such problems, an orientation programme is conducted for students and their parents, during the first week of classes of the college year. Orientation service is a kind of guidance service, which is distinct due to its characteristic features.

Following are some of the objectives of the orientation service:

(1) Acquaint the students with the concerned staff and the student body.

(2) Develop favourable attitudes among the students both towards the school and the staff.

(3) Develop awareness regarding the rules and regulations, functioning patterns and available infrastructural and physical facilities in the school or institution or workplace.

(4) Provide opportunities for the staff members and student body to interact with the new comers.

Orientation Activities: The activities can be broadly classified as follows:

(1) Pre-admission Orientation: Pre-admission orientation helps to acquaint students with the institution, its tradition, purpose, its rules and regulations, curricula, extracurricular activities, the staff and the student body.

Activities: Some of the activities that can be included in pre-admission orientation are:

(i) Issuing handbooks or pamphlets giving information about the school, its courses and activities;

(ii) Visit to schools along with the staff or parents;

(iii) Arranging exhibitions to expose them to the activities that students are undertaking; and

(iv) Arranging conferences and talks with the parents, since they also play a major role.

(2) Post-admission Orientation: This service can be provided throughout the year. It helps the teacher in determining the abilities of students and thereby adopts their teaching styles and activities according to the student needs.

Activities*:* Some of the activities, which can be included in post-admission orientation are:

(i) Arranging group activities, where in the students are provided opportunities to interact with each other and exhibit their abilities.

(ii) Conducting various games like "get-acquainted" games where the student can talk about themselves, such as their interest, hobbies, etc.

Q23. Discuss pupil inventory service as a guidance service. What are its objectives?

Ans. Individual inventory service is an important type of guidance service, which may be recognised often as pupil inventory service. This service is designed to gather all reliable data, information and records, and to assemble and compile these materials for their functional use.

The process of collecting information about each pupil which will mark him/her as a unique personality is a guidance function in most schools. Though counselling as practised in virtually all schools is based upon pertinent data about pupils, it is quite possible that such data might be collected in the absence of a counselling service, or of any intention of establishing one. Some schools may accumulate a vast amount of information about pupils through the use of a cumulative folder, anecdotal records, autobiographies, tests and other devices, little or none of which is used for counselling or other guidance purposes. It would scarcely be correct to describe such an accumulation of information as a guidance activity. In general, the collection of adequate pupil data stems from a desire to use them in assisting pupils to achieve self-understanding and when such is the case, the process may be properly described as a guidance function.

In the problem of collecting, maintaining, interpreting and using the inventory of facts about the pupil or student, certain basic principles have to be considered:

- The collection of the data about each child should be started from the time the child begins his/her schooling.
- Records should grow with the child as s/he progresses in his/her studies.
- Records should be cumulative and inclusive.
- Records should be unbiased, objective and unopinionated.
- Records should be flexible enough to meet the needs of the pupil and the changes of the times.
- The data contained in the inventory should be properly interpreted, well-synthesised and carefully used for the benefit of the child.
- Only the proper tools, techniques and instruments should be employed in the gathering and collecting of necessary information.
- Records should be systematically kept and conveniently filed and should be accessible to the guidance counsellor, to the

principal and to the teacher who may from time to time make good use of the information found therein.

A teacher could provide details of certain behaviour of students by observing them in the classroom situations and making their records. These incidents could be accumulated in the form of anecdotal records.

The objectives of pupil inventory service are as follows:

- To maintain different records concerned with each student and update them periodically; and
- To identify different abilities of students by administration of various tests.

Q24. Explain in brief about occupational information service for students. What are its objectives as a guidance service?

Ans. Occupational information service is a kind of guidance service. The function of the information service is to make available to pupils or students certain kinds of information not ordinarily provided through the instructional programme during the regular period of instruction. It provides a continuous programme about co-operation, opportunities for education and important facts concerning personal and social adjustment. Such information is necessary to guide them in making intelligent vocational or educational choice or in personal and social adjustment.

Information is an essential part of virtually every guidance programme whether we want to assist the students in making better choices or helping them in better adjustment or optimum development. This is the reason that information needs to be organised and utilised as a distinct guidance service so as to:

- Develop in the students a broad and realistic view of life's opportunities and problems at all levels of training;
- Create an awareness of the need and an active desire for accurate and valid occupational, educational and personal-social information;
- assist in learning the techniques of obtaining and interpreting information for progressive self-directiveness;
- promote attitudes and habits which assist in the making of choices and adjustments productive of personal satisfaction and effectiveness; and
- provide assistance in progressively narrowing choices to specific activities, which as approximate to aptitudes, abilities and interests manifested and to the proximity of defined decisions.

The objectives of pupil inventory service are:

- to identify the various abilities of students by administration of various tests; and
- to maintain various records concerned with each student and update them periodically.

Q25. Describe counselling service in guidance programme.

Ans. Counselling is a very important service given in schools and colleges, for the educational, personal and vocational development of each student. Counselling services are considered the 'heart' of the guidance programme. The counselling service must assist the individual to identify, understand and solve challenges and problems that s/he may come across, during education and work. Full-time school and college counsellors should provide counselling in three domains, i.e. academic, career and personal/social. Their counselling services and programmes help students resolve their emotional, social or behavioural problems and help them to develop a clearer focus or sense of direction in their life. Effective counselling services are intended to establish a relationship between the student and the institution, so as to enable the student to achieve optimum adjustment and development, which is important to institutional progress.

When the teacher comes across any student who displays deviant behaviours, s/he can always refer the case to a school counsellor. Further, observations made and recorded by the teacher about certain students can help the counsellor in the counselling process.

This service is intended to establish a relationship between the guidance worker and the student in which the former attempts to assist the latter in achieving optimum educational, vocational, personal-social development and adjustment. The service may be performed by the counsellor, teacher or the administrator provided they are adequately trained. It involves helping the student to:

- understand what he *can* do and what he *should* do;
- understand the choices he faces, the opportunities open to him and the qualifications he possesses for the goal he has chosen;
- handle his difficulties in a rational way and strengthen his attributes;
- make his own decisions and plans on the basis of self-understanding, accept responsibility for his decisions and take action on the plans developed.

Counselling is possible if the counsellor has enough information regarding the individual's assets and liabilities and of the possible courses of action open to him. It consists of an interview or a series of interviews between the counsellor and the counsellee and may involve the administration of certain psychological tests. Being helpful in crystallising the problem and reaching a reasonably good solution, counselling is a distinct guidance service.

Q26. Interpret placement service as a guidance service.

Ans. The Placement Service helps the individual to obtain employment. A guidance programme is incomplete, unless the student is directed towards gainful occupation, or placed in a course, training programme or job; where he can make optimum use of her/his knowledge, attitudes and skills. The Career and Placement Service provides information for all job descriptions submitted by recruiting companies and organisations. It serves as a bridge between the college and the world of employment, maintaining close contact with government offices, community agencies, educational institutions, and industrial firms. These external relations pave the way to finding employment for students who are ready for employment.

This service in the guidance programme intended to help the student in:

- situating himself in the right scholastic track in the proper course;
- finding a suitable place in the post-school environment;
- the fit choice of co-curricular activities available in the school;
- choice of job-oriented courses;
- getting admission in an ITI, polytechnic or college;
- getting part-time jobs during working session and whole-time jobs during vacation and after getting education and training.

Appropriate data from schools should be collected and transmitted to receiving colleges, universities and prospective employers. Close contact with institutions of higher learning as well as with personnel managers in business and industry, co-ordination among teachers and guidance workers are essential to make a success of this service useful for all types of students—the normal, the intellectually gifted the emotionally disturbed, the artistically talented and the mentally retarded to find their appropriate place in an educational or vocational setting.

Hence, a school that provides placement services should be capable to draw upon all the possible resources to assist its students in finding suitable and appropriate jobs. The extent to which the placement service fulfils this purpose is a measure of its effectiveness. This could largely be met by a systematic and proper functioning of the guidance committee. The school committee could also publicise about the placement programme both to the students and community. Within the schools, the information could be published in school magazine, notified in the libraries or announced in student assemblies.

Q27. What is follow-up service? Describe the purpose and steps of follow-up service.

Ans. The Follow-up service begins before the students complete their studies and leave school or college. It seeks to determine the reliability and appropriateness of the educational and vocational adjustment of students. Many students finish their studies without planning their next step into the world. The guidance officer or counselor needs to follow the development of some ex-students, to ensure that they adjusted well in their careers or to know if they need additional guidance and counselling.

Student-Peer-Facilitators are trained to assist a new employee through the 'buddy' approach. Follow-up services in guidance and counselling may be (1) incidental, (2) systematic or (3) flexible in nature. The Follow-up service should be planned and conducted to serve the needs of all students as well as the institutions.

Purpose of Follow-up Service

   (1)   Obtaining information about student-performance after completing their studies.

    (2)   Appraising the school/college educational programme.

    (3)   Appraising the school/college guidance & counselling service.

    (4)   Planning for the improvement of programme and services.

Steps of Follow-up Service

The three steps that are dealt in a follow-up programme are:

    (1)   A systematic gathering of data from the alumni.

    (2)   Interpretation and presentation of that data to all the concerned personnel, i.e. student, parent and community.

    (3)   Suggest a modified framework of educational programme based on the findings made.

Q28. Enumerate some of the necessary preliminary tasks to organise a guidance programme.

Ans. Some of the preliminary tasks needed to be undertaken to organise a guidance programme are:

- Formation of a guidance committee, which comprises of at least seven to eight members. The committee would be constituted of various personnel such as at least two parents, two teachers, a counsellor and a career master. The principal could be the chairperson of the committee.

- Decisions and arrangements must be made regarding the allotment of budget for conducting the various services. The expenses could be determined also keeping in view the payment of honourarium for guest lectures, conveyance to specialists or professionals such as educationists, doctors, etc.

- Suitable arrangements need to be made to acquire minimum infrastructural and physical facilities such as a guidance cell or room, tables, chairs various psychological tests and other required literature.

- Support from the parents and community could be obtained by orienting them to the significance of a guidance programme.

- The school staff and students also need to be briefed about the purpose and importance of the guidance programme and encouraged to participate.

Q29. Write down the essential steps to plan a guidance programme. Also, explain the role of the principal in guidance programme.

Ans. The following steps are necessary to be undertaken to plan the guidance programme:

    (1)   First make a survey of the available guidance services existing in the school or institution.

    (2)   Identify the student needs (or) areas where assistance is required.

    (3)   Obtain the opinion of the staff members and ascertain the extent of assistance possible from them.

    (4)   Statement of explicit objective for the guidance programme on the basis of the student needs.

(5)   Specification of the various functions of each guidance service.
(6)   Assignment and defining of duties to each personnel, who are the members of the guidance committee.

Role of the Principal

The principal occupies a key position in the school guidance programme. In the regular guidance programme, the principal has to play a great constructive role. His attitude towards guidance or pupil development may determine whether mere lip service is rendered to the programme or whether the guidance of pupil development is basic to the whole school programme.

Apart from that appropriate action needs to be taken by the principal to make suitable arrangements for the procurement of psychological test materials, literature, documents and arranging sufficient budget. Further, monitoring of the guidance activities are also been done by the principal.

Q30. Enumerate objectives of secondary school students with their services and activities.

Ans. This stage, which includes students of class IX and X, requires guidance activities to be focussed on the needs of three groups of students. They include those who intend to:

- Continue in higher education (graduation)
- Take up vocational or professional courses (polytechnics; professional education like medicine, etc.)
- Enter a job

The objectives are listed here:

- Help them to make effective adjustments in the family, school and society.
- Provide information about various educational and vocational opportunities and the essential requirements.
- Enable them to make realistic educational and vocational choices.
- Help the students to understand and accept the physiological changes in one self.
- Enlighten parents and teachers about the importance of this stage especially adolescent and create appropriate situations for effective learning and development.
- Identify, develop and strengthen their abilities and interests.

Table 2.2: Services and their activities for secondary school students

Service	Activities
Orientation	• organise school visits, talk by the other school staff. • Arrange parent-teacher meetings (PTMs) to orient the parents.
Pupil	• Collect data on abilities, aptitudes, interests,

Inventory	achievement and other psychological variables through administration of tests. • Maintain student cumulative records. • Identify under-achievers and dropouts from the school records.
Counselling	• Refer the cases to counsellor. • Counselling activities to develop one self. • Organise and conduct group activities, discussions, role-playing to develop personal and social skills. • Arrange talks by professionals such as doctors, educationists on matters like health, addiction, personal habits, sex education and other educational issues. • Conduct activities on social service and arrange for camps.
Occupational information	• Organise career exhibitions and career conferences. • Arrange field trips. • Arrange career talks. • Orient the parents regarding various courses after class X. • Prepare activities showing self-employed persons. • Conduct programme to interact with self-employed persons.
Placement	Provide placement: • For drop-outs • For students who terminate their formal education and get into some vocational course. • For students who are completing school education.
Follow-up	• Obtain and document the addresses of the school-leaving students and drop-outs. • Administer questionnaires or interviews to obtain students opinion about the school guidance programme. • Arrange meetings like "old student association or Alumni".

Q31. Enlist objectives of senior secondary students with their services and activities.

Ans. The senior secondary students cover two classes, i.e. XI and XII and the age of the students usually ranging from 16 to 18 years. The objectives of guidance programme at this stage are:

- Help them to plan their career based on the choice of course.
- Guide them in the area of personal-social adjustment.

- Help students to make appropriate choice of course(s) in accordance with their abilities and interest.
- Help them make decisions.
- Make them aware of various job opportunities related to various courses.
- Help them develop self-confidence.

Table 2.3: Services and their activities for (+2 students) senior secondary students

Service	Activities
Orientation	• obtain pamphlets/handbook of various educational institutions. • orient parents and teachers about various educational institutions. • arrange talks by the school/institution staff, employees.
Pupil Inventory	• administer various tests to measure abilities, and other psychological variables. • Maintain the records of the students and constantly update them.

Counselling	• conduct sessions to develop self-confidence in students.
	• conduct sessions on role playing, e.g. attending an interview; communication skills; and leadership qualities.
	• Arrange debates, group discussions, and drama on various social and educational issues such as:
	  ➢ Discipline in workplace;
	  ➢ career choices and lifestyles;
	  ➢ making decision and alternatives in planning career goals; and
	  ➢ strategies to cope with stress and anxiety.

Occupational information	• Organise
	  ➢ career conferences;
	  ➢ field visits; and
	  ➢ career talks.
	• establish communication with the staff at employment exchanges and related agencies.
	• conduct classroom sessions on:
	  ➢ "Resumes, Applications and Interview"
	  ➢ "Employment Trends"

Placement	• arrange for in-campus interviews • advertise vacancies and college information on the school notice board and address or announce during

	the assemblies.
Follow-up	• form a students' association of the school leaving students • administer follow-up questionnaires to students periodically. • arrange meetings to invite old students.

Q32. What is the need for evaluation in guidance programme?

Ans. Evaluation is needed to determine various aspects like:

- quality of guidance services provided;
- the other activities and techniques need to be adopted in order to make the service effective;
- effect of various guidance services on the behaviour of students; and
- adequacy and feasibility of the guidance services provided.

In general, it contributes to the sum total of useful knowledge in the guidance field.

Research and evaluation are simultaneous activities. Therefore, in every aspect of the guidance service, a research component is essential. The results derived from research and evaluation have implications for both the improvement of guidance programme and also for the school curriculum. A qualified guidance worker must always be encouraged to evaluate and simultaneously undertake research. The guidance committee could discuss the findings with the other staff members, parents and students, thereby facilitating a better co-ordination, and hence, leading to improvement in the guidance services. Unless the existing programmes are evaluated, the worth of it cannot be established.

Q33. What are the various steps included in evaluation of guidance programme? Discuss.

Ans. Following are the steps included in evaluation of guidance programme:

(1) **Identification of Objectives:** The first step is to list out the objectives of the guidance programme. The objectives need to be clearly defined, such that they are specific and measurable.

(2) **Criteria for Measurement:** After the identification of objectives, the criteria for measuring them must be established. This is followed by the determination of the appropriate methods and techniques to collect the required data based on the criteria selected.

(3) **Implementation of the Plan:** Once the design of the plan is prepared, it requires to be implemented. Before its implementations, the expert's opinions and suggestions from other guidance personnel could be obtained subsequently. The activities could be organised and conducted in a systematic way.

(4) **Interpretation of Findings:** Maximum efforts must be made to check that the data collected is reliable. The data must first be compiled and later interpreted accurately. The findings must be summarised and shared with the school personnel and guidance worker. Further, steps must also be taken to implement these findings.

Q34. Describe the methods of evaluation in guidance programme.

Ans. Based on the criteria of evaluation, the methods of evaluation have to be decided. Some of the methods are suggested below:

(1) **Survey Method:** This method is used in an evaluation study when data are required to be obtained from a large group of stakeholders such as students, parents, teachers, etc. receiving any group guidance or counselling programme. Through this method, we can collect data about the perception of students, teachers, parents and others about the guidance and counselling programme using questionnaire/rating scale/interview schedule. Survey method is used most widely in evaluation of guidance and counselling programme/activity because it is flexible and conducted on the total target group or on the representative sample of it.

(2) **Experimental Method:** For scientific evaluation of any programme or intervention, experimental method is the most appropriate method to determine the worth and effectiveness of programme activities and in improving guidance and counselling programme. This method is a planned attempt to study the effect of intervention on one or more groups of students/individuals. Experimental method needs a systematic procedure to follow and sometimes it is difficult for a counsellor to arrange all these conditions. However, this method can be used for some services/activities. There are two designs, which are generally followed by an experimenter: (i) pretest-posttest design and (ii) experimental-control group design.

(3) **Case Study Method:** In this method, the progress made by an individual in achieving the desired modifications after receiving the Guidance and Counselling programme is recorded. Case study method is individualistic and time consuming, but it can provide in-depth information about the progress made due to intervention. Although generalisation of data obtained through this method is not possible but it may be used for specific groups and specific categories.

Q35. Define group guidance. What are its advantages?

Or

What are the advantages of group guidance in schools?

[June-2018, Q.No.-3 (d)]

Ans. Group Guidance is a phrase that has been around as long as the guidance movement; Frank Parsons (1909), the founding father of the guidance movement, used the phrase early in his writings. Group guidance is considered to be an approach aimed at providing helpful personal, emotional, and/or occupational and vocational information to groups of individuals.

Definitions of Group Guidance

Jones: "Group guidance is any group enterprise or activity in which the primary purpose is to assist each individual in the group to solve problems and to make his adjustments."

Crow and Crow: "Guidance in group situations usually is thought of as referring to those guidance services that are made available by school personnel to large or small groups of people."

In schools, where group guidance is promoted, students are able to avail the following benefits through participation in them:

    (1) Information Regarding
- (i) Higher education prospects
- (ii) Occupational opportunities and vocational preparation
- (iii) Leisure time activities
- (iv) Social and civic conditions.

    (2) Experience in Cooperative Living Leading to the Development of
- (i) Interpersonal skills
- (ii) Good sportsmanship
- (iii) Understanding of the self and others
- (iv) Social skills

    (3) Development of Individual's Abilities and Interests through
- (i) Participation in group projects
- (ii) Organisation of student initiated activities
- (iii) Special services and programmes in schools and other institutions.

Advantages of Group Guidance

    (1) It is Economical and Efficient: Through meetings with a group of students, the counsellor can convey information in much less time than if s/he gave the same information to each student individually. The time, thus, saved can be utilised for the more difficult and complex problems of the students. Also, it is economical to collect general background information about the students and their problems in a group, while more specific information about the student can be collected individually.

    (2) It Aids the Normal Student: As schools are organised today, counselling will continue to be largely remedial and deal with problems after they have arisen. No matter how well planned the counselling programme is, there is need for group guidance for the normal student to give him/her information and the direction that s/he needs and wants. With such assistance, s/he can move from there to manage his/her own affairs better.

(3) It Helps in Making Contacts with Students: The counsellor can have many more contacts with a large number of students through group guidance. During these contacts, s/he observes each student's behaviour in the group situation and, thus, increases his/her knowledge of that student.

(4) It Offers Students the Opportunity to Discuss Common Problems: Under expert leadership, students within a group can determine what their common problems are. They can then work towards general agreement as to the best way to solve them.

(5) It Helps to Improve Students' Attitudes and Behaviour: Group discussion provides opportunities for free exchange of opinions and realistic analysis of attitudes. These can help the participants of the group to achieve balanced judgements and desirable behaviour.

(6) It Focuses Collective Judgement on Problems that are Common to the Group: Students are often willing to discuss in group problems that they are unwilling to discuss in individual interviews. It gives them an opportunity to express their anxieties and relieve their pent up feelings. Group suggestions may help them resolve their problems.

(7) It Provides an Opportunity for Observation: The guidance worker can study each student as he reacts in a group situation and know some elements of his/her personality not revealed in any other way. This helps in the thorough understanding of the student.

(8) It Helps in the Development of Wholesome and Helpful Awareness of Unrecognised needs and Problems of the Students: This lays the foundation, develops the need and prepares the way for individual counselling.

Q36. Enumerate certain considerations to be kept in mind to organise group guidance effectively.

Ans. Following are certain considerations to be kept in mind if one is to organise group guidance effectively.

- The identified/selected groups should have the common needs and problems. For example, if class talk is delivered on "Effective Career Planning" for the students of class VI, it is going to be a futile exercise because they are too young to realise its importance.
- The size of the group should not be very large.
- It is a team work. It requires the co-operation of the students, teachers, and administrative staff in the school setting.

- Group guidance must be a continuous activity of the school so that its impact is realised by the students.
- It is not a substitute for individual guidance, but both types are complementary to each other.
- It requires active participation of all the team members. So, such methods should be employed so that the students feel curious to ask questions/issues, etc., e.g. while organising class talks, individuals should be encouraged to express their personal experiences.

Q37. Describe orientation to the students in group guidance activities.

Ans. Students should be given proper orientation about their role while working on the learning tasks. Learning points are to be discussed collectively. Everyone should help each other in performing the learning task and ensure that each one is benefited by the learning tasks. The performance of the group will not be evaluated individually.

Information about the institution, its physical layout, personnel and administrative arrangement, help students become acquainted with the new settings. The newly admitted students can be given information about the school, the various facilities available, the rules and regulation, the course curriculum, what is expected of them, etc. They can be asked to introduce themselves. Further, a small get together with the teachers can be arranged for. Orientation, thus, begins when the parents first takes a child to a nursery school. This is not the end. Orientation should be provided for everyone moving into the school during the term as s/he moves into the new class.

Orientation programme will not be the same for elementary, secondary and senior secondary students. It has to be different at different levels depending on the need.

Q38. Explain in brief about career conferences in group guidance activities. Also, enlist guidelines while planning a conference.

Ans. Career conferences are series of meetings in which professional experts from different vocations share their expertise with the students. These are organised by educational institutions once a year. Special arrangements must be made and the programme should be well drawn up. Parents too can be invited. Separate sessions should be organised for different classes and courses of study. Personnel from Bureau of Educational and Vocational Guidance should also be invited to speak in such conferences. Topics should be selected according to the needs and interests of the students keeping in mind their economical and social background. In this conference, complete information about a particular field should be given along with its allied branches. Through these career conferences, students will be able to gain detailed information about a variety of vocations from the experts themselves.

Following are certain guidelines, which can be drawn while planning a conference:

- Through the checklist, the occupational interest of the students may be determined so that speakers can be chosen from those areas.
- The conference dates should not conflict with examination dates.
- Charts could be prepared for displaying the topic/theme of the career conference.
- The students should be informed beforehand about the purpose of the conference.
- Duties should be assigned to the staff members and volunteer students.
- The names of the guest speakers should be suggested in the meeting and the person who is going to take the charge be appointed.
- Prepare pamphlets for due publicity. A note should be sent to the parents informing about the conference.
- The schedule of talks, discussion groups, film shows, etc. should be announced in advance.

Q39. Write the major steps involved in planning a conference.

Ans. The career conference requires months of planning in advance. The following steps are involved in planning a conference:

(1) The idea of organising the conference should be presented at least 45 days in advance. Once approval has been obtained the students can be informed about it. Informing the students beforehand is very much required because then they can offer themselves as volunteers.

(2) A list of the volunteer teachers and students to be made and duties to be assigned to them like arranging for the mike, lectures, refreshment, distribution of pamphlets, etc.

(3) Information should be sent to the principals of other schools and parents. The aim of the career conference and a brief outline of the plan should be sent to them.

(4) Draft invitation letter for guest speakers.

(5) A detailed programme schedule of talks, discussion, films and charts to be made.

(6) The session-wise programme schedule should be decided well in time and intimated to the students and other participants.

(7) Prepare a list of speakers for each session. It is generally good to have 2 or 3 speakers for each session so that in case of unavailability of one, the other can be invited. The resource persons could be the parents, alumni and staff members.

(8) Brief the speaker about the theme and the objectives of the conference.

Q40. Write a note on class talks in group guidance.

Ans. Class Talk is a talk on topics of common interest of students. The topics are of general interest and dealt within the whole class group. It is given for creating awareness, promoting interaction among students and seeking further clarifications. It helps in identification and diagnosing the problem of students and further referral. Some of the topics of common concerns could be improving study skills and study habits, time management, forming and maintain friendship, enhancing self-confidence, conflict resolution, self-understanding, hobbies, interview taking, managing stress, peer pressure, etc.

Certain points are to be kept in mind while organising a class talk.

- The topic selected should be according to the need and level of students.
- It should be presented in simple terms with lots of examples and illustrations from daily life. Use of difficult words should be avoided.
- Ensure the participation of students.

This can be done by asking questions, or by encouraging students to give examples from their life. This will make the students feel interested and involved in the talk.

- Charts, posters, pamphlets, etc. can be used to highlight the major points more effectively.
- Tables/figures, etc. can be prepared.
- The talk should not be very long.
- The number of students should not be more than 40.
- The students should be informed in advance about the schedule, theme, venue and other details of the talk.
- Supplementary materials like charts, posters and films are to be kept handy.

Class talks can be on topics such as time management, study habits, how to prepare for examinations, life skills, healthy eating habits, healthy living, social skills, etc.

Q41. Describe in brief about career talks in group guidance. Also, give additional guidelines while preparing career talk.

Ans. The aim is to provide relevant information to the class/group regarding a particular career. It includes nature of work, working conditions, work requirements like age, educational qualifications, institutions for training, special skills required, personal attributes, job opportunities, pay bands, avenues for promotion, sources of further information, etc. The school can invite professionals from different fields such as defence, medicine, banking, insurance, film, media, etc. for delivering career talk on concerned career.

While preparing the career talk, the general points are the same as for the class talks. Certain additional guidelines while preparing the career talk are:

The future prospect of the career, educational qualifications required, the institution offering the course, duration of the course, mode of selection, hostel facilities, positive and negative points associated with the career, etc. should be clearly stated while delivering a career talk.

Career talk should include topics on a variety of careers to accommodate the interests of all students present.

Q42. Define plant tours in group guidance programme. Also, enlist its steps.

Ans. Plant tours provide an excellent opportunity to the students to be aware of the various occupations available. These tours to industrial and business establishment for class groups can be arranged as part of group guidance programme. These include visits to commercial establishments, industries, professional colleges, research institutions, etc. All these should be arranged as these provide the students with direct and firsthand experience of the work done and the physical and social environment in which it is done. Visit should be followed by group discussion, and so on.

The main purpose of the plant tours is to increase the career awareness of the students by their interaction with people at work in occupation.

Fig. 2.1: Plant Tour

Steps of Plant Tours

(1) **Organisation of a Plant Tour:** The idea of the plant tour should be first discussed with the principal.

(2) **Selection of Venue:** The place to visit should be the one where most students are likely to work. It should be planned keeping in consideration the socio-economic status and other variables of the group, e.g. few places could be hotels, telephone company, banks, etc.

(3) **Selection of Transport Mode:** Another important question is 'How to plan for such tours?' How do you get permission from companies for the visit? Parents can act as a resource person. The parent who is involved in specific type of job can be of potent help. Or else a direct call to the director of the company can be a help. State to him/her clearly the purpose of your visit and size of the group.

(4) **Preliminary Arrangements:** Following points should be kept in mind in making the arrangements, whether through visit, letter or telephone:

    (i)   Explain clearly the purpose of the tour.

    (ii)   Number, size, level and interest of the group(s), number of facilitating teachers with the group.

    (iii) Fix the starting- returning time.

    (iv) Arrange for a question/discussion period before and after the tour.

    (v)   Arrange transportation.

    (vi) Secure the parent's consent if necessary.

(5) Orientation of the Students: Some do's and don'ts one has to keep in mind are:

    (i)   Be appreciative. It costs time and money to entertain you.

    (ii)   Don't act like labour inspector.

    (iii) Don't criticise

    (iv) Don't be too loud

    (v)   Don't disrupt the company work.

    (vi) Don't ask irrelevant questions.

    (vii) Avoid comparisons.

    (viii) Don't try to educate or socialise with the employees or the management.

    (ix) Move with the group.

(6) What to Observe: Inform students beforehand what they are expected to make a note of. They should be asked to pay attention to the nature of work rather than on the talks that are exchanged among the workers.

Q43. Interpret group discussion in group guidance activity.

Ans. A group of students meet together to discuss informally and deliberate on a topic of mutual concern, which helps them to be aware of the various problems and its solutions.

In group discussions, students define their working relationships and be associated with an accepting group of people of their own age who face problems similar to their own.

Certain norms must be formed while inviting participation from students in group discussion:

- The topic should be of interest to them.
- Each one should present their own views.
- Criticising, leg pulling should not be encouraged. In such a situation, counsellor should intervene.
- The points for discussion should be limited to the topic only. The discussion should not deviate from the original topic.

In the group discussion, the topic to be selected and presented should follow certain principles:

- Topic should match with the maturity level of students in the group.
- The topic should be based on problems of real importance to students. The topic should represent matters of concern to the majority of students. This will lead to more participation from the students.

A few students, sometimes, dominate a discussion. So, the group may be divided into 3-4 smaller groups of 5 students each. To introduce a topic or to "warm up" the group, a buzz session is a useful method. The teacher writes a thought provoking question/issue on the blackboard. Then divides the class into subgroups of 3-4 students and prompt them to discuss. This is known as the buzz session.

During the group discussion, many personality traits of the individual can be observed like the leadership qualities, co-operation, submissiveness, dominating behaviour, etc.

Q44. Explain socio drama and psycho drama. Also, enumerate its procedure and role play activities.

Ans. Socio drama an Psycho drama were developed by J.L. Moreno *et al.* to provide spontaneous situations wherein people could gain insights by dramatising their conflicts, In psycho drama, the greater emphasis is upon to promote personalised work of individual whereas in socio drama a problem common to many or a group is taken, for example, how to persuade one's parents about one's decision for selection of humanities stream rather than science stream is a case of psycho drama while persuading the society against unstability, dowry, etc. are some of the issues of socio drama.

Psycho drama is defined as, "the method by which a person can be helped to explore the psychological dimensions of his problems through the enactment of his conflict situations, rather than by talking about them" (Blatner, H., 1973, p. 6). Psychodrama usually takes place in a group, however, it focuses on one individual – the "protagonist".

Socio drama is useful in school situation. The plan is to create a situation, assign roles to players and act out a planned sequence of events. For example, a skit may be prepared showing a party situation. The aim is to make the participants learn various social graces and manners. Such socio-drama could take place in front of a group of receptive audience.

Fig. 2.2: Socio drama and psycho drama

Procedure: Some prerequisites for conducting a socio drama are as follows:

(1)   Describing clearly and specifically through discussions, situation common to the group members. The situation should be appropriate to group characteristics.

(2)   Breaking down the situation into sequences.

(3)   Obtaining volunteers to play the various roles. Creating a feeling of reality about the situation by making the players familiar with the persons whose role(s) they are planning.

(4)   Carrying out the socio dramatic situational sequences.

Role Play Activities

Role playing is a learning structure that allows students to immediately apply content as they are put in the role of a decision-maker who must make a decision regarding a policy, resource allocation or some other outcome.

For example, if the student is having difficulty with his/her father, s/he may be placed in the role of the father while a fellow student plays the role of the son. In human relations, valuable insights can develop through role-playing. Role-play can also be utilised to demonstrate how to attend a job interview, how to accept disappointments, etc.

Some suggestions, for counsellor who plan to use this technique:

(1)   Whenever the counsellor senses that a student is having trouble describing his/her problems and telling how s/he feels about them, the counsellor should respond to the student's feelings of inadequacy in the situation. S/he may suggest role-play as a technique. But s/he should also stress that it is not effective unless the student volunteers to play the role.

(2)   The scene to be acted out should be described by the member who had the problem.

(3)   A counsellor must encourage students to act the scenes whenever a student wants to know how others perceive one's conflict and how they react to one's proposed actions.

(4)   When the group has finished discussing on the first role-playing of the situation, some members of the group may suggest re-playing the scene with re-assignment of roles. Such repeating the scene with the players in new roles usually results in new insights.

Example of a Role Play

Mona (a standard X girl) brought a beautiful wall hanging with mirrors on the top of it. She got it for the crafts exhibition in the school. Unfortunately during the show, it fell down and all the mirrors broke down. Mona started crying. The counsellor tried to console her.

After about half an hour, when Mona was slightly balanced, she suggested her to make an outline for the play depicting the entire story. She agreed. Her other classmate also volunteered to help her in the role play. The outline and the scene was described.

The opening scene was the one in which Mona described her broken doll. The play covered a number of conflicting situations including the one in which Mona demanded that her classmates help her find the culprit and make her pay for the wall hanging. The scene also showed how, when they could not identify the person who had broken the wall hanging, Mona came to accept the idea that her classmates were responsible and they should not be expected to pay for her loss. She was able to accept her loss in a more mature way.

Q45. Write short notes on the following:
(i) Visit to Career Fair/Exhibition

Ans. Career fair enables visitors to gather greater knowledge about various courses and programmes and allows greater interaction between participating institution representatives and students. In a career fair, various stalls are put up by different institutes offering different courses. For example, Institute of Fashion Technology, Institute of Hotel Management or various Universities. They give information about the courses offered by them. Students get a chance to get information about various courses at one place itself.

These institutions sometimes use video cassettes, slide show, films, etc. to show the nature of work related to that career. They distribute information booklets or pamphlets free to the visitor. These fairs save time and effort. The students need not go from one institute to another to get information about the courses. But precaution must be taken and find out if these courses are recognised by the concerned regulatory body. If the courses are not recognised, they may not lead to any job later on.

(ii) Career Quiz Session

Ans. Career quiz sessions are a useful way of giving information pertaining to career. This activity motivates the students to get information so that they can participate in the quiz. Such quizzes of short duration can be made a regular feature of the extracurricular schedule. One-word answers, true or false statements can be given:

- State the full form of N.I.F.T., I.T.I., M.B.A., B.Ed., IIM, BITS, N.I.D., N.I.I.T., N.D.A., etc.
- State the educational qualification for entering into N.D.A.
- Which stream is required for joining the navy wing of defence force?

Such short questions can be asked. For reference, they can be told to see the newspapers and the information displayed on the bulletin board from time to time.

Another way in which many students can participate is to make it at the class level. Later on, it could be on the basis of sections. It can be held in each class separately and the winner can participate in the inter class quiz competition.

(iii) Student Council Meeting

Ans. Participating in Student Council will help students develop decision-making and problem-solving skills. Student Council also provides experience to students about the functioning of participatory democracy. Student Council can be formed with 2-3 students representing each class, 2-3 teachers, counsellor and the principal. The counsellor and the teachers should orient the student members about the functioning of the SC and their responsibilities. The student representatives can discuss the problems faced by the student community, provide ideas about improving academic achievement, request for additional service to facilitate student welfare, etc. in the SC and find solutions. Meetings can be held periodically, say twice a month as per convenience.

Such council meetings help in knowing the students' problems and building a rapport with the students and the management. Further, students feel responsible and important. They play an active role in the decision-making.

Q46. Discuss the aids to guidance in group situations.

Ans. The numerous kinds of supplementary materials are now available to aid counsellors in motivating group interest in pertinent topics of discussion. These materials need to be used with discretion, however.

Supplementary group guidance materials include appropriate books, newspapers, films, film strips, radio and TV programmes, charts posters, pamphlets, brochures, etc.

(1) **Books:** Various books have been written dealing with career related topics or improving one's personality.

Some of the books are:

(i)   Choose your career   by Dr. Phalachandra and Anita Bhadaria

(ii) After 10+2 what   by Dr. Kumkum Tandon

(iii) Career Planner I & II   by Dr. Kumkum Tandon

Certain books aiming at personality grooming are:

(i)   How to start a conversation and make friends?

(ii) How to stand up for yourself?

(2) **Newspaper:** Various newspapers are coming out with topics related to careers. Some of the newspapers are Times of India, Hindustan Times, Indian Express, Dainik Jagran. They publish articles related to career regularly on a weekly basis. They provides latest upto date information. If you happen to get one week's Hindustan Times, you will find it provides an additional supplement 'careers' every week, fast track is a corner which gives information about the various courses with the last date of filling up the application forms and on Youth and Career which tells about different careers. Not only this it takes up topics pertaining to personality development also.

Similarly, other newspapers also provides such information.

(3) **Magazines:** Certain magazines like Competition Success Review, G.K. Today, Mukta, Target also provide information about careers and on topics related to personality development. School magazine can also be made use of for providing information about scholarships, various colleges giving information pertaining to career. It can provide helpful supplementary service.

(4) Prospectus of different institutes offering courses, pamphlets, brochures are also invaluable sources of getting information.

(5) Audio Visual Aids: Motion pictures, Films, TV programmes, video cassettes, etc. depicting life situations used as aids for guidance in group situation for students and parents, e.g. the nature of work of a person in defence service can be comprehensively grasped if the students are shown a documentary film depicting the adventurous life they lead.

While making use of a movie or video film in group guidance the following points are to be kept in mind.

(i)   Select an appropriate movie relevant to the topic. The movie should not be an outdated one.

(ii) The time duration is noted beforehand.

(iii) Check the print.

(iv) Inform the group beforehand about the film and the purpose of showing it.

(v)   Encourage discussion after the film show is over.

More and more states and cities are sponsoring local radio and TV programmes for educational and vocational purposes.

One such radio programme which started is "Phone in Programme". They advertise about it in the newspapers. E.g., if a programme is organised on "Chartered Accountancy as a Career". 2-3 experts will be called from that area at the radio station who are going to answer the questions. The question can be asked by anyone, you also could be one of the participant on the telephone. Such question will be answered immediately and can be heard by others on the phone. The programme is of one hour duration.

Television has also started with certain career related programmes. 'Hum Honge Kamyab' a Zee TV production is a regular feature.

'Television Job Watch' a programme started in 1994 is another step by Doordarshan to provide people with the information about the jobs available in companies. It also provides a comprehensive information about the job prospects.

Such programmes reach a large number of people thus saves time and effort.

(6) Bulletin Board Displays: Information, which should reach a large number of students, can more efficiently be imparted through bulletin boards. Advertisement about careers, articles of general interest, charts and posters providing information can be put on the display board. Such bulletin boards should be put at place, which is common for the students.

(7) Activity: In the school situations, bulletin board display competition can be organised in schools. For example, the students of class IX are divided into 5-6 smaller groups. Each group is given a different topic for the display. Let us say the topics are Hotel Management, Designing, Defence Services, Business Administration, Law, etc. Each group is supposed to collect material related to the topic (pictures, pamphlets, etc.). A general guideline can be given to them:

(i) Meaning (Job profile)

(ii) Present scope and future prospects

(iii) Qualifications

    (a) Educational

    (b) Professional

    (c) Age limit

(iv) Mode of selection

(v) Various departments specifying the type of work carried out in each department.

(vi) Few clips of advertisement related to this field.

(vii) Pictures showing work of people in different departments.

The students are required to put the above information alongwith the pictures on the display board.

Each group will put up the display material for one week. They can be evaluated and by the end of one round, the group with the best presentation can be given certificates.

This actually has been found to be successful in imparting guidance. Certain quiz related to the displays can be held during the assembly time.

(8) Career Query Boxes: Usually, there is only one full time counsellor in the school and the work load is much on him/her, so it is not possible for him/her to devote time to the career related questions individually. Moreover, many questions are common, therefore, the counsellor doesn't need to address them separately.

In such cases, 'Career Query Box' can be used. A wooden box of approximately 12×12 inches can be taken. There is a small cut on the top of the box from where papers can be slipped in (like the ballet boxes). It can be locked. Students can put their questions related to career with name and class. A day in a week can be decided to open it. The answer can be written on slips of papers with the question and put up on the display board. The help of the students can be taken for writing the answers.

Q47. Enumerate the limitations of group guidance activities.

Ans. Following are the various limitations of group guidance activities:

- Group activities though serve a useful purpose, cannot be taken as a substitute for individual counselling.

- Group activities serve many of the objectives of the school guidance programme, but not all of them.
- It helps the students with their common problems but individuals differ in the amount of assistance they need to work through their difficulties.
- Further, students may feel hesitant to come out with their personal problems in the group. So, in such cases group guidance cannot be of help.
- Group activities are not taken seriously by some of the students.

Despite the limitations, group activities save time and efforts. It helps in making the individual counselling easy. It is complementary to individual counselling.

Q48. Write down the problems in organising group guidance activities.

Ans. Group guidance activities serve useful purpose specially saving in time and effort. While organising these activities, some problems that a counsellor may face are mentioned below:

- Lack of adequate funds is a major problem.
- A rigid type of administration is another major cause of trouble. Generally, when the counsellor asks for slot in the timetable for conducting these guidance activities, s/he may get a discouraging reply, the time table is already full. Then the counsellor is left with no other choice than to take the substitute/arrangement period.
- Lack of co-operation on part of the administration as well as the staff members may also create problems in organising such activities. Teachers may feel that guidance activity is an additional burden.

If tackled with a bit of planning, patience and boldness, these problems can be overcome. For instance, the problem of timetable, which does not have a period for guidance activities, one may take work experience/S.U.P.W. classes. Further, co-curricular activity classes can be taken in rotation every week. Career quizzes can be arranged with no difficulty if the entire plan has been discussed with management.

Further, the use of guidance in teaching and reducing the problem of truancy and indiscipline, underachievement can be conveyed to the teachers. Once they find a positive correlation between the two, they will be most willing to help. As far as the inadequacy of funds is concerned, the management needs to be convinced about the minimum requirement.

Q49. Enlist and explain various counselling skills.

Ans. Since counselling is a conversation or dialogue between the counsellor and client, the counsellor needs certain communication skills in order to facilitate change. The counsellor needs the following basic communication skills to do effective counselling:

(1) **Active Listening:** Listening refers to the ability of counsellors to capture and understand the messages clients communicate as they tell their stories, whether those messages are transmitted verbally or non-verbally.

Active listening involves the following four skills:

(i) Listening to and understanding the client's verbal messages. The counsellor has to listen to the mix of experiences, behaviour and feelings the client uses to describe his/her problem situation. Also, "hear" what the client is not saying.

(ii) Listening to and interpreting the client's non-verbal messages. Counsellors should learn how to listen to and read non-verbal messages.

(iii) Listening to and understanding the client in context. The counsellor should listen to the whole person in the context of his/her social settings.

(iv) Listening with empathy. Empathic listening involves attending, observing and listening ("being with") in such a way that the counsellor develops an understanding of the client and his/her world. The counsellor should put his/her own concerns aside to be fully "with" their clients.

(2) **Attending:** Attending refers to the ways in which counsellors can be "with" their clients, both physically and psychologically. Effective attending tells clients that we are with them and that they can share their world with us. Effective attending also puts us in a position to listen carefully to what our clients are saying. The acronym SOLER can be used to help us to show our inner attitudes and values of respect and genuineness towards a client (Egan).

S: Face the client squarely; that is, adopt a posture that indicates involvement.

O: Adopt an open posture. Sit with both feet on the ground to begin with and with our hands folded, one over the other.

L: As we face our client, lean towards him/her. Be aware of their space needs.

E: Maintain eye contact. Looking away or down suggests that we are bored or ashamed of what the client is saying. Looking at the person suggests that we are interested and concerned.

R: As the counsellor incorporates these skills into the attending listening skills, relax.

(3) **Paraphrasing:** A paraphrase is a restatement of the meaning of a text or passage using other words. This is restating or rewording the content (what is said by the client) back to the client. This should not be mere parroting the words back to the client. Paraphrasing involves reflection of the content and feelings of the client. Paraphrasing and reflection help in confirming with the client if the counsellor has understood the problem as narrated by the client.

(4) Empathy: Empathy is the capacity to understand or feel what another person is experiencing from within their frame of reference, i.e. the capacity to place oneself in another's position. Use of empathy is one of the most vital elements in the counselling. Empathy is the counsellor's ability to experience the client's world as if it were our own without ever using the quality.

(5) Asking Questions: Counsellors ask questions for fact finding and engaging with the client. Fact-finding questions are used for collecting data such as age, occupation, family status, etc. regarding a new client. Open-ended questions help in engaging and establishing a relationship with the client. Open-ended questions are used to elicit a response from the client, probe and expand a response given by the client or explore deeper into the client's problem.

(6) Immediacy: This involves a counselor's understanding and communicating of what is going on between the counsellor and client within the helping relationship. There are two types of immediacy: (i) Relationship immediacy. (Between client & counsellor); (ii) "Here & Now" immediacy focuses on some particular event in the session.

(7) Self-disclosure: Self-disclosure is an important way to let clients know the counsellor as a person. Self-disclosure at a moderate level is seen more positively by clients than disclosure at a high or low level (Edwards & Murdock, 1994). In moderation, it is helpful for the counsellor to disclose facts about himself, if it serves the needs of the session/client. Self-disclosure takes the following forms:

(i)   The counsellor's own problems;

(ii)   Facts about the counsellor's role;

(iii)   The counsellor's reactions to the client (feedback); and

(iv)   The counsellor's reactions to the counselor-client relationship.

(8) Summarising: It is sometimes useful for the counsellor to summarise what was said in a session so as to provide a focus to what was previously discussed, and so as to challenge the client to move forward. Summaries are particularly helpful under the following circumstances:

(i)   At the beginning of a new session. A summary of this point can give direction to clients who do not know where to start; it can prevent clients from merely repeating what they have already said, and it can pressure a client to move forwards.

(ii) When a session seems to be going nowhere. In such circumstances, a summary may help to focus the client.

(iii) When a client gets stuck. In such a situation, a summary may help to move the client forward so that s/he can investigate other parts of his/her story.

(9) Goal Setting: After assessing the problem, the counsellor works with the client to set realistic goals or behavioural changes the client wants to accomplish. It is important to set goals that are achievable. Goals are set depending on the nature of the problem and the client's ability to engage in the helping process. Time bound specific goals give a sense of purpose and accomplishment to the client.

(10) Ending Sessions and Follow-up: Setting boundaries is important in a counselling relationship. Counsellors should begin and end sessions on time. Clients should be informed about the rules of the counselling contract and counsellors should not be lenient if the client is late for the session. The message to the client should be, being late means forgoing the session. This is necessary because it is the client's responsibility to work towards the set goals or behavioural changes. When ending each session, the counsellor may encourage the client to carry on the new behaviour learnt in the session in the outside world. This may be followed up at the beginning of the next session by enquiring about the client's accomplishments in the world outside.

(11) Termination of Counselling: Termination is an important, though, often misunderstood phase of counselling. This is often ignored or taken for granted. Yet successful termination is vital for the well-being of client as well as counsellor. Termination is the end of the professional relationship with the client when the session goals have been met. It is a phase of counselling that can determine the success of all previous phases and must be handled skillfully. A formal termination serves three functions:

(i) Counselling is finished and it is time for the client to face their life challenges.

(ii) Changes which have taken place have generalised into the normal behaviour of the client.

(iii) The client has matured and thinks and acts more effectively and independently.

Q50. Discuss behavioural interventions to counselling. What are the various techniques for behavioural counselling?

Ans. Behaviour provides satisfying experience and such behaviour that approved or reinforced through childhood is likely to be repeated. Similarly, if a behaviour is discouraged, not approved or not reinforced, it tends to disappear. Therefore, if behaviour is learned, it can be unlearned in a similar way. Behavioural learning theories can, thus, help us understand behavioural patterns exhibited by the clients and modify them. There are positive and negative reinforcements. A reward (stimulus) that is presented during the behaviour or immediately after the behaviour is called a positive reinforcement. In similar kind, if the stimulus is withdrawn or not given after the behaviour, it is considered a negative reinforcement. Therefore, behaviour counselling is based on the understanding that reinforcement strengthens the behaviour, which means positive reinforcement leads to the behaviour occurring in the future whereas negative reinforcement resulting either in behaviour modification or dropping of the behaviour. Behavioural counselling aims at developing desirable behaviour and modifying or removing undesirable behaviour.

The behavioural ABC method is a useful mnemonic for functional analysis. A stands for antecedents, B stands for 'behaviour', C stands for consequences.

The counsellor, after the functional analysis of the behaviour, would assess if change in 'A' would result in a new (desirable) or modified behaviour (B). Alternatively, the counsellor would assess if removing or change in (C) would develop a new behaviour (B). The focus of the behavioural intervention is in developing a new behaviuor; strengthening a newly developed behaviour; weakening a problem behaviour; or modifying the problem behaviour (B). For designing a behavioural intervention plan, we need to collect baseline data related to the problem behaviour of the client. We may ask the client to keep a self-monitoring diary that will provide information about the frequency, length and intensity of the problem behaviour. In a school or any other educational institution, teachers can observe learners (client's) regarding the problem behaviour and maintain a diary. We can seek report from parents, teachers and peer group about the learner's (client's) behaviour.

Behavioural Counselling Techniques

Techniques in behavioural therapies apply the learning principles to change maladaptive behaviours (Weiten, 2007). The techniques do not focus on clients achieving insights into their behaviour; rather the focus is just on changing the behaviour. For example, if a behavioural therapist is working with a client, that has an alcohol problem, the behavioural therapist will design a programme to eliminate the behaviour of drinking — but there would be no focus on the issues or pathological symptoms causing the alcohol problem.

There are a number of techniques used in behaviour therapy that have been scientifically validated as being successful approaches to treating symptoms:

(1) **Exposure Therapies:** Exposure therapies are designed to expose the client to feared situations similar to that of systematic desensitisation (Corey, 2005). Exposure therapies are used to reduce disabling feelings and emotions such as anxiety, fear, anger, phobia, etc. The client is gradually exposed to the problem situations or in imagination under the

supervision of the counsellor. The behavioural assessment should clearly indicate that the problem behaviuor is irrational and inappropriate which means the problem behaviour is not because of the inadequacy of skills. For example, if a child is fearful of swimming, it should not be due to the lack of swimming skills.

Exposure therapies are based on classical conditioning, which include systematic desensitisation, _in vivo_ desensitisation, flooding and implosion. All these are discussed as follows:

(i) **Systematic Desensitisation:** Systematic desensitisation was developed by Joseph Wolfe and was designed for clients with phobias. This treatment follows a process of "counterconditioning" meaning the association between the stimulus and the anxiety is weakened through the use of relaxation techniques, anxiety hierarchies and desensitisation (Weiten, 2007). The systematic desensitisation is done in the following steps:

(ii) **Constructing Anxiety Hierarchy:** The client (here, learner) is asked to list all the situations or events that induce anxiety and arrange it in increasing order of intensity. In the anxiety hierarchy, the client may be asked to construct 10-12 episodes/scenes that produce anxiety. The first scene produces the least anxiety and the last scene produces anxiety of the highest intensity. For instance, a list of anxiety hierarchy created by a client fearful of spiders is given as follows.

(a) Hear someone mention spider.

(b) See picture of spider.

(c) See a small spider on the wall.

(d) See a small spider crawling on the floor.

(e) See a big spider on the wall.

(f) See a big spider crawling on the floor.

(g) Spider crawling on the desk.

(h) Spider crawling on the arm of the chair he is sitting.

(i) Spider crawling on shirt sleeve.

(j) Spider crawling on bare foot or arm.

(iii) **Training in Relaxation:** A relaxation technique (also known as relaxation training) is any method, process, procedure or activity that helps a person to relax; to attain a state of increased calmness; or otherwise reduce levels of pain, anxiety, stress or anger. Relaxation techniques are often employed as one element of a wider stress management programme and can decrease muscle tension, lower the blood pressure and slow heart and breath rates, among other health benefits.

Counsellors use a variety of relaxation techniques to help their clients deal with anxiety. In this, the counsellor provides training to the clients in relaxation. Clients receive training to relax different muscle groups in the order starting with the small muscles (toes, feet) to the larger muscle groups (shoulder, neck, face).

Mental imagery is another relaxation technique in which the client is asked to imagine herself/himself in a place or situation that is associated with pleasant memories. The pleasant imagery helps the client to move into a state of relaxation. When the client is in a state of relaxation, the physiological changes that happen are opposite to the physiological responses induced by anxiety. In relaxation state, the heart beat and the respiration rate start returning to normalcy, and muscle tension begins to loosen.

Shavasana is yoga posture that can be practiced for relaxation. In this yoga posture, the client is asked to maintain the posture of a corpse and instruct the body to relax gradually from toe to head. *Vipassana* is a meditation technique which can be used for relaxation. *Pranayama,* the breathing technique which many of us are familiar with, is another relaxation technique.

Relaxation activity has to be done in a calm environment and in a comfortable posture in a chair or mat.

(iv) Desensitising the Anxiety-inducing Stimulus: The final and last step in systematic desensitisation is 'desensitising the anxiety inducing stimulus'. Following the counsellor's instructions, the client enters into relaxation state. When the client is in deep relaxation state, s/he is presented with the least anxiety provoking scene from the list constructed by the client earlier. The client is instructed to visualise each item in the list. Even if a scene produces tension, it would not be lasting as relaxation and tension cannot go together. However, if the tension stays longer, the client is instructed to move away from the scene and asked to relax further. Once again when the client is in deep state of relaxation the scene that provoked anxiety is presented. The process is repeated with each scene till the time the most anxiety provoking scene fails to provoke anxiety in the client. When the client stays calm and relaxed while imagining the high anxiety provoking scene, there is little chance that the corresponding event in real life would provoke anxiety. Remember the state of equanimity is not achieved in one sitting but through a series of sessions, usually 8-10 sessions. Therefore, the counsellor must make the decision after assessing the severity of the case about the approximate number of sessions that would need for the desensitisation therapy. The counsellor should also review the progress of the desensitisation process periodically and make changes, if required.

(v) **In Vivo Desensitisation:** This can be used in the case where systematic desensitisation fails. In vivo desensitisation, the client is actually exposed to the phobic stimulus. In in vivo desensitisation, the client is gradually introduced to the real life anxiety provoking stimulus. Here too the client is asked to develop a hierarchy of fear inducing stimulus. The client receives training in relaxation techniques. When the client is in relaxation state, the counsellor gradually presents the fear producing actual stimulus. Some counsellors provide positive reinforcement in place of relaxation.

(vi) **Flooding:** Flooding involves the client being exposed to the actual or imagined fearful situation for a prolonged period of time. The example of the client with the spider fear would be that the client would be exposed to the spider or the thought of a spider for a prolonged period of time and uses relaxation techniques to cope.

There may be ethical issues in using these techniques with certain fears or traumatic events and the client should be provided with information on the techniques before utilising them so he or she understands the process. This technique is usually used when the systematic and in vivo desensitisation processes fail. As in the desensitisation process, in flooding too the client is given training in relaxation. A few sessions are used for learning the relaxation techniques. The client may practice the relaxation techniques at home too. After the client has learned the relaxation techniques, the counsellor exposes the client abruptly to the anxiety provoking stimulus. Due to classical conditioning, the client has learnt to associate fear with the stimulus. In flooding technique, the same principle is used to extinguish the fear response by replacing it with a feeling of relaxation. Unlike the systematic desensitisation process, in flooding the exposure to the fear inducing stimulus is rapid, abrupt and direct. Flooding is applied in real situation and the client cannot escape from the situation.

(iv) **Implosion:** Implosion is a process in which objects are destroyed by collapsing (or being squeezed in) on themselves. Flooding is done in real situation whereas implosion is done using imagery. For example, a learner may be asked to imagine a scene in which spiders are crawling around the room. The counsellor continues with exaggerated details of the scene that the spiders are crawling on his/her face and entering his/her nose. In implosion treatment, the client may show strong emotional reactions. The treatment is continued till the client is assessed to have eliminated the anxiety behaviour associated with spider.

In another situation like, if a learner is fearful of public speaking; s/he doesn't ask questions in the class; and even when the teacher asks question, s/he doesn't say the answer although s/he knows it. In implosion therapy, s/he is asked to imagine a scene in which s/he is addressing the school assembly, fumbling for words, students laughing, whistling and hooting, noise becoming louder, and principal and teachers angry and scolding him/her. S/he goes through a few more sessions of intensive anxiety evoking imagery of public speaking till his/her public speaking phobia is eliminated.

(2) Stimulus Control by using Reinforcement and Punishment: Therefore, systematic use of reinforcement and punishment for stimulus control is based on the principles of operant conditioning. In stimulus control technique, the focus is on the antecedent to the occurrence of a behaviour. In a school situation, stimulus control can be understood through an example.

A teacher named Riddima teaches English in class IX. After the class is over, if the students have any academic problem, they would go to her and discuss. She would listen and help them to deal with their problems. Another teacher named Madhuri teaches Science to the same group of students. But the students do not go to Madhuri although they experience difficulty in the subject. Initially, when students would approach Madhuri to discuss their subject related problems, s/he would scold them for not being attentive in the class. Gradually, students stopped going to her. As Riddima listens and provides reinforcement to the students whenever they approach her, they continued to meet her and discuss their subject related problems. Here, Ridhima's presence is an antecedent to the behaviour of the students which is discussing their academic problems. Or we can say Ridhima's presence is serving as stimulus control for the behaviour of the students. As Madhuri did not reinforce the behaviour of the students, it gradually stopped occurring.

(3) Role Play: A role-playing game is a game in which the participants assume the roles of characters and collaboratively create stories. Participants determine the actions of their characters based on their characterisation, and the actions succeed or fail according to a formal system of rules and guidelines. Within the rules, they may improvise freely; their choices shape the direction and outcome of the games.

Role-playing can also be done online in the form of group story creation, involving anywhere from two to several hundred people, utilising public forums, private message boards, mailing lists, chatrooms, and instant-messaging chat clients (e.g., MSN, Yahoo and ICQ) to build worlds and characters that may last a few hours, or several years. Often on forum-based role-plays, rules, and standards are set up, such as a minimum word count, character applications, and "plotting" boards to increase complexity and depth of story.

There are different genres of which one can choose while role-playing, including, but not limited to, fantasy, modern, medieval, steam punk, and historical. Books, movies, or games can be, and often are, used as a basis for role-plays (which in such cases may be deemed "collaborative fan-fiction"), with players either assuming the roles of established canon characters or using those the players themselves create ("Original Characters") to replace — or exist alongside — characters from the book, movie, or game, playing through well-trodden plots as alternative characters, or expanding upon the setting and story outside its established canon.

Counsellors use role play technique to modify a behaviour. Role play can also be used to learn a new behaviour. In role play, the counsellor and the client assume specified roles and enact a problem situation. Initially, the counsellor plays the role of the client and the client does the role of the other actor (parent, teacher or principal) in the problem situation. In the following session, they exchange the roles which means the client plays his/her role and the counsellor plays the role of the other actor. In the second session, where the client is playing his/her original role in the problem situation, s/he attempts to model his/her behaviour on the behaviour demonstrated by the counsellor in the first session. Over time in subsequent sessions of role exchanges and modeling, the client learns a new behaviour or modifies the existing behaviour so that the situation is no more problematic. For instance,

Harish is a class X student. His academic performance is very good. He is also an excellent classical singer. He wants to pursue a career in classical music and become a vocalist. His parents are doctors and own a hospital. They want him to pursue a career in medicine and eventually run the hospital when they retire. They are now planning to get him admission in an expensive coaching centre to prepare for the medical entrance exam after the 12th class. He has been so far unsuccessful in telling his mother about his desire to pursue a career in classical music. As soon as he begins to talk to mother about his future career plans, his mother would block him by saying that he is going to become a doctor and there was nothing more to discuss. Harish doesn't want his parents to be unhappy but he doesn't want medicine for a career either. But he has so far not succeeded in presenting his case to the parents. He feels unhappy and distressed. That is how he approached the school counsellor and discussed the problem. The counsellor suggested role play to Harish for dealing with the situation. Harish agreed to the suggestion. To begin with Harish was asked to enact his mother's role and the counsellor played Harish's role. In the next session, Harish assumed his own role and the counsellor played his mother. In this session Harish was expected to incorporate what he has learnt from the counsellor's behaviour while playing Harish. Initially, it was not very easy for Harish to model his behaviour on the behaviour of the counsellor as Harish in the earlier session. Because, he felt nervous confronting his mother. In subsequent sessions involving exchange of roles and modeling by the counsellor, gradually Harish has learnt to confront his mother and assert himself.

(4) Token Economy: A token economy is a system for providing positive reinforcement to a child or children by giving them tokens for completing tasks or behaving in desired ways. Rules are established prior to the start of the treatment which specify the behaviour to be modified and the reward to be given. Each time the client exhibits the desired behaviour, it results in the reward of a token.

Token economies are used as a method of strengthening a behaviour, or increasing its frequency, because the tokens are a way of "paying" children for completing tasks and the children can then use these tokens to buy desired activities or items (Miltenberger, 2008).

The basic principle of token economy is that a child earns a certain number of tokens by engaging in desired behaviours (called "target behaviours") and can then exchange these tokens – effectively using them as payment – to gain access to backup reinforcers.

Q51. What are the various applications of different behavioural and cognitive interventions as a counsellor? Discuss.

Ans. Aaron Temkin Beck (born July 18, 1921) is an American psychiatrist who is professor emeritus in the department of psychiatry at the

University of Pennsylvania. He is regarded as the father of cognitive therapy, and his pioneering theories are widely used in the treatment of clinical depression. Beck also developed self-report measures of depression and anxiety, notably the Beck Depression Inventory (BDI) that became one of the most widely used instruments for measuring depression severity.

Psychologist Aron Beck developed the cognitive therapy concept in the 1960s. Cognitive approach to counselling is based on the understanding that human behaviour is influenced by cognition or thought process. Therefore, when individuals respond to events or situations, they do so depending on their beliefs, attitude, or expectations. This means there is a pattern of thinking behind our manifested behaviour. That ineffective behaviour is due to distortion in the thinking process. So if maladaptive behaviour has to be unlearnt, modified or a new behaviour has to be learnt, changing the thinking pattern is essential. Therefore, the client is helped to examine the rationality of assumptions behind his/her behaviour. Most counsellors combine behavioural and cognitive therapy to deal with client dysfunctions or problems.

The goal of cognitive therapy is to get such an individual to recognise the illogical and self-defeating patterns within his thought, and through a variety of measures cease to think that way. Each of the cognitive distortions is illogical, that each does in fact exemplify a specific or general logical fallacy.

(1) **All-or-Nothing Thinking:** This cognitive distortion exemplifies the fallacy of *false dilemma*, presuming that only two alternatives exist when in fact there are more than two (Schick & Vaughn, 2002, pp. 299-300). The student who believed she had to either keep a 3.5 grade point average or else drop out of school was certainly setting up a false dilemma. There were, of course, other alternatives. It is in this way, then that the cognitive distortion of all-or-nothing thinking is illogical—it involves the fallacy of false dilemma.

(2) **Over-generalisation:** This cognitive distortion exemplifies the fallacy of hasty generalisation, drawing a conclusion about all or most things of a certain type on the basis of evidence concerning only a few things of that type (Bassham, *et al.*, 2002, pp. 172-73). The person who engages in overgeneralisation sees a single event as a sign of a never-ending pattern of defeat. The high school senior who concludes on the basis of not getting into the college of her choice, that all of life will be a series of disappointments is engaging in over-generalisation, and in the language of logic is committing the fallacy of hasty generalisation. On the basis of one important event being disappointing she reasons that all future important events will be disappointing.

(3) **Mental Filter:** This cognitive distortion exemplifies the fallacy of *suppressed evidence*. This fallacy occurs when an arguer unjustifiably overlooks or slights relevant evidence that warrants a quite different conclusion than the one drawn by the arguer (Kahane & Cavender, 1998, pp. 54-56, slightly adapted). When, through the cognitive distortion of mental filter, we allow a single negative detail to colour our vision of all reality we commit the fallacy of suppressed evidence. The new car owner who allows the small paint chip to so disturb his life is committing the fallacy of suppressed evidence. He is dwelling obsessively on this one negative reality, while ignoring other positive realities in his life. Obviously this person has let things get away from him, has let a small negative fact dictate conclusions that are simply unwarranted.

(4) **Disqualifying the Positive:** This cognitive distortion also exemplifies the fallacy of *suppressed evidence*. Consider the depressed man who discounts his wife's statement that "I like you, the children like you, and your friend Bob likes you" in order to persist in his negative thought that "no one likes me." This individual is unjustifiably ignoring or downplaying evidence that is inconsistent with his conclusion, and thus commits the fallacy of suppressed evidence.

(5) **Jumping to Conclusions:** This cognitive distortion exemplifies the general fallacy of *insufficient evidence*. The person who "jumps to conclusions" often makes a negative interpretation of facts that are inconclusive. An old friend tells me that he does not have time to talk on the phone at the moment. I have no good evidence that he doesn't want to talk to me, but I nevertheless assume this to be the case. A strong candidate for a job concludes she will not get the position, essentially because she assumes the worst about herself. The depressed individual is nearly always inclined to draw negative or self-critical conclusions from evidence that more objective observers would find to be inconclusive or supportive of a less negative conclusion.

(6) **Magnification or Minimisation:** Magnification and minimisation typically involves the general fallacy of *unacceptable premise*. Clearly, the woman who believes that her new promotion is not a big deal and that breaking her diet makes her a failure is drawing conclusions from premises that are not reasonable or warranted.

(7) **Emotional Reasoning:** This cognitive distortion exemplifies the general fallacy of insufficient evidence. The distortion occurs when an individual believes, without good reason, that his or her negative feelings reflect the way reality is. Thus, for example, a depressed individual who reasons that he is worthless because he feels worthless commits the fallacy of insufficient evidence by drawing an unwarranted conclusion from insufficient evidence.

(8) Should Statements: This cognitive distortion commonly exemplifies either the specific fallacy of false dilemma or the general fallacy of unacceptable premise. In one variant of this distortion, a depressed individual may reason something like this:

Example I

(i) I must stay on my diet, or else I'm worthless and must punish myself.

(ii) I didn't stay on my diet.

(iii) Therefore, I'm worthless and must punish myself.

Since the first premise poses a false either/or choice, this argument commits the fallacy of false dilemma. In the second common variant of the distortion, a depressed individual draws a conclusion based on a false and unrealistic "should" statement. That is:

Example II

(i) Anyone who feels angry with his or her kids is a bad parent and should feel guilty.

(ii) I sometimes feel angry with my kids.

(iii) Therefore, I am a bad parent and should feel guilty.

In this example, the first premise is unrealistic and unwarranted. Thus, the arguer commits the fallacy of unacceptable premise.

(9) Labeling and Mislabeling: This cognitive distortion illustrates the general fallacy of _insufficient evidence_. A depressed individual who reasons for example, "I didn't get the promotion, therefore I'm a loser," is guilty of drawing an excessively self-denigrating conclusion from insufficient premises. Similarly, a person who labels his wife a "bitch" after a series of minor disagreements commits the fallacy of insufficient evidence by attaching a harsh and inappropriate label that is not warranted by the evidence.

(10) Personalisation: This cognitive distortion exemplifies the fallacy of _false cause,_ the error of supposing two events are causally connected when they are not (Bassham, _et al.,_ 2002, pp. 171-72). Personalisation is, in fact, one of the leading ways in which we mistakenly assume a causal connection. Perhaps because we would like to think we have more control over things than we actually do, we assume personal responsibility for things that are not actually our fault. The teacher who feels like a failure because a certain student is failing may well be involved in the cognitive distortion known as personalisation, and so may well be committing the fallacy of false cause. A dedicated as competent teacher cannot reasonably assume she is the cause of failure in the case of a lazy or mediocre student.

Most people can see this easily, but the depressed individual often cannot.

A counsellor can help clients identify and correct cognitive distortions in their thinking process. Cognitive behavioural therapy (CBT) uses different techniques to help clients examine their dysfunctional thoughts to understand their non productive or self-destructive behaviour.

CBT Technique

Cognitive Behavioural Therapy is a therapy, which takes a psycho-therapeutic approach to solving problems associated with behaviour, dysfunctional emotions and cognition. In the cognitive behavioural therapy, a systematic and goal-oriented process is followed. The basic idea around which CBT techniques revolve is that no external factors but inherent ones are responsible for the behaviour we exhibit and feelings we experience; in short, our thoughts guide our behavioural patterns. CBT techniques are executed in a time-bound manner. On an average, 16 sessions are needed to complete this therapy.

The cognitive behavioural therapy exercises help in modifying a person's behavioural patterns. Behavioural patterns are modified for bringing about positive changes in the patient's personality. These techniques are as follows:

(1) **Cognitive Rehearsal:** In this technique, the patient is asked to recall a problematic situation from his/her past. The therapist and patient work on the problem to find a solution for it. The therapist asks the patient to rehearse positive thoughts in his/her mind; rehearsing positive thoughts helps in making appropriate changes to the patient's thought processes. The power of imagination proves to be of great help when you are doing such type of exercises.

(2) **Validity Testing:** In this technique, validity of thoughts of the patient are tested by the therapist; the patient is allowed to defend his/her viewpoint with the help of an objective evidence. The faulty nature or invalidity of beliefs held by the patient is exposed if s/he is unable to produce any kind of objective evidence.

(3) **Writing in a Journal:** It is a practice of maintaining a diary to keep an account of the different situations encountered by patients in day-to-day life. Thoughts associated with these situations and behaviour exhibited in response are also mentioned in the diary. The therapist and patient review what all is written in the diary and try to identify the patient's maladaptive thought patterns. The discussion which takes place between patient and therapist is helpful for finding the different ways in which behaviour of the patient gets affected.

(4) **Guided Discovery:** The purpose behind using this technique is to help patients to understand their cognitive distortions. Patients are offered the necessary assistance and

guidance by therapists to understand how they process information. It allows patients to alter the way they process of information. Upon completion of this treatment, the patient's perception of the world undergoes a profound change and s/he starts seeing things with a new outlook. A change in perception enables the patient to modify his/her behavioural patterns.

Rational Emotive Behavioural Therapy

Rational emotive behaviour therapy (REBT) is an active-directive, philosophically and empirically based psychotherapy, the aim of which is to resolve emotional and behavioural problems and disturbances and to help people to lead happier and more fulfilling lives. REBT was created and developed by the American psychotherapist and psychologist Albert Ellis, who was inspired by many of the teachings of Asian, Greek, Roman and modern philosophers. REBT is the first form of cognitive behavioural therapy (CBT) and was first expounded by Ellis in the mid-1950s; development continued until his death in 2007.

According to Ellis, the commonly held irrational beliefs are as follows:

(1) Something potentially dangerous or harmful should be a cause of great concern and should always be kept in mind.

(2) It is essential to be loved and approved by every significant person in one's life.

(3) There is always a right answer to every problem, and a failure to find this answer is a disaster.

(4) To be worthwhile, a person must be competent, adequate and achieving in everything attempted.

(5) A person must depend on others and must have someone stronger on whom to rely.

(6) A person should get upset over the problems and difficulties of others.

(7) Some people are wicked, bad, villainous, and should be blamed or punished.

(8) It is terrible and disastrous whenever events do not occur as one hopes.

(9) The past determines one's present behaviour and thus it cannot be changed.

(10) Running away from difficulties or responsibilities is easier than facing them.

(11) Unhappiness is the result of outside events and a person has no control over such despair.

Ellis used the A-B-C-D-E therapeutic approach to help clients resolve their problems.

(A) The activating event or stimulus, paired with the (B) belief about the activating event, causes a (C) consequence (the emotional and behavioural response) (D) is the disputing intervention that is introduced to change the (B) belief. After which a new (E) effect (more appropriate belief) becomes associated with the original (A) activating event. Lastly new (F) feelings arise which are associated with the new beliefs about ourselves.

Q52. What is transactional analysis? Describe the behavioural models of ego state.

Ans. Transactional analysis (TA) is a psychoanalytic theory and method of therapy wherein social transactions are analysed to determine the ego state of the patient (whether parent-like, child-like, or adult-like) as a basis for understanding behaviour. In transactional analysis, the patient is taught to alter the ego state as a way to solve emotional problems. The method deviates from Freudian psychoanalysis, which focuses on increasing awareness of the contents of unconsciously held ideas. Eric Berne developed the concept and paradigm of transactional analysis in the late 1950s.

Transactional analysis helps us to understand the effective and ineffective aspects of our personality. As a counsellor, we can train our clients to apply TA to improve their intra-personal and inter-personal effectiveness.

(1) **Ego States:** According to TA, we have three sides or 'ego-states' to our personality – the Parent, Adult and Child ego states.

An ego state is a way of us experiencing the world. It is an entire system of thoughts, feelings, and behaviours from which we interact with one another (and even with ourselves in our internal conversations). Our thinking, feeling and behaviour when we are in each ego state is consistent.

Please note that each ego state is given a capital letter to denote the difference between ego states and actual parents, adults and children.

The ego states are drawn in diagrammatical form as follows:

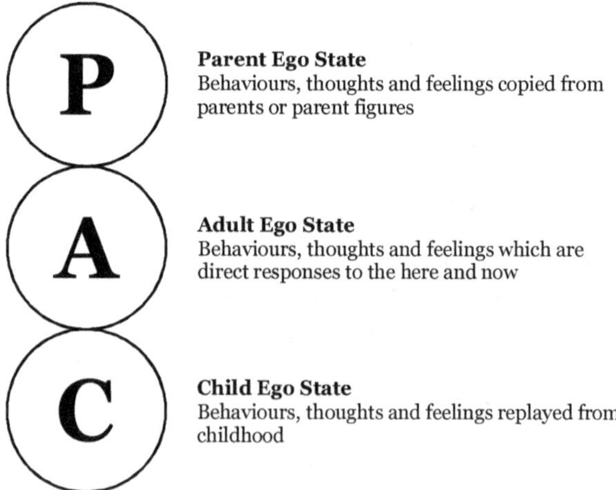

Fig. 2.3: Structural Diagram

(i) **The Parent Ego State:** This is a set of feelings, thinking and behaviour that we have copied from our parents and significant others.

As we grow up we take in ideas, beliefs, feelings and behaviours from our parents and caretakers. (If we live in an extended family then there are more people to be influenced by and learn from). When we do this, it is called introjecting and it is just as if we take in the whole of the care giver. For example, we may notice that we are saying things just as our father, mother, grandmother may have done, even though, consciously, we don't want to. We do this because we have lived with this person for so long that we automatically reproduce certain things that were said to us, or treat others as we might have been treated by them. It's as if someone has pressed 'play' on a recording and we play back what we saw and heard without question. The Parent ego state is rooted in the past.

There are two types of parent we can play:

(a) **The Nurturing Parent:** This Parent type is caring and concerned and may often appear as a mother-figure (though men can play it too). They seek to keep the child contented, offering a safe haven and unconditional love to calm the Child's troubles.

(b) **The Controlling (or Critical) Parent:** This Parent type tries to make the Child do as the Parent wants them to do, perhaps transferring values or beliefs or helping the Child to understand and live in society. They may also have negative intent, using the Child as a scapegoat.

(ii) **The Adult Ego State:** The Adult ego state is the 'grown up' rational person who talks reasonably and assertively, neither trying to control nor reacting aggressively towards others. The Adult is comfortable with him/herself and is, for many of us, our 'ideal self'.

The Adult ego state deals with the here and now reality. It is the processing centre and important because it is the only ego state that is not connected to the past. The Adult ego state is able to deal with current things in ways that are not unhealthily influenced by our past. If you were asked how to make a paper airplane you would probably reply from your Adult ego state.

The Adult ego state is about being spontaneous and aware, with a capacity for intimacy. The Adult is able to see people as they are, rather than what we project onto them. The Adult asks for information, rather than staying scared or making assumptions.

In the structural model, the Adult ego state circle is placed in the middle of the Parent and Child ego states to show how it needs to orchestrate between these two. For example, the Parent may criticise the Child, saying "You are no good, look at what you did wrong again, you are useless". The Child may then respond with "I am no good, look how useless I am, I never get anything right". (Most people don't hear their internal dialogue as it goes on so much they just believe life is this way). An effective Adult can intervene by stating that this kind of parenting is not helpful and asking if it is prepared to learn another way. Alternatively, the Adult can just stop any negative dialogue and decide to develop another positive Parent ego state perhaps taken in from other people they have met over the years.

(iii) **The Child Ego State:** The Child ego state is rooted in the past and plays back thoughts, feelings and behaviours that we experienced as a child. For example, if the boss calls us into his or her office, we may immediately get a churning in our stomach and wonder what we have done wrong. If we explored the reason for this automatic thinking, we might remember the time the head teacher called us in to tell us off. In the same way, we might go into someone's house and smell a lovely smell and remember our grandmother's house when we were little, and all the same warm feelings we had as a six-year old may come flooding back.

There are three types of Child we can play:

(a) **The Natural Child:** This child type is largely un-self-aware and is characterised by the non-speech noises they make (yippee, whoo-hoo, etc.). They like playing and are open and vulnerable.

(b) **The Little Professor:** This child type is the curious and exploring Child who is always trying out new stuff (often much to their Controlling Parent's annoyance). Together with the Natural Child they make up the Free Child.

(c) **The Adaptive Child:** This child type reacts to the world around them, either changing themselves to fit in and so being very good, or rebelling against the forces they feel and so being naughty.

Both the Parent and Child ego states are constantly being updated. For example, we may meet someone who gives us the permission we needed (but did not get) as a child, to be fun and joyous. We then use that person in our imagination "I wonder what X would say now?" to counteract our old ways of thinking and give us new permissions. So instead of thinking that we must work longer and longer hours to keep up with everything, we relax and take some time out. Subsequently, rather than beating ourselves up for what we did or did not do, what tends to happen is we automatically start to give ourselves new permissions and take care of ourselves.

(iv) **The Adult Ego State:** The Adult ego state behaviour is reflected as our concern with information, facts and data about the here and now of our living. In the Adult ego state, we collect, analyse and evaluate the old and new data. We formulate hypotheses and test them. Unlike the other two ego states, the Adult ego state deals with facts and data, not with feelings and emotions. There are two aspects to the Adult ego state, the Photographic Adult (PA) and the Combining Adult (CA).

    (a)   **Photographic Adult(PA):** It is that part of our personality which records what is happening around us, remembers and reports it. In this functioning of the Adult ego state, our brain perceives the surroundings like a camera, clicks it, records it, and reports on it when needed. For example, when you tell someone that you had met her last Sunday at the theatre, you are using your photographic Adult ego state.

    (b)   **Combining Adult (CA):** The Combining Adult part of our personality analyses and evaluates the data collected by the Photographic Adult and what is stored in the memory.

It is interesting to note that TA psychotherapy involves much work to update the Adult ego state with new information, and challenge the Child or Parent ego state ideas.

The given figure shows the three ego states:

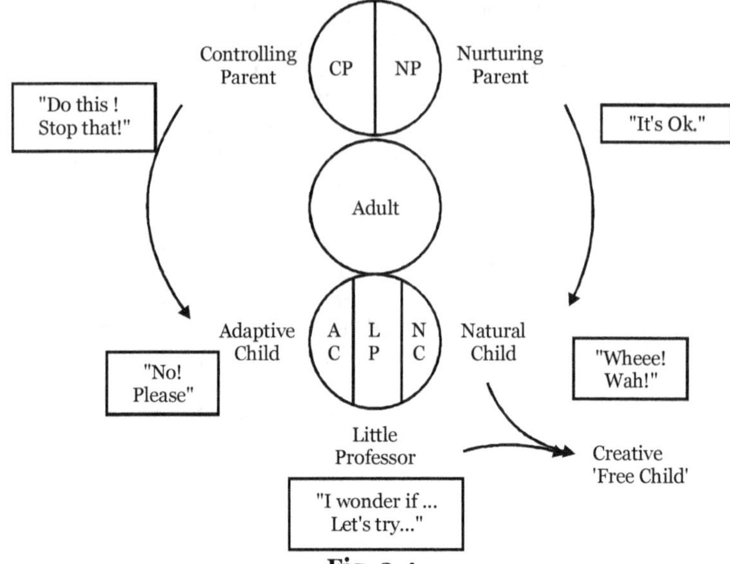

Fig. 2.4

Part of TA therapy also involves encouraging the client to grow their less developed ego states so that the three ego states are more in balance.

(2) **Contamination of Ego States:** There can be disturbance in the integrated functioning of the ego states when ego states boundaries are crossed and functional autonomy of an ego state is restricted by the other ego state or ego states.(When ego states overlap, it causes confusion, lack of clarity, and develops blind areas in our personality. This is known as contamination of the ego states.) Contamination occurs when the Parent or Child ego states intrude into the boundary of the Adult ego state and inhibits its objective thinking. For example, when you say boys have superior intelligence compared to girls, you are operating from a contaminated Adult ego state. Here you have accepted the cultural prejudice of male supremacy as afact. This means your Parent ego state has contaminated your Adult. Let us take another example of contamination of the ego state. In the case of Ruhi cited earlier, say she takes up the medical profession although that is not what she wished to do. Because she thinks this way she can please her parents and she is happy to take up medical profession. When she was a little girl, her mother would say, be a good girl and do as told because she knew what was best for Ruhi. Here, Ruhi's Parent ego state has contaminated her Child ego state. And the Child ego state has contaminated the Adult ego state when she says she is happy joining the medical profession although classical music is her passion.

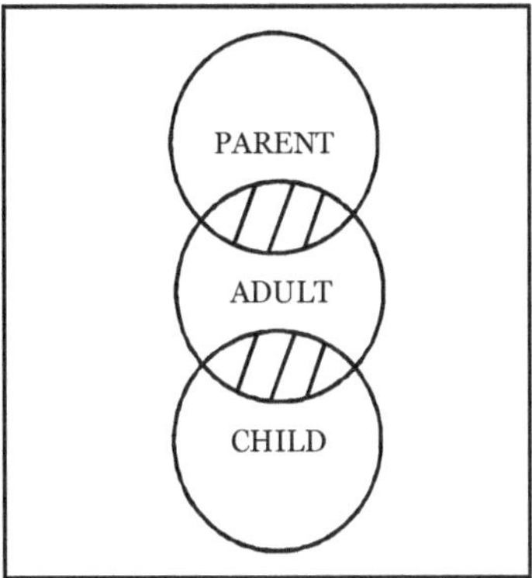

Fig. 2.5: Double Contamination

(3) **Exclusion of Ego States:** Some people function as though one or two ego states are missing from their personality. This is known as exclusion of the ego states. A common example is a parent or a caretaker who is expected to look after everyone in the family and does not have any time for herself. Here the caretaker has excluded her Child ego state and operates from the Parent ego state. Another example is a parent who does not look after and provide for the family. This person has decommissioned his/her Parent and Adult ego states.

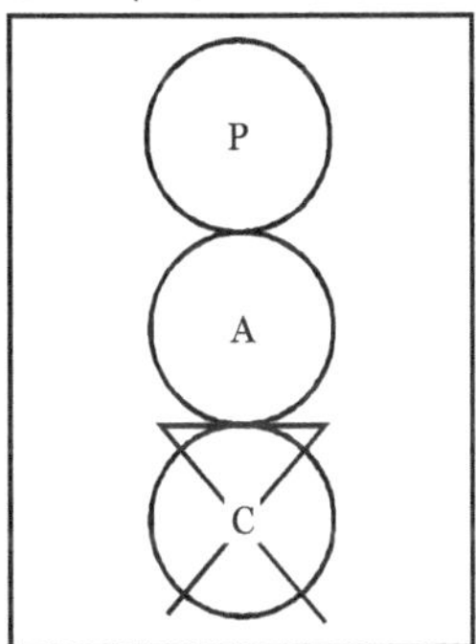

Fig. 2.6: Exclusion

Q53. Explain the professional as well as personal qualities of an effective counsellor.

Or

Discuss professional as well as personal qualities required to be an effective counsellor.

Ans. The personal and professional qualities of counsellors are very important in facilitating any helping relationship. A counsellor must be well equipped to assist individuals to make adjustments and live a happy and harmonious life. The adjustment can be with regard to the school and curriculum, vocation and personality. For effective counselling, the counsellor must be equipped with two kinds of data. First he must have data relating to the counsellee's background aptitudes, achievements, interests, plans, etc. Further, he must have the skill to interpret this data. Secondly, the counsellor must have information about the areas in which the counsellee may seek his assistance. These areas may be educational or personal. With these two kinds of information, he assists the counsellee to match his individual patterns of potentiality with appropriate opportunity. As the process of counselling develops, both the counsellor and counsellee must arrive at a common ground.

Counsellor's who continually develop their self awareness skills are in touch with their values, thoughts and feelings. They are likely to have a clear perception of their own and their client's needs and accurately assess both. Such awareness can help them be honest with themselves and others. They are able to be more congruent and build trust simultaneously. Counsellors who possess this type of knowledge are most likely to communicate clearly accurately.

Three other characteristics that make counsellors initially more influential are perceived expertness, attractiveness and trustworthiness. Expertness is the degree to which a counsellor is perceived as knowledge able and informed about his or her specialty. Counsellors who display certificates and diplomas in their offices are usually perceived as more credible than those who do not and as a result, are likely to be effective. Clients went to work with counsellor who appears to know profession well. The main aim of GPH book is to provide knowledge as well as good marks in exam.

Attractiveness is function of perceived similarly between a client and counselor. Councellors can make themselves attractive by speaking in clear, simple, jargon free sentence and offering appropriate self disclosure.

All the counsellors are not alike. They differ in various ways. Their personal characteristics, as well as, their personality differ quite substantially. A number of research organisations have tried to ascertain the personal qualities of a counsellor, which are essential to bring about therapeutical transformation in another person (i.e. the client). Three researchers namely Carkuff, Truax & Carl Rogers came up with the under mentioned characteristics of a school counsellor, which are as follows:

- **Empathy:** The empathic behaviour is the ability of a counsellor to stand in the shoes of the client, i.e. to see the things from the point of view of the client. The quality of empathy is a must for the counselling process to succeed. Empathy calls for 'forgetting oneself so that the counsellor surrenders himself completely towards the client. The process of empathisation is never total or complete, which leaves a lot to be desired, for the counselling process of succeed. Several empathy enhancing activities helps in enhancing the quality of empathy in a counsellor.
- **Genuineness:** Rogers as well as Truax considered genuineness, as very important part of counselling. The employees of various public services are well trained to meet the public at large, in a

very cordial and friendly manner. "Genuineness" is synonymous with good or honest intentions. A genuine interest in the client is a must for the counselling process to succeed.

- **Warmth:** Personal warmth or being warm is a controversial issue. There is a hairline difference between being warm or being dubbed as 'sickliness'. The quality of being warm refers to a situation, where a person shows interest in other individual/group. 'Cold' individuals rarely become good counsellors. A word of caution here, a too warm counsellor may lead towards the development of over-dependence on the part of the client. The ideal feeling of being warm is the one which demonstrates that the counsellor is non-judgemental and is honestly interested in his/her client. Care should be taken to see that the counsellor does not try to dominate the process of counselling.

- **Concreteness:** It can be termed as a type of skill. It is an ability to listen, to what is being said by the client, instead of what is being implied. Concreteness in counselling is essential, if the counselling process has to succeed. A counsellor possessing the skill of 'concreteness' does not go for details (regarding psychological explanations) of what the client is speaking about, but instead tries to understand what the client is trying to express. Any quick, preconceived or initial judgement about what the client is saying will not be particularly helpful. In fact, it will be counterproductive. The concept of concreteness almost integrates all the important elements of the counselling process. A concrete counsellor, invariably, listens to and accepts what the client is saying and does not quickly make his judgements.

- **Unconditional Positive Regard:** Rogers came up with a term called, 'unconditional positive regard' to refer to 'necessary and sufficient conditions for therapeutic change' in the counselling relationship. Rogers emphasised that the counsellor's positive feeling for the client must never be conditional in nature. He further suggested that the counsellor should feel warmly disposed towards the client, irrespective of the client's feelings or emotions, which is almost impractical or unreal. This is impossible. Further, it is important that a counsellor is broad minded and initially non-judgemental. Also positive general disposition towards the client is a must for the counselling process to succeed.

- **A Tragic Sense:** In order to get involved with a client's problem a 'tragic sense of life' must be developed. All human beings have some limitations. A tragic sense helps the counsellor to remain humble. It also inducts a sense of humanity in him. Counsellors are not people with better brains, but are the people who readily listen to the problems of their clients. The book you can most believe—GPH book.

- **A Sense of Humour:** A sense of humour comes quite handy, in rescuing most of the sensitive or delicate situations. It does not means that a counsellor should resort to a comedian's tactics. It also does not mean that a counsellor should start taking the conversation during counselling session lightly. But, it means to help a client to regain the sight of the larger picture of a problem. It helps in calming down the tense atmostphere, that builds up because the clients generally blow the things out of proportion. Even subjects dubbed as 'taboos', can be easily confronted with the help of a sense of humour.

- **Self-awareness:** It means to being aware of oneself, i.e. to be aware of one's own limitations and strengths. It means to explore oneself. It is a realistic attempt of comparing oneself with other people. It means to explore one's own life situations.

  A MAN is literally what he thinks, his character being the complete sum of all his thoughts. –James Allen in "As a Man Thinketh"

A good counsellor is also:

- a positive influencer
- enthusiastic
- caring
- supportive
- trusting
- focussed
- goal-oriented
- knowledgeable
- attentive
- clear and concise
- patient
- observing
- responsive

✍ ✍ ✍

Career Development

INTRODUCTION

Career development is an important and life long process in an individual's life. It is influenced by a number of factors like family, personal values, interests, aptitudes and society. Career development is a lifelong process of getting ready to choose, and generally continuing to make choices from among the many occupations available. Each person going through this process is influenced by a large number of factors including family, personal values, interests, aptitudes and societal context. The word "career" is to be distinguished from other interchangeably used words such as vocation, job, or profession. Career patterns are developmental in nature. They must be understood in terms of life stages. Many genetic, social, economic and environmental factors influence the determining of career patterns. Life adjustment process, to a large extent, depends upon vocational adjustment. Therefore, the career planning is very important for everybody, and sooner one realises this, better it is. Hence, the role of teachers is very important in the planning of career of students.

Q1. Describe the different motivational needs for which people work.

Or

Explain psychological and social needs under motivation to work.

Ans. Following are the motivational needs of the people, which could be satisfied by work:

(1) Social Needs

(i) **Independence:** Whenever a person gets involved into a group, it is very rare that his/her relationship is of an equal level. Mostly, the person assumes either a position of a subordinate or that of a superior. Thus, within the limits of their own preferences, the workers tend to enjoy a certain degree of independence. If the job does not allow them the freedom they would like to have in execution of their duties, they feel uncomfortable.

(ii) **Provision for Emergencies/Welfare Activities:** Workers expect to be treated fairly in exchange for their service time, abilities and merit. The fair treatment involves fair pay for their expertise, level of experience and fulfilment of security needs. When an employee falls sick or is incapacitated s/he expects the organisation to compensate so that s/he can survive. If the individual's assessment of the treatment s/he receives on the job is not satisfactory, s/he is not happy with the job.

(iii) **Status of the Individual:** The work gives social status to the worker. The status, which a job offers, varies from one occupation to another. It may be high in case of professions, managerial and other occupations like this. Semi-skilled and unskilled jobs confer a lower social status on the worker. However, the satisfaction of the individual from his/her job and the status depends on his/her own pattern of needs acquired in his/her typical environment.

(2) Economic Needs

(i) **Present Income:** The satisfaction with the present income level is affected by the level of the aspiration of the person and the parity between his/her income, and that of others who are similar to him/her in education, income and experience. Workers feel satisfied when they get income similar to that of fellow colleagues. But if s/he feels that s/he is not being treated fairly and is given lesser income than others similar to him/her in experience and competence s/he feels dissatisfied.

(ii) **Job Security:** Workers are not simply satisfied with a job that provides satisfactory income and helps them to maintain a social status at par with people similar to them in education, age and experience. They would like to be ensured of a future income too.

The jobs involving high accident rates or those offering seasonal employment leave the employee insecure about future income. The jobs, which offer pension or other post-retirement benefits, will be preferred by those whose financial resources are limited to salaries. The retired persons may also likely to take up a job, which requires less physical effort and responsibility to earn income and be able to retain the job.

(3) Psychological Needs: The psychological needs are given below:

(i) Self-esteem: Self-esteem relates to one's evaluation of oneself. It is the way one feels about oneself, and the extent to which an individual values oneself. To be able to do something and to be a productive member of society could be highly satisfying to the individual.

However, different individuals are differentially affected by the work they are doing. It depends on their own self-concept, which will influence his/her expectations from self, and others' expectation from him/her.

(ii) Identity: Work gives an identity to the individual, especially in the present day society, where people are known more in terms of work. The existence of the individual, his/her lifestyle, his/her environment, all are influenced by the work s/he engages in.

(iii) Self-expression of Skills and Competence: Work offers opportunities to express various abilities, interests, skills and even the values and attitudes they have acquired. The work becomes satisfying if the individuals are able to exercise the competence and the skills they possess. If the work provides opportunities to use the special training or the skills or knowledge that a person has acquired over the years, the person feels good about it.

(iv) Commitment and Self-worth: Another dimension of work, which motivates a person, is his/her own commitment to the work. The feeling of having a personal mission to be completed, or a goal to be achieved, could be highly energising and motivating. The self-worth of the person also depends on this feeling of fulfilment of his/her commitment, values and preferences.

Q2. How does work affect the lifestyle of the individuals? Discuss.

Ans. The lifestyle of a person is usually determined by the work s/he does. Different jobs or occupations make different demands on the time of the individual. High-level jobs do not end within the office hours. Business keeps a person on the work for longer hours than the office work. It is not only the time but social status of the person is also influenced by the occupation. Although social status is complex and is influenced by many factors, work is a strong influence that determines the status in the current society.

- **Occupation and the Status:** The occupation could be classified in a hierarchical manner according to prestige, the income, skill or training requirement, educational level, interests and the ability. One such classification divides occupations into the categories like professional, proprietary and managerial, clerical and sales, skilled and supervisory, semi-skilled and unskilled. The difference between the status at various levels is clear. The higher an individual is earning, the higher is his/her occupational hierarchy.

- **Work Routines and Occupation:** Normally, the white collar workers finish work in regular office hours while the professional people (like professors, advocates, tax consultants, etc.) work beyond office hours also. Either they may have to spend time in improving their technical skills or they are working for their professional development. Since, the time spent on the job is different, the time a person will be able to devote for leisure, family and other hobbies will be automatically structured according to the occupational demands.

- **Work Influences Attitudes and Values:** Jobs differ in terms of the status, leisure, work activity, time routine, income and even the persons one meets. Different people have preferences for different activities, work routines and leisure. The status or the income may also be differently valued. Therefore, people generally tend to choose occupation according to their values and attitudes. But all of them do not succeed in entering an occupation of their choice. Therefore, in an occupation, there are people with different preferences, likes and dislikes.

- **Social Climate:** Usually, it is the social situation that determines the people with whom one may come in contact with. The limited number of people available from same type of occupation, interest and hobbies tend to change the person in ways similar to that of the job.

- **Dress and Language:** Besides interest and hobbies, occupation also influence the dress, language and conduct. The persons inadvertently, subconsciously and incidentally learn to express himself/herself in language which is typical of that used by people in that occupation. The language associated with the white collar jobs is very different from that used in manual jobs. The professional people employed in outdoor jobs dress up differently than those in indoor occupations. The choice of formal and informal dress is also different to a great extent.

Q3. Define career development. Also, explain its planning and importance.

Ans. Career development is defined as an organised, planned effort comprised of structured activities or processes that result in a mutual career plotting effort between employees and the organisation. Career development is an ongoing process by which individual's progress through a series of stages, each of which is characterised by a relatively unique set of issues, themes and tasks.

Following are the main definitions of Career development:

According to **Schuler**, "It is an activity to identify the individual needs, abilities and goals and the organisation's job demands and job rewards and then through well-designed programmes of career development matching abilities with demands and rewards."

In the words of **Mansfield**, "Career development is a process in which personnel experience, concept and publicly observable aspect of career interact to precipitate each successive stage of occupational statuses."

According to **Middlemist, Hill and Greer**, "Career development is a process of planning the series of possible jobs one may hold in an organisation over time and development strategies designed to provide necessary job skills as the opportunities arise."

Planning of Career Development

As both, the individual and the organisation, have interests in individual's career, career planning is a deliberate process of being aware of self, available opportunities, existing constraints with the alternative choices and sequences. It also involves, identifying career related goals and undertaking work education and related developmental exercises to provide the right direction, proper timings and sequences to attain a specific career goal. Career planning is an ongoing process by which an individual sets his/her career goals and identifies the means and ways to achieve them. The way people plan for their life's work is considered as career planning. It propels and sometimes compels an individual to explore, choose and strive in order to derive satisfaction with one's career objective. Hence, career planning has significance in individual's life.

Importance of Career Development

Career development provides the framework with skills, goals, awareness, assessment and performance, which helps an individual to move in the right direction and achieve the goals one has in one's career. Once a child has grown into adolescence, his/her interests, abilities, values, etc. have already been influenced in certain directions. Choices have already been made which will direct the future career. Therefore, these early or timely decisions have to be made consciously and objectively. In order to help children plan consciously and base their educational and vocational choices on factual information, it is important that they have access to career related information which will help them plan judiciously. It is not only career information they need but also information related to the educational and personal development, so that they get opportunity to develop and be able to choose from a repertoire of choices.

Q4. Discuss theory of career development as propounded by Super (1953).

Ans. Super's Career Development Theory posits that there are five life stages in career development. He specified a duration or age bracket for each stage, but these are not fixed, at least not in the sense that people within that age group are undergoing only the corresponding stage. The biological age of the person does not necessarily have to correspond to the development stage. Individuals may be experiencing (and re-experiencing) some stages even when they do not belong in the specified age range. These stages are as follows:

(1) **Growth Stage (Coverage: 0 to 14 years old):** This is when the development of one's self-concept begins. The child will start developing attitudes, recognising his needs and preferences, and gain a general understanding of the world of work.

This is where the person starts learning how to relate to other people. Along with developing a realistic self-concept, or an identity that they deem to represent his true self, s/he will also be faced with his limitations, and will start accepting them.

We have often heard it said that acknowledging own faults, flaws and limitations is a sign of growth. This stage in the theory reinforces that idea.

(2) **Exploration Stage (Coverage: 15 to 24 years old):** The teenager or young adult finds his/her hobbies and interests. S/he starts to approach skills acquisition activities tentatively, trying out classes and coursework. This is also the point where s/he will be testing the waters and gain work experience.

S/he will take an active role in seeking and learning about opportunities. S/he is eager, although apprehensive. Later on, s/he may find the opportunity that appeals to him/her, and will grab it with both hands. This also involves the search and identification of new tasks to work on once they are done with what a previous task.

(3) **Establishment Stage (Coverage: 25 to 44 years old):** Things start to get more serious, and so is the individual. S/he will be more determined and focussed in honing his/her work chops, so as to speak, and actively seek out entry-level skill building opportunities. S/he will also be looking for more work experience, one that is stable and offers fewer uncertainties.

It is at this point that s/he makes a decision on which field or career path to take, and s/he will get started on it. Once s/he finds that position that s/he wants, and that matches him/her, s/he will settle into it. Along the way, s/he will actively pursue new learning and development of new skills, practically anything that will make him/her improve.

(4) Maintenance Stage (Coverage: 45 to 64 years old): At this point, the main concern of the individual is to keep his position and improve it. Mostly, what s/he will be doing is to learn continuously and make adjustments whenever and wherever necessary.

At some point in one's life, s/he may start questioning his/her past choices and decisions. Did s/he choose the right path? Is s/he following the career path that s/he really wants? In this stage, s/he will re-evaluate his occupational choices and perform verification and confirmation. If s/he realises that it is not the right occupation for him/her, s/he may have to go back to the Exploration stage.

If, however, s/he ascertains that s/he is on the right track, s/he will make efforts to make his/her position even more secure. After all, as s/he goes up the career ladder, there will be more challenges and, along with them, more competition. S/he will have to take steps to ensure that s/he can hold his own against the competition and remain firmly in his spot. During this time, some people will live through a mid-life crisis.

(5) Decline (Coverage: 65 years old and above): Output is visibly reduced, and productivity is lower. At this point, the person is getting ready for retirement, and to completely leave the workplace.

S/he will most likely be decreasing his/her participation in activities that demand a lot of him/her. His/her focus will be on the essentials, or what s/he deems important, instead of the trivial matters such as competing for a position, accomplishing a task that s/he knows is beyond his/her stamina or capability.

Q5. Discuss the theory of personality development and career choice as given by Roe.

Or

State Roe's proposition on the origin of needs and interests.

Or

Describe different parenting styles of child rearing by Roe.

Ans. Anne Roe's (1956) theory is on possible relationships between career development and personality. The theory views the whole range of occupations in terms of their relationship to individual. The theory views the whole range of occupations in terms of their relationship to individual, differences in backgrounds, physical and psychological variables and experiences. From her findings, Roe concluded that major personality differences exist between people who join diverse occupations. These differences are centred around the type of interactions they have with people and things. Another conclusion she arrived at was that the personality differences that exist are partly the result of influences of child rearing practices.

Thus, due to dissatisfaction with available classifications of occupations, Roe developed a list of eight occupational groups, which are discussed as follows:

- **Service:** These occupations are primarily concerned with serving and attending to the needs and welfare of other persons. This group includes occupation such as social work, guidance, domestic and protective services. The important element is a situation in which one person is doing something for the other (Examples include counsellor, social workers and police personnel).

- **Business Contact:** These occupations are primarily concerned with the face-to-face sale of commodities, investments, real estate and services. The person to person relation is important, but it is focussed on persuasion to a course of action, rather than on helping. The persuader will profit if his/her advice is followed (Salesman, Public Relations Officers, Brokers and Insurance Agents).

- **Organisation:** These are the managerial and white collar jobs in business, industry and government. The occupation is concerned primarily with the organisation and efficient functioning of commercial enterprises and of Govt. activities. The quality of person to person interaction is very formal (Industrialists, Bankers, Financial Executives, Cashiers).

- **Technology:** This group includes occupations concerned with the production, maintenance and transportation of commodities and utilities. Hence, there are occupations in engineering, crafts, and the machine trades, as well as in transportation and communication. Interpersonal relations are of relatively little importance and the focus is on dealing with things (Ship Captains, Chief Engineers, Applied Scientists, etc.)

- **Outdoor:** This group includes the occupations primarily concerned with the cultivation, preservation and gathering of crops, marine or inland water resources, mineral resources, forest products and other natural resources and with animal husbandry. Interpersonal relations are largely irrelevant. Because of the increasing mechanisation of some of these occupations, a number of jobs previously classified in this group have moved to group-4. For example, Consulting Specialists, Architects, Scientists, Forest Rangers.

- **Science:** These are the occupations primarily concerned with scientific theory and its application under specified circumstances other than technology (Research Scientists, Medical Specialists and Medical Technicians).

- **General Culture:** These occupations are primarily concerned with the preservation and transmission of the general cultural heritage. Here, interest is in human activities rather than in individual persons. This group includes occupations in education, journalism, linguistics and the subjects usually called the humanities. Most elementary and high school teachers are placed in this group. At higher levels, teachers are placed in groups by subject matter, e.g. teachers of science or of art or of humanities (Justice of Supreme and High court, Lawyers, Teachers and Scholars).
- **Arts and Entertainment:** These occupations include those concerned with the use of special skills in the creative arts and in entertainment. The focus in them is on a relationship between one person (or an organised group) and a more general public. The interpersonal relation is important but neither so direct nor of the same nature as that in group 1 & 2 (Adapted from Roe and Klos, 1972). Creative artists, performers of skill, athletes, designers, conductor of music, interior decorators, etc., are placed in this group.

Levels of each Occupational Group

- **Professional and Managerial (Independent responsibility):** It refers to independent responsibility and involves important and varied responsibilities, policy-making and education, and includes top management, administration and professional jobs which, when a high level of education is required, often include individuals with doctorates, such as international bankers or industrialists in the organisation occupational group.
- **Professional and Managerial:** It is similar to the first level, but which involves relatively less independence and less important decisions, policy interpretation rather than policymaking, and may require a bachelor's or higher degree, but not a doctorate, including, for example, business and government executives and union officials.
- **Semi-professional and Small Business:** This involves a low level of responsibility for others, application of policy, and usually requires high school or technical school education including, for example, employment managers and business owners.
- **Skilled:** This includes occupations requiring apprenticeships or special training or experience, including, for example, cashiers, sales clerks and warehouse supervisors.
- **Semi-skilled:** This includes occupations requiring some training or experience, but less than is required in skilled occupations, for example, filing clerks and typists.

- **Unskilled:** This includes occupations in which no special training or experience is required, for example, messengers in organisations.

Roe's Proposition on the Origin of Needs and Interests

Proposition on the origin of needs and interests by Roe is discussed as follows:

- Genetic inheritance sets limits on the potential development of all characteristics.
- Whether these inherited characteristics will achieve, surpass or under achieve, their potential is determined not only by the experiences unique to the individual, but also such factors as race, sex, social and economic position of the family and general cultural background.
- The direction of development of interests, attitudes and other personality variables, which have relatively little genetic control, is determined entirely by individual experiences.

The following are the possible variations:

- Needs that are satisfied routinely as they appear do not become unconscious motivators.
- Needs for which even minimum satisfaction is rarely achieved will, if of a higher order, become eliminated, if of a lower order, prevent the appearance of higher order needs and will become dominating and restricting motivators.
- Need for which satisfaction is delayed, but eventually accomplished, will become unconscious motivators, according to the degree of satisfaction felt.
- The eventual pattern of psychic energies, in terms of attention directedness, is the major determinant of interests.
- The intensity of these needs and of their satisfaction, and their organisation, are the major determinants of the degree of expressed motivation.
- Anne Roe then suggested that individual's genetic background underlines abilities and interests, which in turn are related to vocational choice. A combination of genetic factors and need hierarchies exerts influence on the selection of a vocation later in life. The intensity of desire to achieve vocational success is dependent upon the strength of the individual's need structure. In others words, given equal genetic endowments the differences in occupational achievements between two individuals may be a result of the discrepancies in their motivation levels. And these differences in the strength of the need structure and motivation, Roe suggested, was due to differences in need satisfaction during childhood. Consequently, Roe proposed that child-rearing practices related directly to the motivational behaviour expressed by adults later in life.

Modes of Child Rearing

Roe proposed that the manner in which parents interact with the child is one of the major influences on the motivational intensity of the child.

Different parenting styles will produce distinctive behaviour patterns in children. She conceptualised them as follows:

- **Emotional Concentration on the Child:** This could take the form of being either over-protective or over-demanding. The over-protective parent will fully and quickly satisfy the child's lower needs but may hesitate in gratifying the higher order needs of love and esteem, at the same time, will reward behaviour that is socially desirable. This type of interaction will make the child to over emphasise the immediate or quick gratification of physiological demands. For the satisfaction of higher order needs, s/he exhibits a dependency on others and a willingness to conform to socially desirable behaviour. These higher order needs could be a need to be loved, esteem, or a sense of belongingness. The over demanding parents have many similarities to over-protective parents. The over-protective parents will gratify the physical needs promptly and adequately. The over-demanding parents lay down conditions of conformity to their values, and social achievement in return for the love offered to the child. The child's needs of self-actualisation are indulged in if they are in accordance with parental aspirations for the child.

- **Avoidance of the Child Expressed Either as Emotional Deprivation or Neglect:** Roe put forward that parents who neglect merely the physical wellbeing of the child were not causing as harmful an effect as those parents who neglected the emotional needs of the child. This emotional rejection of the child leads to slower emotional development, though it may not cause miss-proportioned development.

- **Acceptance of the Child, Either Casually or Lovingly:** The accepting type of parents will satisfy their children's needs at most levels in slightly different ways and in varying degrees. The personality that develops in children of accepting parents is capable of seeking gratification of needs at all levels.

  Roe then hypothesised that people have two basic orientations either towards or not towards persons. These orientations were dependent upon childhood experiences, and they in turn affected the vocational choice.

Q6. Elucidate Holland's theory of vocational personalities and work environment. Also, explain its nature and assumptions.

Or

Delineate Holland's theory of vocational personalities and work environment.

Or

Enlist and explain six models environment by Holland.

Or

Discuss the implications of Holland's theory for counselling.

Ans. The theory of vocational choice developed by John L. Holland is one of the most widely researched and applied theories of career development. Based on the premise that personality factors underlie career choices, his theory postulates that people project self- and world-of-work views onto occupational titles and make career decisions that satisfy their preferred personal orientations. The theory incorporates several constructs from personality psychology, vocational behaviour, and social psychology, including self-perception theory and social stereotyping.

Applications of Holland's theory of vocational choice involve assessing individuals in terms of two or three prominent personality types and then matching the respective types with the environmental aspects of potential careers. The theory predicts that the higher the degree of congruence between individual and occupational characteristics, the better the potential for positive career-related outcomes, including satisfaction, persistence and achievement.

Nature

Holland's theory of vocational personalities and work environment is structural – interactive in nature. It means that it provides explicit links among various personality characteristics and corresponding job titles. According to Holland, the description of different structural-interactive approaches includes:

- The choice of an occupation is an expression of personality and not a random event, although chance plays a role.
- The members of an occupational group have common personalities and similar histories of personal development.
- Because people in an occupational group have similar personalities, they respond to any situations and problems in similar ways.
- Occupational achievement, stability and satisfaction depend on congruence between one's personality and job environment.

Its focal point is personality and its typology. He contends that each individual, to some extent, resembles one of six basic personality types. Just as there are six types of personalities, there are six types of environments, which, like personalities, can be described according to certain characteristics. Environments are characterised by the people who occupy them. For example, the personality type of persons in a theatre differs from persons working with computers. Similarly, teachers working at primary level differ from their counterparts working at colleges/universities.

Assumptions

This theory is based on four assumptions. They are:

- "In general, most persons can be categorised as one of six types: realistic, investigative, artistic, social, enterprising or conventional."

- "There are six kinds of environments, i.e. realistic, investigative, artistic, social, enterprising or conventional."
- "People search for environments that will let them exercise their skills and abilities, express their attitudes and values, and take on agreeable problems and roles." This assumption is well expressed in the saying "Birds of a feather flock together."
- "Behaviour is determined by an interaction between personality and environment."

Six Models of Environment

Originally, Holland believes that the individual could be categorised as belonging to a single one of the six types. He suggests that while one of the six types usually predominates in people, there are also sub-types or personality patterns. Each environment is dominated by a given type of personality, and each environment is typified by physical settings posing special problems and opportunities. Following are the six models of environment as proposed by Holland:

- **Realistic Environment:** Realistic environments emphasise concrete, practical activities and the use of machines, tools and materials. These behavioural tendencies of realistic environments lead, in turn, to the acquisition of mechanical and technical competencies and to a deficit in human relations skills. People in realistic environments are encouraged to perceive themselves as having practical, productive and concrete values. Realistic environments reward people for the display of conforming behaviour and practical accomplishment.

- **Investigative Environment:** Investigative environments emphasise analytical or intellectual activities aimed at the creation and use of knowledge. Such environments devote little attention to persuasive, social and repetitive activities. These behavioural tendencies in investigative environments lead, in turn, to the acquisition of analytical, scientific and mathematical competencies and to a deficit in persuasive and leadership abilities. People in investigative environments are encouraged to perceive themselves as cautious, critical, complex, curious, independent, precise, rational and scholarly. Investigative environments reward people for skepticism and persistence in problem solving, documentation of new knowledge, and understanding solutions of common problems.

- **Artistic Environment:** Artistic environments emphasise ambiguous, free and unsystematised activities that involve emotionally expressive interactions with others. These environments devote little attention to explicit, systematic and ordered activities. These behavioural tendencies in artistic environments lead, in turn, to the acquisition of innovative and creative competencies, i.e. language, art, music, drama, writing- and to a deficit in clerical and business system competencies. People in Artistic environments are encouraged to perceive themselves as having unconventional ideas or manners and possessing aesthetic values. Artistic environments reward people for imagination in literary, artistic or musical accomplishments.

- **Social Environment**: Social environments emphasise activities that involve the mentoring, treating, healing or teaching of others. These environments devote little attention to explicit, ordered, systematic activities involving materials, tools or machines. These behavioural tendencies in social environments lead, in turn, to the acquisition of interpersonal competencies and to a deficit in manual and technical competencies. People in social environments are encouraged to perceive themselves as cooperative, empathetic, generous, helpful, idealistic, responsible, tactful, understanding and having concern for the welfare of others. Social environments reward people for the display of empathy, humanitarianism, sociability and friendliness.

- **Enterprising Environment:** Enterprising environments emphasise activities that involve the manipulation of others to attain organisational goals or economic gain. These environments devote little attention to observational, symbolic and systematic activities. These behavioural tendencies in enterprising environments lead, in turn, to an acquisition of leadership, interpersonal, speaking and persuasive competencies, and to a deficit in scientific competencies. People in enterprising environments are encouraged to perceive themselves as aggressive, ambitious, domineering, energetic, extroverted, optimistic, popular, self-confident, sociable and talkative. Enterprising environments reward people for the display of initiative in the pursuit of financial or material accomplishments, dominance and self-confidence.

- **Conventional Environment:** Conventional environments emphasise activities that involve the explicit, ordered, systematic manipulation of data to meet predictable organisational demands or specified standards. The behavioural tendencies in conventional environments lead, in turn, to the acquisition of clerical, computational and business system competencies necessary to meet precise performance standards and to a deficit in artistic competencies. People in conventional environments are encouraged to perceive themselves as having a conventional outlook and concern for orderliness and routines. Conventional environments reward people for the display of dependability, conformity and organisational skills.

People search for environments that will let them exercise their skills and abilities, express their attitudes and values and take on agreeable problems and roles. Realistic types seek realistic environments. Social types seek social environments and so on. To a lesser degree, environment also searches for people through friendship and recruiting practices. The person's search for environment is carried on in many ways, at different levels of consciousness, and over a long period of time.

The above key assumptions are supplemented by several secondary assumptions that can be applied to both persons and environments. The purpose of the secondary concepts is to retain or modify the predictions or explanations that are derived from the main concepts.

- **Consistency:** Consistency refers to the assumption that adjacent pairs of types on the hexagon are most related and accordingly most consistent. For example, career clients whose tests show social and artistic as their two highest codes are considered to be more consistent than if they tested social and realistic as their two highest codes.

- **Differentiation:** Differentiation addresses a person's purity of type or whether that person clearly resembles one or perhaps two types, yet clearly does not resemble the other types. For example, a person is considered highly differentiated if s/he measures high on conventional and measures significantly low on all the other types. That same person could also measure highest on Conventional, next highest on Enterprising, significantly lower on all the other types and have both a consistent (due to adjacent codes) and well-differentiated profile.

- **Identity:** Identity deals with the clarity of one's whole typological picture. A clear sense of one's career picture that includes an understanding of one's interests, goals and talents as well as movement towards an accurate career environment is an indication of a firm career identity. Degrees of identity are highly related to the concepts of consistency and differentiation.

- **Congruence:** Congruence refers to the degree of match between one's type and the type of the work environment that s/he ultimately chooses. For example, persons who measure artistic as their highest type would be most congruent in an environment that incorporates artistic activities, that allows for artistic expression, and that attracts other artistic people.

Vocational Choice as an Integration between Major and Secondary Assumptions

The individual will seek an occupational environment that corresponds to the orientation, if one orientation is clearly dominant over others. However, a very low percentage of people, in actual implementation, would fall in this category. Often, it is possible that two or more orientations are of nearly the same strength, other being much weaker, or just on the periphery. In such a case, an individual will vacillate in the selection of an occupation. Here is where factors like consistency, differentiations and identity come into play. A person, who is artistic and social, will find it easier to select a vocation than a person who is artistic and conventional. When a particular orientation is well-differentiated than the others in a person, vocation selection is quick, decisive and appropriate. On the other hand, a person exhibiting all orientations in almost equal intensity would be confused, indecisive and unsure about vocation selection. The smoothness of decisions is affected by the clarity of the structure of developmental hierarchy. Other environmental factors will also influence the ease with which an occupational environment is selected. Some of these could be family factor, such as aspirations and occupational history, financial resources, general economic conditions in society, educational opportunities, which might result in pressures towards a particular occupational environment. Not only does the particular dominant personal orientation influence the career choice a person makes, but the pattern of the orientations within the individual's hierarchy exerts a significant influence. That is, two students with the same major orientation will choose similar fields, but the stability of their choice is a function of the order of the other five orientations in their personal hierarchy. If the order is consistent, and all other factors are constant, the choice is likely to be stable. If the pattern is inconsistent for that occupational environment, then the choice is likely to be unstable. For instance, a dramatist with the hierarchical order artistic, investigative, realistic, social enterprising and conventional is likely to be more stable in the pursuit of his/her dramatic creations than another dramatist whose hierarchy is artistic, realistic, investigative, social enterprising and conventional.

Implications for Counselling: Holland has given detailed descriptions of people with different orientations in order to help students or adults knowing their personal orientations. To have a concrete measure to learn about personal orientations, Holland researched and developed the Self-Directed Search Inventory, which provides scores on the six parameters. At the end, a code gives the dominant orientations of the person. Using this information and the occupation finder (developed by Holland), which classifies occupations according to various codes; the most suitable occupations could be short-listed. The classification of the various occupational environments could be used by the counselor to orient a person to the world of work. It gives a person better understanding of what to expect and what is expected of him if he joins a particular occupation. By virtue of the extensive data that Holland has given about the features of people possessing different personal orientations, a counselor already has a considerable body of information about a client simply by virtue of knowing his/her major personal orientation to life. This helps the counselor in making some educated guesses about the client's background, parents, the client's goals, values, social relations, motivators and distracters.

Q7. **Briefly explain about four significant variables involved in vocational choice of Ginsberg's theory. What are the major periods of the vocational development process?**

Or

Describe in brief about variation in the pattern of vocational process.

Or

Discuss the general concept of Ginzberg's theory. Also, explain its implications for counselling.

Ans. According to Ginzberg, there are important components that help the individual in arriving at an adequate vocational choice. If majority of these ingredients fail to develop properly, an individual's vocational development process is bound to suffer.

Ginzberg's another significant concept is the child's ability to identify with suitable models at appropriate times during the career development process. This identification with adults at the various stages of vocational development gives a direction to students and help by making it easier to follow realistic mode.

The two basic personality types exist with respect to work are another characteristic features of this theory. This personality types exist are the work oriented type and the pleasure oriented type. This does not imply that people have either this or that kind of personality, but that one mode is more characteristic of an individual's approach to life. The work oriented individual can be identified by the ability to delay gratification, nothing or very little can distract him/her in the pursuit of his/her career goals. Whereas the pleasure oriented person is unlikely to postpone gratification for work and is susceptible to distraction by other alternatives that may seem reasonably attractive, e.g. a vocational course or another opportunity away from his/her central line of work.

On the basis of earlier research, Ginzberg and his associates found that four significant variables were involved in vocational choice. These four variables are as follows:

- **Reality Factor:** This pressurises the individual to take into account various environmental factors while exercising one's vocational choice.
- **Influence of the Amount and Quality of Education:** This would broaden or narrow the scope of a vocational decision.
- **Personality and Emotional Make-up of the Individual:** This would have fallouts for vocational inclination.
- **Individual Values:** These were considered significant since different careers gave opportunities to practice different values.

Ginzberg proposed vocational choice as a developmental process, occurring in reasonably clearly marked periods and characterised by a series of compromises the individual makes between wishes and possibilities.

The Major Periods of the Vocational Development Process: Following are the major periods of the vocational development process:

- **Fantasy Period:** During the fantasy phase of career development, the child has little awareness of how one attains career goals. The youngster's thinking about career, largely the result of daydreaming and the wish to be an adult, is relatively untempered by any consideration of reality factors. As children grow older, however, they begin to take reality into account.

In the early-stage of this period, children state vocational preferences, which are dominated primarily by the pleasure principle. This principle implies that very young children show interest in activities for the sake of pleasure. As the child learns about the world of work, s/he expresses choices that have potential for extrinsic rewards such as success and its money with which to buy material possessions and so on. Coupled with the above developmental change is also the hypothesis that a child experiences frustration due to their small size and ineffectiveness as compared to adults. In order to overcome this sense of helplessness, the child finds relief in playing adult roles, which are clearly manifested in their work roles. It also helps the child internalise the values of the adult. During the fantasy period, children ignore reality, abilities and potential, and the time perspective, which are very important ingredients of the vocational choice process, according to Ginzberg.

- **Tentative Period:** It starts at approximately the age of 11. It is characterised by the individual's recognition of the problem of occupational choice.

  The tentative period consists of four substages, i.e. the interest, capacity, value and transition stages. In this period, the individual have in career choice. Then, in sequence, s/he focuses on capacities and values as factors to be considered. Finally, in the transition substage, the necessity for making a career choice is faced, and the individual becomes increasingly aware of the complex of factors, which must be considered in choosing a career.

- **Realistic Period:** The last phase of the developmental sequence is the realistic period, which is subdivided into the exploration, crystallisation and specification stages. In the *exploration stage*, the preliminary career decisions are tested in a realistic context, e.g. an entry job or college courses in a field or fields of interest. In the *crystallisation stage*, the individual evaluates his/her successes and failures and evolves a more specific notion of his/her career goals. When this process is complete, the *final stage of specification* is attained, during which a specific career choice is made.

Variation in the Pattern

Everyone adheres to the given framework is not possible, though attempts have been made to describe the pattern of the vocational process by assigning different age groups to different periods and stages. Individual variations occur in the broad pattern due to biological, psychological and environmental reasons. Such differences will occur in two possible behavioural areas.

Firstly, people will vary with regard to occupational choices they express over time. Some people would display a wide variety of choice before selecting one. There may be others who are more focussed on one choice to the exclusion of others. So they settle quicker for their particular occupational choice.

The other sphere is with regard to the timing of the crystallisation stage. There may be a wide range relating to the surfacing of crystallisation. In some, it may surface towards the end of the tentative period, and in some, it may materialise only in the mid or late twenties.

Ginzberg also mentions that there may be deviant patterns in the development, which differ from the normal process. Some of the probable reasons could be severe emotional disorders, limited exposure of the child to different activities, unusual personal and financial circumstances, etc.

Implications for Counselling

Ginzberg and his associates proposed the theoretical framework, which can be used in two important ways in counselling students in their vocational development. These ways are as follows:

- This information can be well utilised by arranging experiences and activities for students so that this could facilitate their progress through different stages. The developmental tasks of every stage could be highlighted and brought to the attention of teachers and parents, so that they could gather or compile their efforts to help the students attain them.

- The theoretical framework can also be used by the teacher to anticipate problems that might be encountered by the students at predicted stages of development. This would help the teacher to develop preventive procedures to encounter the problems. For example, in the interest stage, the teacher could encourage the parents and the child to devote time to various activities, give the child adequate exposure before s/he can narrow down her/his interests to two or three. Similarly, in the capacity stage, he can caution the parents and students against reading more than required in a test or a sports performance, etc. emphasising that ability has to be measured with that of others in the same field.

Q8. Define social learning theory of career development. Enumerate the four factors of career development of individuals suggested by Krumboltz, Mitchell & Jones (1976).

Ans. The social learning theory of career decision-making proffered by Krumboltz and his colleagues was first formulated in 1976 (Krumboltz, A.M. Mitchell & Jones, 1976). The theory and a significant restatement published by Mitchell, Jones and Krumboltz in 1979 was the first adaptation of Bandura's (1977) social learning theory to the career field. This theory was also one of the first to address both the content and process of career decision-making, although Hesketh and Rounds (1995) have commented that the theory has a stronger emphasis on process than content.

The social learning theory of career decision-making (SLTCDM) aims to explain how people become employed in the wide variety of available occupations. It extends trait and factor theory in its attempt to explain the process of person-job congruence. Holland (1982) commented on the importance of learning theory in supporting the content of his typology. The theory is based on learning principles, and suggests that individuals learn about themselves, their preferences and the world of work through direct and indirect experiences. They then take action based on these knowledge-and skills-based learning.

In particular, there are four categories of factors, which influence an individual's career decision-making process:

(1) Genetic Endowments and Special Abilities
  (i) Inherited qualities that may set limits on individual career opportunities

(2) Environmental Conditions and Events
  (i) Factors of influence that are often beyond the individual's control
  (ii) Certain events and circumstances influence skills development, activities and career preferences

(3) Learning Experiences
  (i) Instrumental learning experiences and associative learning experiences
  (ii) Negative and positive reactions to pairs of previously neutral situations

(4) Task Approach Skills
  (i) Sets of skills the individual has developed, such as problem-solving skills, work habits, metal sets, emotional response and cognitive responses
  (ii) Modified as a result of desirable or undesirable experiences

Krumboltz and associates place a lot of importance on unplanned and chance events in determining the career choice of individuals. The consequences of these events can be positive or negative. According to this theory, unplanned events and chance encounters are a result of earlier decisions and behaviour rather than being a random occurrence. Career counsellors can help clients learn from these events and use them as a tool for taking actions or making decisions relevant to their career development. Genetic and environmental factors influence career development but they are beyond the control of the individual.

Q9. Discuss social cognitive theory of career development.

Ans. Social Cognitive Career Theory (SCCT) is a relatively new theory that is aimed at explaining three interrelated aspects of career development: (1) how basic academic and career interests develop, (2) how educational and career choices are made, and (3) how academic and career success is obtained. The theory incorporates a variety of concepts (e.g. interests, abilities, values, environmental factors) that appear in earlier career theories and have been found to affect career development. Developed by Robert W. Lent, Steven D. Brown and Gail Hackett in 1994, SCCT is based on Albert Bandura's general social cognitive theory, an influential theory of cognitive and motivational processes that has been extended to the study of many areas of psychosocial functioning, such as academic performance, health behaviour and organisational development.

Three intricately linked variables – self-efficacy beliefs, outcome expectations, and goals – serve as the basic building blocks of SCCT. Self-efficacy refers to an individual's personal beliefs about his/her capabilities to perform particular behaviours or courses of action. Unlike global confidence or self-esteem, self-efficacy beliefs are relatively dynamic (i.e. changeable) and are specific to particular activity domains. People vary in their self-efficacy regarding the behaviours required in different occupational domains.

Lent, Brown and Hackett have presented three interlocking models of career development, which are:

- model of interest development,
- model of career choice, and
- model of performance.

The findings are organised as twelve sets of propositions. These sets are given below:

- An individual's occupational or academic interests at any point in time are reflective of his/her concurrent self-efficacy beliefs and outcome expectations.
- An individual's occupational interests also are influenced by his/her occupationally relevant abilities, but this relation is mediated by one's self-efficacy beliefs.
- Self-efficacy beliefs affect choice goals and actions both directly and indirectly.
- Outcome expectations affect choice goals and actions both directly and indirectly.
- People will aspire to enter occupations or academic fields that are consistent with their primary interest areas.
- People will attempt to enter occupations or academic fields that are consonant with their choice goals, provided that they are committed to their goal and their goal is stated in clear terms, proximal to the point of actual entry.
- Interests affect entry behaviours indirectly through their influence on choice goals.
- Self-efficacy beliefs influence career/academic performance both directly and indirectly through their effect on performance goals. Outcome expectations influence performance only indirectly through their effect on goals.
- Ability (or aptitude) will affect career/academic performance both directly and indirectly through its influence on self-efficacy beliefs.
- Self-efficacy beliefs derive from performance accomplishments, vicarious learning, social persuasion and physiological reactions

in relation to particular educational and occupationally relevant activities.

- As with self-efficacy beliefs, outcome expectations are generated through direct and vicarious experiences with educational and occupationally relevant activities.
- Outcome expectations are also partially determined by self-efficacy beliefs, particularly when outcomes (e.g. success, failures) are closely tied to the quality or level of one's performance (Lent, Brown and Hackett 1994).

Q10. Define the term 'Occupational Information'. What are its purposes and sources?

Ans. Occupational information is one of the major components needed to make effective career decisions. Occupational information refers to the collection of details about occupational and educational opportunities. Gathering and using occupational information is essential if an individual is to select options that fit his/her interests, values, aptitudes and skills. Occupational information can include details about the employment outlook, salary, related occupations, education and training, and job duties. Following are some definitions of occupational information:

According to **Shartle**, "Occupational Information is the accurate and usable information about jobs and occupations".

Hoppock says, "Occupational Information includes any and all kinds of information, regarding any position, job or occupation, providing only that the information is potentially of a person who is choosing an occupation.

Purposes of Occupational Information: Occupational information service serves the following purposes:

- To create an awareness of the need for accurate and valid occupational, educational and personal-social information.
- To promote attitudes and habits which assist in making career choices and adjustment.
- To develop a broad and realistic view of life's opportunities and problems at all levels of training.
- To provide assistance in narrowing choices progressively to specific activities, which are appropriate to attitudes, abilities and interests manifested.
- To assist in the mastery of techniques of obtaining and interpreting information for progressive self-direction.
- To provide an understanding of the wide scope of educational, occupational and social activities in terms of broad categories of related activities.

Sources of Occupational Information

Types of occupational information required for career planning may be classified as quantitative and qualitative. Quantitative information implies occupational distribution trends and employment opportunities.

Qualitative information implies nature of work performed, qualifications required, conditions of work and the returns to the worker.

Sources are basically of two types. They are primary sources and secondary sources that regulate employment. Primary sources of occupational information may include employer of an organisation, employee in an organisation, government organisations, agencies or official bodies.

Some of them are listed below:
- Central Institute of Research and Training in Engagement Service (CIRTES), DGET, Ministry of Labour, New Delhi.
- Association of Indian Universities (AIU), New Delhi.
- National Council of Educational Research and Training (NCERT), New Delhi.
- Union Public Service Commission (UPSC), New Delhi.
- Directorate of Audio Visual Publicity (DAVP), New Delhi.
- Planning Commission, New Delhi.
- Ministries – Annual Reports.
- Central Statistical Organisation (CSO), New Delhi.
- Institute of Applied Manpower Research (IAMR), New Delhi.

Q11. Delineate the types and methods of occupational information.

Ans. The types and methods of occupational information are as follows:

Types of Occupational Information: Following are the various types of occupational information:
- **Biography:** An account of the life of a man or woman successful in a given field of endeavour portraying the problems the subject faced in preparing for and advancing in his/her career.
- **Occupational Brief:** It covers the various types of specialisations in an occupational field in general terms. It is not as extensive as monograph but yet describes all job opportunities.
- **Job Series:** It offers broad coverage of an entire occupational area giving brief accounts of all job opportunities in the field. It may be in book, manual or article form.
- **Career Fiction:** An account portrayed through the experiences of one or more fictional characters of an occupation, which may encompass duties, qualifications, preparations, conditions, nature of work and advancement.
- **Occupational Abstract:** It is a concise summary of a job in an occupational area citing the duties and nature of employment in general terms. It may be in narrative or outline form.
- **Business and Industrial Descriptive Literature:** It gives an account of specific industry of business and the major occupations are represented in it.
- **Occupational Guide:** It presents general information about various phases of an occupation but doesn't describe any specific job.

- **Occupational Monograph:** It offers extensive coverage of all phases of an occupation including details, comprehensive analysis of related occupations.
- **Poster or Chart:** These are pictorial and schematic portrayal of occupational information in the direction of catching the attention of target groups and sustaining the same.
- **Community Survey, Economic Report and Job Analysis:** It is an account of accurate, highly statistical, comprehensive report made as a result of local, national or industrial studies.
- **Occupational or Industrial Description:** It describes the principal opportunities of an occupation in an industry or occupations in several industries.
- **Audio-Visual Material:** These are in the form of motion pictures, still pictures, video films, audiotapes, audio skits, video skits, etc.
- **Article or Reprint:** An account of an occupational phase of an occupation or person performing the occupation.
- **Recruitment Literature:** It is in the form of recruitment procedures, nature of work, financial benefits helpful to students and youth who seek employment.

Methods of Occupational Information: We may employ the following methods to collect occupational information.

- We may call on both primary and secondary sources personally to the possible extent or depute someone who can do the job.
- We may address letters to both primary and secondary sources requesting them to procure your occupational information.
- We may contact both primary and secondary sources on telephone and collect required information.
- We may cull out occupational information from newspapers, periodicals, magazines, journals, websites, etc.
- Combination of two or three strategies indicated above may be employed for deriving better results.

Q12. **Classify the occupational information. What are the various characteristics of a good filing system?**

Ans. Classification of the occupational information is given below:

- Jobs may be classified according to their function such as: research, finance, manufacturing, distribution and education.
- Jobs may be classified according to the employer such as GEC, Bosch, TATA, Railways, etc.
- Jobs may be classified according to school subjects such as Mathematics, Languages, etc.
- Jobs may be classified based on National Classification of Occupations, a document published by DGET, Ministry of Labour, New Delhi.
- Jobs may be classified based on National Industrial classification published by Ministry of Statistics.

- Jobs may be classified according to the expressed interest patterns and measured interest patterns such as artistic, computational, etc.
- Jobs may be classified according to the activities involved such as selling, teaching, typing, etc.
- Jobs may be classified based on International Standard classification of occupations published by International Labour Organisation.
- Jobs may be classified according to the product, which they produce such as automobiles and chemicals.
- Advertisements relating to broad fields of occupation, training, apprenticeship, job-oriented courses, etc. are classified based on Guidance Code Numbers (GCOs) which comprise two components namely interest area and educational level.
- Jobs may be classified based on International Standard Industrial Classification published by the United Nations.

Characteristics of a Good Filing System: Following are the characteristics of a good filing system of occupational information:

- A latest list of files needs to be maintained,
- Files should be classified into:
  General files
  Personal files
  Confidential files, etc.
- Filing should be done on a daily basis, preferably in the evenings, to avoid backlog & waste of time in retrieving a document.
- Sort the papers to be filed in the order the files are maintained, i.e. in the alphabetical order or numerical order.
- Before filing, pins/clips, etc. should be removed and instead the papers can be stapled, if necessary.
- After sorting, arrange the documents in strict chronological order placing the latest one on the top.
- Start new files for new subjects, and if the papers are not of a recurring nature, just put them in a folder which can either be disposed of at a later time or put in a file covers if they accumulate.
- One should not take more than 3 minutes time to retrieve a paper or information from a file.
- Filing should be so systematic that in case we hand over the charge of filing to a 2nd person, the handing over process should take the minimum time to explain and understand.

Q13. Describe about International Standard Classification of Occupations (ISCO-08). Also, explain its conceptual framework, classification structure and code scheme.

Ans. The International Standard Classification of Occupations 2008 (ISCO-08) provides a system for classifying and aggregating occupational information obtained by means of statistical censuses and surveys, as well as from administrative records. It is a revision of the International Standard Classification of Occupations 1988 (ISCO-88), which it supersedes.

ISCO-08 is a four-level hierarchically structured classification that allows all jobs in the world to be classified into 436 unit groups. These groups form the most detailed level of the classification structure and are aggregated into 130 minor groups, 43 sub-major groups and 10 major groups, based on their similarity in terms of the skill level and skill specialisation required for the jobs. This allows the production of relatively detailed internationally comparable data as well as summary information for only 10 groups at the highest level of aggregation.

Conceptual Framework

The framework and the concepts underpinning ISCO-08 are essentially unchanged from those used in ISCO-88. The definitions of these concepts have been updated and guidelines for their application to the design of the classification have been strengthened and clarified, where necessary, to address deficiencies in ISCO-88.

The framework used for the design and construction of ISCO-08 is based on two main concepts, i.e. the concept of job, and the concept of skill.

A job is defined in ISCO-08 as, "a set of tasks and duties performed, or meant to be performed, by one person, including for an employer or in self employment".

Occupation refers to the kind of work performed in a job. The concept of occupation is defined as a "set of jobs whose main tasks and duties are characterised by a high degree of similarity". A person may be associated with an occupation through the main job currently held, a second job, a future job or a job previously held.

Skill is defined as the ability to carry out the tasks and duties of a given job. For the purposes of ISCO-08, two dimensions of skill are used to arrange occupations into groups. These are skill level and skill specialisation.

Skill specialisation is considered in terms of four concepts:
(1)   the field of knowledge required;
(2)   the tools and machinery used;
(3)   the materials worked on or with; and
(4)   the kinds of goods and services produced.

Within each major group, occupations are arranged into unit groups, minor groups and sub-major groups, primarily on the basis of aspects of skill specialisation.

Skill Level 1: Occupations classified at Skill Level 1 include office cleaners, freight handlers, garden labourers and kitchen assistants.

Skill Level 2: Occupations classified at Skill Level 2 include butchers, bus drivers, secretaries, accounts clerks, sewing machinists, dressmakers, shop sales assistants, police officers, hairdressers, building electricians and motor vehicle mechanics.

Skill Level 3: Occupations classified at Skill Level 3 include shop managers, medical laboratory technicians, legal secretaries, commercial sales representatives, diagnostic medical radiographers, computer support technicians, and broadcasting and recording technicians.

Skill Level 4: Occupations classified at Skill Level 4 include sales and marketing managers, civil engineers, secondary school teachers, medical practitioners, musicians, operating theatre nurses and computer systems analysts.

Table 3.1: Mapping of ISCO-08 major groups to skill levels

ISCO-08 major groups	Skill level
Managers	3+4
Professionals	4
Technicians and Associate Professionals	3
Clerical Support Workers	2
Services and Sales Workers	
Skilled Agricultural, Forestry and Fishery Workers	
Craft and Related Trades Workers	
Plant and Machine Operators, and Assemblers	
Elementary Occupations	1
Armed Forces Occupations	1+2+4

In the above table, formal education and training requirements are used as part of the measurement of the skill level of an occupation, these requirements are defined in terms of ISCED-97.

Table 3.2: Mapping of the four ISCO-08 skill levels to ISCED-97 levels of education

ISCO-08 Skill Level	ISCED-97 groups
4	6 Second stage of tertiary education (leading to an advanced research qualification)
3	5a First stage of tertiary education, 1st degree (medium duration)
2	5b First stage of tertiary education, (short or medium duration)
	4 Post-secondary non-tertiary education
	3 Upper Secondary level of education
	2 Lower Secondary level of education
1	1 Primary level of education

Classification Structure

International Standard Classification of Occupations 2008 (ISCO-08) has arranged occupations into one of 436 unit groups. Each unit group is made up of several 'occupations' which have similarity in skill level and skill specialisation. Unit groups are arranged into minor groups, minor groups into sub-major groups, and sub-major groups into major groups based on skill level and skill specialisation.

Table 3.3: Number of groups at each level of ISCO-08

Major group	Sub-Major Groups	Minor Groups	Unit Groups
Managers	4	11	31
Professionals	6	27	92
Technicians and Associate Professionals	5	20	84
Clerical Support Workers	4	8	29
Services and Sales Workers	4	13	40
Skilled Agricultural, Forestry and Fishery Workers	3	9	18
Craft and Related Trades Workers	5	14	66
Plant and Machine Operators, and Assemblers	3	14	40
Elementary Occupations	6	11	33
Armed Forces Occupations	3	3	3
Total ISCO-08	**43**	**130**	**436**

Code Scheme

ISCO-08 provides a code number, a title and brief description for each group classified at the four skill levels. The code number for each group is denoted as follows:

(1)	Major group	—	One digit
(2)	Sub- major group	—	two digit (comprising the major group code plus one digit)
(3)	Minor group	—	three digit (comprising the higher level code plus one digit)
(4)	Unit group	—	four digit (comprising the higher level code plus one digit)

The following are the six sub-major groups in major group 2 with their code number.

21. Science and Engineering Professionals
22. Health Professionals
23. Teaching Professionals
24. Business and Administration Professionals
25. Information and Communication Technology Professionals
26. Legal, Social and Cultural Professionals

In the sub-major group, it may be noticed that the 'Teaching Professionals' is given the code number 23 (2 digit) in which 2 indicates the major group and 3 indicates the serial order in the sub-major group.

The sub-major group is further divided into minor groups (3 digit) and unit groups (4 digit) as given below:

23 Teaching professionals

    231 University and Higher Education Teachers

        2310 University and Higher Education Teachers

    232 Vocational Education Teachers

        2320 Vocational Education Teachers

    233 Secondary Education Teachers

        2330 Secondary Education Teachers

    234 Primary School and Early Childhood Teachers

        2341 Primary School Teachers

        2342 Early Childhood Educators

    235 Other Teaching Professionals

        2351 Education Methods Specialists

        2352 Special Needs Teachers

        2353 Other Language Teachers

            2354 Other Music Teachers

            2355 Other Arts Teachers

            2356 Information Technology Trainers

            2357 Teaching professionals Not Elsewhere Classified

This is a comprehensive classification of the sub-major group 23: Teaching Professionals. In this classification, we have seen that the sub-major group 23: Teaching Professionals is divided into five minor groups and each minor group is further divided into one or more unit groups.

Q14. Briefly explain about National Classification of Occupations-2015. Also, discuss its design and structure.

Or

Discuss design and coding structure of National Classification of Occupations-2015.

Ans. National Classification of Occupations – 2015 (NCO-2015) is a revised version of NCO – 2004 in line with ISCO-08 and National Industrial Classification 2008 (NIC-2008). The NCO-2015 is a comprehensive repository of national occupations. The main objectives of updating the NCO 2004 were to:

(1) make NCO-2015 compatible to ISCO-2008 so that it is relevant for international reporting, comparisons, and exchange of statistical and administrative information about occupations.

(2) create a useful model of the development of National Classifications of Occupations (NCO).

Design and Structure: The skill level of the occupation in NCO-2015 is defined as follows:

**Table 3.4: Skill level and educational requirements –
ISCO-08 & NCO-2015**

Skill Level	ISCO-08 Educational Requirements	NCO-2015 Educational Requirements
I	Primary Education	Upto 10 years of formal education and/or informal skills
II	Secondary Education	11-13 years of formal education
III	First University Degree	14-15 years of formal education
IV	Post-Graduate University Degree	More than 15 years of formal education

The NCO-2015 has classified occupations into nine divisions in tune with skill levels as defined in Table 3.4.

Table 3.5: NCO-2015 Division, Title, Skill Level

NCO-2015 Divisions	Title	Skill Level
1	Legislators, Senior Officials, and Managers	Not Defined
2	Professionals	IV
3	Associate Professionals	III
4	Clerks	II
5	Service Workers and Shop & Market Sales Workers	II
6	Skilled Agricultural and Fishery Workers	II
7	Craft and Related Trades Workers	II
8	Plant and Machine Operators and Assemblers	II
9	Elementary Occupations	I

We may have noticed that skill level is not defined for Division 1 comprising of Legislators, Senior Officials and Managers.

Coding Structure

Based on the ISCO-08 and the factors impacting skill and labour environment in India, the NCO-2015 coding framework was created.

The coding structure of NCO-2015 is as follows:

Table 3.6: Coding structure NCO-2015

Coding Structure NCO-2015 Digits	Representation	Corresponding Mapping to ISCO-2008
The first digit	Division	Major Group
The first two digits	Sub-Division	Sub-Major Group
The first three digits	Group	Minor Group
The first four digits	Family	Unit Group

The first two digits after the decimal	Occupation	
The last two digits after the decimal	QP NOS	

(1)   The first digit of NCO-2015 represents the Division (Major Group in ISCO)

(2)   The first two digits of NCO-2015 represent the Sub-Division (Sub-Major Group in ISCO)

(3)   The first three digits of NCO-2015 represent the Group (Minor Group in ISCO)

(4)   The first four digits of NCO-2015 represent the Family (Unit Group in ISCO)

(5)   A decimal is introduced after the first four digits in order to create a distinction between the Families and individual Occupations.

(6)   The first two digits after the decimal of NCO-2015 represent the different occupations that can be combined under the given Family.

(7)   The last two digits after the decimal of NCO-2015 represent the availability of a QP NOS for the job role (QP means Qualification Pack or sector specific competency framework. NOS means National Occupational Standards)

(8)   The value of the last two digits would depend on two scenarios:

   (i)   If QP NOS is available, then the value of the last 2 digits after the decimal will be between 1-99 (arranged sequentially).

   (ii)   If QP NOS is unavailable, then the value of the last two digits after decimal will remain 00. Coding structure is illustrated in Table 3.7 below.

Table 3.7: Coding Structure

Code: 2330.0100 Job Title: Senior secondary and secondary school teacher, Arts		
2	Division	Professionals
23	Sub-Division	Teaching Professionals
233	Group	Secondary Education Teachers
2330	Family	Secondary Education Teachers
2330.0100	Occupation	Senior secondary and secondary school teacher, Arts

Here, the first digit '2' in the code stands for Division (Professionals), '23' stands for sub-division (Teaching professionals), '233' stands for Group (Secondary Education Teachers), and '2330' denotes Family. Therefore, the occupation code for the job titled: Senior Secondary and Secondary School Teacher, Arts is '2330.0100' (8 digits). The first two digits after the decimal in the occupation code represent the different occupations under the same Family. The last two digits (00) after the decimal in the occupation code indicate that QP NOS is not available for the given occupation title (senior secondary and secondary school teacher, Arts).

Occupation codes for other job titles under the same family (2330) are given below:

2330.0200   Senior Secondary and Secondary School Teacher, Science

2330.0300   Senior Secondary and Secondary School Teacher, Commerce

2330.0400   Language Teacher, Senior Secondary and Secondary School

2330.9900   Senior Secondary and Secondary School Teachers, Other

Source: NCO-2015, Vol. 1, PP. 15-65 GOI, www. ncs.gov.in

Q15. Discuss the classification of economic activities by industry with their structure and codification.

Ans. In occupational information, the classification of economic activities by industry with their structure and codification is available at the international and national level.

International Standard Industrial Classification (ISIC Rev. 4)

The International Standard Industrial Classification of All Economic Activities is published by the Department of Economic and Social Affairs (Statistic Division) of the United Nations.

Structure and Codification: The fourth revision of ISIC provides substantially more detail at all levels than the previous versions of the classification. This increased detail responds to requests by both producers and users of statistics. However, the basic coding system of the classification has not been changed. The ISIC Rev. 4 structure consists of 21 'sections' identified by letters A-U, 99 'Divisions' represented by two digits, 990 'Groups' represented by three digits and 9900 'Classes' represented by four digits.

Table 3.8: ISIC Rev. 4 Sections, Divisions, Descriptions

Section	Division	Description
A	01-03	Agriculture, forestry and fishing
B	05-09	Mining and quarrying
C	10-33	Manufacturing
D	35	Electricity, gas, steam and air conditioning supply
E	36-39	Water supply; sewerage, waste management and remediation activities
F	41-43	Construction
G	45-47	Wholesale and retail trade; repair of motor vehicles and motorcycles
H	49-53	Transportation and storage
I	55-56	Accommodation and food service activities
J	58-63	Information and communication
K	64-66	Financial and insurance activities

L	68	Real estate activities
M	69-75	Professional, scientific and technical activities
N	77-82	Administrative and support service activities
O	84	Public administration and defence; compulsory social security
P	85	Education
Q	86-88	Human health and social work activities
R	90-93	Arts, entertainment and recreation
S	94-96	Other service activities
T	97-98	Activities of households as employers; undifferentiated goods- and services-producing activities of households for own use
U	99	Activities of extraterritorial organisations and bodies

As we can see from table 3.8, Education comes under 'Division 85' in 'Section P'. Now we examine the detailed structure and coding scheme for the 'Description' Education.

Table 3.9: Section P Education

Division	Group	Class	Description
Division 85			Education
	851	8510	Pre-primary and primary education
	852		Secondary education
		8521	General secondary education
		8522	Technical and vocational secondary education
	853	8530	Higher education
	854		Other education
		8541	Sports and recreation education
		8542	Cultural education
		8549	Other education
	855	8550	Educational support activities

The 'Group' code is a three digits number. For example, the 'Group' code for secondary education is 852, the first two digits represent the 'Division' 85 Education, the third digit represents the hierarchical order in the 'Group'. There are two classes under Group 852. General secondary education is represented by the numerical code 8521 and Technical and vocational secondary education is represented by the numerical code 8522. In both cases, the fourth digit represents the class in the hierarchical order.

National Industrial Classification 2008 (NIC-2008)

NIC-2008 is the revised version of NIC-2004 in line with the ISIC Rev. 4. The NIC-2008 provides a basis for the standardised collection, analysis and dissemination of industry wise economic data for India.

Structure and Codification: All the activities under NIC-2008 are grouped into several "activity groups" or "tabulation categories" in a hierarchical manner. Activities are first grouped into 'section' alphabetically coded from A through U, every section is divided into 'division' with 2-digit numeric code, every numeric code, every division into 'group' with 3-digit numeric code, every group into 'class' with 4-digit numeric code and every 4-digit class into 5-digit 'sub-class'. The structure is illustrated below:

Table 3.10

Level	Description
Section P	Education
Division 85	Education
Group 852	Secondary Education
Class 8521	General Secondary Education
Sub-Class 85211	General School Education in the first stage of the secondary level (upto Xth standard) without any special subject pre-requisite

The structure of NIC-2008 is identical to the structure of ISIC Rev. 4 up to 4- digit level *'class'*.

Classes were then divided into 5 digit 'sub classes' according to national requirements. NIC-2008 has 21 sections, 88 divisions, 238 groups, 403 classes and 1304 sub-classes.

Uses: The uses of occupational classifications are as follows:

- ISCO and ISIC provide an understanding of occupation/job descriptions and economic activities prevalent at an international level.
- NCO and NIC provide data for international comparison. These data can be used for studying the socio-economic development taking place in the country.
- Counselors can use the classification of occupations for career counselling.
- ISCO and ISIC serve as model for countries developing or revising their national classifications of occupations.
- Counselors can make students aware of the skill level needed for various occupations.
- NCO and NIC are used by the government agencies, industry associations and researchers for administrative, analytical and research purposes.
- NCO and NIC provide a national picture of occupational classifications and economic activities in alignment with the ISCO and ISIC.
- Counselors can use the occupation descriptions to make the students aware of the tasks and duties involved in an occupation.
- Employment exchanges use these data for registering employment seekers.

Q16. What do you understand by guidance code number?

Ans. A Guidance Code Number is an indication of an applicant's interests and educational level. Training, apprenticeship and admission notifications are advertised, based on two-factors, namely – interest area followed by educational level. In the guidance code number, first interest area code is written, followed by the educational level code. These codes are used in the case of educated freshers and these are not used in the case of occupationally set or semi skilled categories of students or unemployed youth.

The following educational levels are assigned code numbers indicated against them.

- Post-Graduate – 1
- Graduate – 2
- PUC/+2 – 3
- Matric – 4
- Middle – 5
- Others – 6

The following codes are allotted to interest areas.

Interest Area	**Code**
Technical	0
Health	1
Scientific	2
Welfare	3
Teaching	4
Clerical	5
Business Contact	6
Manual	7
Literary	8
Artistic	9
Protective	10

For instance, 'X' showing interest in the area of teaching and is a graduate is assigned Guidance Code Number 4.2; and 'Y' showing interest in the area of Business Contact and is a matriculate is assigned Guidance Code Number 6.4.

The assignment of Guidance Code Number to educated fresher's is done with a view to prepare a comprehensive programme from the view point of providing systematic occupational information.

Q17. Why is it important to update occupational information?

Ans. It is important to update the already collected information and collect latest information so as to keep with current trends. We have to maintain a master copy at our level wherein we effect changes in the same as and when we notice change in the information either by way of collecting information from individuals, institutions, associations, industries, employers or by way of collecting from publications of different kinds including mass media like Newspapers, Magazines, Radio, TV, etc.

While updating occupational information, the obsolete occupational information should be weeded out by conducting reviews periodically and the master copy should be updated to provide latest information.

We can gather information from any part of the country or the world at the click of a mouse with the World Wide Web/internet available today. Another important highlight that would emerge out of this is the need for professionals to develop software in this regard. We need to develop ourselves professionally in taking up this challenge.

Q18. What are the various tools through which occupational information can be collected and updated?

Ans. Following are the various tools through which occupational information can be collected and updated:

- Biography;
- Occupational Abstract;
- Business and Industrial Descriptive Literature;
- Posters;
- Occupational monographs;
- Career Fiction;
- Community Surveys, Economic Report or Job Analysis;
- Computer;
- Charts;
- Occupational Brief;
- Occupational and Industrial Descriptive Literature;
- Occupational Guide;
- Audio Visual Aids;
- Article of Reprint;
- Recruitment Literature; and
- Job Series.

Q19. What are the various methods to disseminate occupational information?

Ans. We may employ any of the following methods to disseminate occupational information:

- Display of career literature of different kinds for the benefit of students, unemployed youth, non-governmental organisations, employer's associations, parents and community members at large.
- Arranging discussions so as to interact with different target groups in the context of placing world of work before them.
- Delivering class talk, career talk, address by Non-Governmental Organisations, Parent Teacher Associations, Teachers Associations and similar gatherings.
- Conducting Mock Interviews in order to prepare candidates either for admission to specialised courses or for entry into different occupations.
- Screening career films on need based topics for the benefit of different target groups.

Q20. Enumerate some strategies to disseminate occupational information.

Ans. We should equip ourselves with the strategies which have emerged in the recent past and which would help us to keep pace with current trends. Following are some of the strategies explained briefly:

- Organisation of career fairs where, apart from display of career literature, experts are available to clarify doubts on the part of those who participate in the fairs.
- Organisation of Entrepreneurial Awareness Campus in order to apprise the potential employment seekers about the existing realities prevailing in the wage-paid labour market and to enable them to have exposure to avenues available in launching their own enterprises in terms of Governmental Schemes, Financial assistance available, Traits that are required to take up self-employment, managerial inputs that are required and so on.
- Screening of career-oriented film to inform the target groups.
- Conducting Rozgar Bazar/Rozgar Mela implies arranging face-to-face meet between employers and potential employment seekers to provide opportunity to clarify each other's point in arriving at consensus about the extent of suitability or otherwise on the part of employment seekers.

Q21. How does the evaluation of occupational information material take place? Discuss.

Or

Describe the criteria for evaluating occupational literature.

Ans. Evaluation of occupational information material is a continuous procedure and we should undertake the same periodically so as to enhance the quality of the material. This can be done by raising relevant issues in terms of time, venue, people, reason and the method, which have direct bearing upon copyright date of book/material, geographical limitation, quality of authorship, purpose and modus operandi of collection and presentation of factual information, respectively.

Criteria

While evaluating occupational literature, following criteria may be kept in mind:

- Occupational literature can be evaluated in terms of the comprehensiveness of the content, presentation of textual and tabular material and availability of the latest data in tune with the international and national level data.
- Tabular and graphic materials should be accompanied by a well-integrated discussion.
- Tabular material should be set up-in proper form.
- Text or footnotes should indicate the source of quoted or paraphrased material.
- Transition between parts of the text should make clear interpretations.

- Occupations should be presented in their social and economic setting.

Methods Used for Collecting Data

Evaluation in terms of what organisation, group or individual sponsored it is required. Indication of data when material was gathered, bear evidence of methods used in gathering the data, bear evidence to prove findings are validated and tryout with consumers or target groups.

Style and Format

It must be observed that the data of publication is always given and style should be clear, concise and interesting but not too verbose. While considering format, it should be pleasing, attractive and typography reader friendly. A table of content, index and bibliography should invariably find a place in the publication. Provision for revision should be made when original publication is issued.

Q22. What are the various mobilising resources for setting up occupational information service programme.

Or

Elucidate the categories of mobilising resources required to organise occupational information service.

Ans. The mobilising resources for setting up occupational information service programme can be broadly classified as money, material and manpower. All these three are discussed as follows:

- **Money:** One of the most crucial input for the effective conduct of various activities in the context of any endeavour and more so in the case of occupational information service programme is nothing but 'money'. In order to mobilise this input, we are required to bring about awareness among all those who are in a position to make contributions financially. Apart from this, we need to make them appreciate the importance of the activities in the context of their own professional development so that the programme becomes need based and sustainable.

- **Material:** In the form of publications like Newspapers, Magazines, Periodicals, Journals, Annual Reports, Video Films, Audio Tapes, Television, Video Cassette Recorder, Tape Recorder, Projector, Computers, etc., a lot of materials are required to set up occupational information service programme. These materials have to be mobilised for effective dissemination of information.

- **Manpower:** We need to mobilise other appropriate individuals and institutions as manpower resources, besides harnessing our potentialities as vital manpower resource. Community members should be harnessed as resources for conducting different activities under occupational information service programme. Trained guidance personnel, teachers, community members specialised in different areas can also be utilised in the conduct of various activities of occupational information service.

As far as mobilising of this input is concerned, community members with philanthropic mind and non-governmental organisations can come to our rescue in a big way.

Publicity measures through Mass Media have to be initiated so that financial, material and manpower contributors on one hand and different target groups on the other hand would effectively involve in the endeavour of development of well-articulated occupational information service programme.

Q23. Define career patterns. Also, distinguish the term career patterns from other related terms.

Ans. The pattern emerging in the job movement of a group of individuals is termed as career pattern. Firstly, in the field of sociology, the term career pattern was originated. A career is something with long-term goals for which we make money. Career development is part of all round development of the individual. Today, career has emerged out as one of the most significant areas of concern for those who advocate education for national development. The dramatic increase in interest to develop this potential through education and work among all sections is visible if we scan various publications related to career. Career patterns refer to sequence of occupations in the life of an individual or group of individuals.

Traditionally, only a few professions – doctor, lawyer, minister, statesman, and the like – were considered to have careers. More recently however, the concept of career has been extended to include many other work-related roles. A distinction can be made between a job or occupation and a career. The concept of a job focuses on aspects external to the individual; it can be described separately from the person. A career includes these external aspects. However, it simultaneously demands consideration of internal (to the individual) or subjective aspects including individual attitudes and self-concepts. A career, then, it experienced by a person and like any other experience, is both similar to the experiences of others but also different because of individual variations.

Using these ideas, we can state that a career consists of the sequence of work-related activities an adventure that an individual experiences, perceives, and acts on during a lifetime. A career is individually experienced, perceived, and is associated with workrelated activities. However, it is influenced by, and exercises influence on, all other life activities – familiar and social included. It cannot be observed at a single point in time; rather it is a process that covers the lifetime of the individual.

There are a number of commonly held views that are not necessarily associated with the concept of a career. A career need not imply upward mobility. There are liner careers, to be sure, but also other types-doctor, lawyers, etc. that do not necessarily lead to progression up a hierarchy. Careers are not associated with one organisation. Although some people spend their entire working life in one company, many others are highly mobile and will pursue their careers in many different organisations. Finally, career success cannot be externally measure by such things as rank, salary, and speed of promotion. Although these factors may affect an individual's self-perceptions of career success, there are many other factors that might affect individual perceptions. For example, one person may see her career primarily as the means to provide money to have a particular life style while another person may view it as an end in itself. These two individuals would likely evaluate career events differently.

The concept of a career being individually perceived and experienced raises the idea of free choice. This right of choice, however, also carries the responsibility for accepting the consequenes of these decisions. A person has the opportunity and responsibility for career an life choices. Using external criteria as a measurement of career success and waiting for someone else to plan and chart your career is inappropriate. The Concept of personal choice suggests that you and you alone can take this responsibility.

Career Patterns and Other Related Terms

It is better to differentiate career pattern from other related words or terms used interchangeably in order to understand it. These words are job, occupation, profession and vocation.

A job is something short-term that we do for money. We often hear the phrase "dead end job" when people talk about their work. There is no long-lasting fulfilment or happiness from a job.

Occupation refers to denote one's source of livelihood, being most generic lowermost in the pyramid starting from occupation, moving on to vocation and then to profession. According to Merriam - Webster Online Dictionary, occupation means "an activity in which one engages" or "the principal business of one's life".

Occupation also means the work that one does on a long-term basis, but in this case, it may be paid or unpaid. If we spend our days running the local library, because people want us to, but they are unable to pay us, we would describe that as an occupation, but we probably wouldn't describe it as a job. In simple words, 'Occupation' is a person's usual or principal work especially as a means of earning a living. Occupation is also referred to as business, profession, employment, job or vocation. Basically, it is the activity to which one regularly devotes oneself.

A profession is a specialised occupation or vocation characterised by intensive education and training in a specific field of knowledge with an intension to apply and serve the humanity. According to the Oxford English Dictionary, "professions involve the application of specialised knowledge of a subject, field, or science to fee-paying clientele." In other words, the professional provides service to the society on the basis of her/his specialised knowledge and skills, and in turn gets paid for it.

Merriam - Webster Online Dictionary defines vocation as "the work in which a person is regularly employed". It involves a routine activity of some kind – physical or scholarly and needs certain or no skills. Vocation is an occupation that demands practical skills on the part of the individual. A vocation is something to which we all should strive. A vocation is similar to a career but we also get deep satisfaction and fulfilment from our vocation.

Q24. Elucidate the relationship of career patterns with life stages.

Ans. Occupation is a group of similar jobs in which people perform essentially the same task, drawing on the same body of knowledge and using the same basic skills independently of the person pursuing it. The choice of occupation or occupational choice is a lifelong process of decision-making for those who seek major satisfaction from their work. This leads them to reassess repeatedly how they can improve the adjustment between their changing career goals and the realities of the world of work, and lead a productive life in society. All these are related to career pattern. The concept of Career Pattern is closely parallel to the psychological concept of life stages, in which the major events and concerns group themselves. It varies from one stage of life to another, justifying the classification of life into a sequence of characteristic stages. In order to understand this relationship, some psychologists and sociologists have defined the life stages in the following manner:

(1) **Super:** Donald Super developed the theories and work of colleague Eli Ginzberg. Super felt that Ginzberg's work had weaknesses, which he wanted to address. Super extended Ginzberg's work on life and career development stages from three to five, and included different sub-stages. The five life stages as propounded by Super are discussed as follows:

Table 3.11

Stage 1: Growth	Age 0–14	Characteristics: Development of self-concept, attitudes, needs and general world of work
Stage 2: Exploration	Age 15–24	Characteristics: "Trying out" through classes, work experience, hobbies. Tentative choice and skill development
Stage 3: Establishment	Age 25–44	Characteristics: Entry-level skill building and stabilisation through work experience
Stage 4: Maintenance	Age 45-64	Characteristics: Continual adjustment process to improve position
Stage 5: Decline	Age 65+	Characteristics: Reduced output, prepare for retirement

(i) **The Growth Stage (0 to 14 years):** This is the first life stage, the period when children develop their capacities, attitudes, interests, socialise their needs, and form a general understanding of the world of work. This stage includes four major career developmental tasks, i.e. becoming concerned about the future, increasing personal control over one's own life, convincing oneself to achieve in school and at work, and acquiring competent work habits and attitudes.

(ii) The Exploration Stage (14 to 25 years): This is the period when individuals attempt to understand themselves and find their place in the world of work. Through classes, work experience and hobbies, they try to identify their interests and capabilities and figure out how they fit with various occupations. They make tentative occupational choices and eventually obtain an occupation. This stage involves three career development tasks. The first one, the crystallisation of a career preference, is to develop and plan a tentative vocational goal. The next task, the specification of a career preference, is to convert generalised preferences into a specific choice, a firm vocational goal. The third vocational task is implementation of a career preference by completing appropriate training and securing a position in the chosen occupation. This stage is further divided into the following three sub-stages:

(a) Tentative (15 to 17 years): Needs, interests, capacities, values and opportunities are considered at this stage. Tentative choices are made, tried out in fantasy, discussion, courses, work and so on.

(b) Transition (18 to 21 years): Reality considerations are given more weight as the youth enters the labour market or professional training and attempts to implement a self-concept at this age.

(c) Trial (22 to 24 years): A seemingly appropriate field having been located, a beginning job in it is found and tried out as a life role.

(iii) The Establishment Stage (25 to 45 years): This is the period when the individual, having gained an appropriate position in the chosen field of work, strives to secure the initial position and pursue chances for further advancement. This stage involves three developmental tasks. The first task is stabilising or securing one place in the organisation by adapting to the organisation's requirements and performing job duties satisfactorily. The next task is the consolidation of one's position by manifesting positive work attitudes and productive habits along with building favourable coworker relations. The third task is to obtain advancement to new levels of responsibility.

(iv) **The Maintenance Stage (45 to 65 years):** This is the period of continual adjustment, which includes the career development tasks of holding on, keeping up, and innovating. The individuals strive to maintain what they have achieved, and for this reason they update their competencies and find innovative ways of performing their job routines. They try also to find new challenges, but usually little new ground is broken in this period.

(v) **The Decline Stage (over 65 years):** This is the final stage, the period of transition out of the workforce. In this stage, individuals encounter the developmental tasks of deceleration, retirement planning, and retirement living. With a declined energy and interest in an occupation, people gradually disengage from their occupational activities and concentrate on retirement planning. In due course, they make a transition to retirement living by facing the challenges of organising new life patterns. The decline stage has the following two main sub-stages:

(a) **Deceleration (65 to 70 years):** The pace of work slackens, duties are shifted and the nature of work is changed to suit declining capacities. Many find part-time jobs to replace their full-time occupations.

(b) **Retirement (over 70 years):** As with all specified age limits, there are great variations from person to person. But complete cessation of occupation comes for all in due course; to some easily and pleasantly, to others with difficulty and disappointment, and to some only with death.

(2) **Miller and Form (1951):** The five periods in the pattern are preparatory, initial, trial, stable and retirement. Clearly, the first three are most appropriate in the analysis of occupational choice. Each of the periods has a definite set of activities associated with it and in which the individual engages and in which he has to make adjustments. The first and last periods are really non-work periods, thus, the preparatory period is associated with the 'early experiences and adjustments in the home, school and community as the young person develops physical and mental maturity' while the retirement period demands 'new adjustments in the home and community as the work position in the market place is relinquished' (p. 535).

(i) **Preparatory Work Period:** At the preparatory stage of development for work, the child is able to develop a perspective of approach to certain work tasks. While the nature of the rewards at this stage are undoubtedly different from those of the real work situation, certain habits and customs are created at this stage which have an influence on future activities in the work situation. And so it can be argued that the preparatory work period enables the individual to acquire certain skills and perspectives that normally ensure a relatively smooth transition to paid employment. The extent of the success of this phase in developing these skills and perspectives in the individual depends upon factors such as social class, the degree of family cohesion and personality characteristics.

(ii) **Initial Work Period:** At this stage, an amalgam of family, educational and work experiences can be seen. It follows that the longer period of time that is spent in educational involvement, then the longer it will be before the trial work period comes into play. For those in this situation, the initial work period may act as a functional substitute for the trial work period, although it is generally true that those who continue their education into their late teens or early twenties have a wider range of occupations of an 'initial' kind than do those who complete their education at the minimum leaving age.

(iii) **The Trial Work Period:** While the two previous work periods may be regarded as some-what transitional, the trial work period marks the introduction of an element of permanence into the work life of the individual. Nevertheless, it is still somewhat transitional in that the individual is at this stage still seeking a truly permanent position. Indeed, Miller and Form estimate that this period may only last for a matter of months. Nevertheless, it is permanent in that it does indicate a complete break from non-work life.

(iv) **The Stable Work Period (35-60/5):** The stable work period is so named because of its characteristic security in that at this time the individual has found a job and work situation in which he intends to remain. But it should not be assumed that the term stable automatically means that there will be no shifting of occupation or employment until retirement age, nor that this period is without its own peculiar strains and tensions for the individual.

(v) **The Retirement Period (60-65+):** The retirement period is a replica of the decline stage.

Q25.Discuss different types of career patterns as propounded by Davidson and Anderson (1937).

Ans. Davidson and Anderson (1937) found four types of career patterns, which are given below:

• **The Stable Career Pattern:** This pattern is applicable on those persons who have gone directly from school or college into a type of work that they have consistently followed, i.e. they have skipped the trial work period. A person chooses a career and sticks to that till he retires. A few examples of people having stable career patterns can be Defence Services, Banking, Civil Services, Central Services, Income-tax, Teaching, Secretarial Services, Chartered Accountancy and so on.

- **The Conventional Career Pattern:** In this case, the typical progression is from initial through trial to stable employment as Managerial, Clerical, MBA, Computer Engineering, Executives and so on. The person has not taken up a stable career. He tries his fortunes in different careers, before he finally takes up any stable or enduring one, which is satisfying to him.

- **The Unstable Career Pattern:** Here, the sequence trial-stable-trial is followed. In this category, we may consider careers related to various crafts as career in fashion technology, dance, music, etc. The person moves from one to another career or business or part-time job, as Consultant, Property Dealer, etc.

- **The Multiple-Trial Career Pattern:** In this pattern, frequent change of employment takes place with no one type sufficiently prolonged or dominant to justify calling the person established in a career. Examples may be quoted from Consultant, Technical Assistants, etc.

Q26. What are the various determinants of career patterns? Discuss.

Ans. The sequence, frequency and duration of the trial and stable jobs are determined by many factors. Among them, the following are important:

- personality characteristics (needs, values, interests, traits and self-concept);
- individual parental socio-economic level;
- the opportunities to which one is exposed;
- career maturity;
- mental ability; and
- skills.

However, self-concept and socio-economic status are the most important factors as the determinants of career patterns, because they:

- help to shape occupational concepts; and
- tend to open or close opportunities.

Krumboltz (1989) describes the decision process in the choice of an occupation being determined by the following four factors:

- Genetic endowments and special abilities (race, sex, physical appearances and characteristics, intelligence, computing ability, muscular co-ordination).
- Task approach skills (attitudes, knowledge, skills, performance standards and values, work habits, perceptual and cognitive processes, mental sets and emotional response an individual

brings to new situations and tasks). These skills develop readiness to cope with the development tasks.

- Environmental conditions and events (number and nature of jobs, training opportunities, social policies and procedure of selecting trainees and workers, technological developments and change in social organisations).
- Learning experiences (instrumental learning experiences in which antecedent, covert and overt behavioural responses and consequences are present).

Q27. What is meant by career maturity? Also, enlist its characteristics and components.

Ans. Career maturity is defined as the degree to which individuals are prepared to make good educational or vocational decisions. It is usually seen as dependent on their knowledge of themselves and of the world of work, their ability to make decisions, and a positive attitude towards making career decisions. It is developmental in nature, following an individual's growing maturity in all life areas. Frank Parsons, generally considered to be the father of career development, saw career maturity as encompassing a clear understanding about oneself, knowledge of the requirements of different occupations, and true reasoning on the relationships among these. The term career maturity was first promulgated by Donald E. Super, and many authors have used it subsequently in developing career counselling assessment instruments and career counselling processes and procedures.

Usually, career maturity is defined as the individual's readiness to cope with the developmental tasks with which s/he is confronted because of his/her biological and social developments, and because of society's expectations of people who have reached that stage of development. This readiness is both affective and cognitive as shown by research with the Career Development Inventory (CDI). The CDI assesses two affective variables, namely Career Planning (or planfulness), and Career Exploration (or curiosity). It also assesses three cognitive characteristics including:

- Knowledge of the principles of career decision-making and ability to apply them to actual choices;
- Knowledge of the nature of careers, occupations and the world of work; and
- Knowledge of the field of work in which one's occupational preference falls.

A component of career maturity, identified in the Career Pattern Study (CPS) monographs by Super and others (1957) and in Crites (1978) adaptation is Realism. Realism is a mixed affective and cognitive entity. It is assessed by combining personal, self-report and objective data and comparing the aptitude of the individual with the aptitudes typical of people in the occupation to which s/he aspires. Realism is a "Trait". It can be accessed through Career Development Inventory (CDI) or Career Maturity Inventory (CMI). However, no single measure can be called maturity, as any test or inventory score is at best an assessment of one or more aspects of a complex whole.

Q28. Define vocational success. What do you understand by vocational adaptation and criteria of vocational adjustment?

Ans. Career patterns lead to vocational success, which further leads to feelings of autonomy, of being somewhat in control of one's present and even of one's future. Vocational success also leads to the development of interest in the things in which one has been successful. Finding that one can, to some extent, control one's activities helps in the development of self-esteem. At the same time, it leads to an understanding that one can plan for future events and have success in their shaping. Thus, develops the ability to make decisions, to plan, to identify and solve problems.

Vocational Adaptation

Vocational adaptation, also known as vocational adjustment, refers to a condition when a person is relatively unaffected by the job and its challenge. If we glance through our job from the date of joining or compare our roles and responsibilities as a progressive teacher with the teachers taught us in students' days, we can certainly discriminate the expectations from teachers at that time with that of present teachers. At that time, teachers were the only source of information. Presently, teachers have been using other sources such as television programmes, newspapers, computers, CD, ICT, etc. as information providers and thus, teachers had adapted themselves as per the need of the hour.

Criteria of Vocational Adjustment

The career patterns lead to vocational adjustment. This is a function of the degree to which an individual is able to implement his/her self-concept, to play the kind of role s/he wants to play, to meet his/her important needs in his/her work and career. This means self-realisation.

The improvement in other aspects of adjustment is the result of the improvement in vocational adjustment. Plausibly, it should do so, since general adjustment is a synthesis of specific adjustments. By relieving tension, clarifying feelings, gaining insights, achieving success, an individual develops a feeling of competence, which is one important area of vocational adjustment. It is possible to realise the ability of the individuals to cope more adequately with other aspects of living, therefore, bringing about improvement in general adjustment will bring about improvement in others. Assisting a client to use his/her assets to make a better vocational adjustment will result in his/her being able to make a better adjustment in other areas of living.

Individuals having genuine problems of vocational adjustment, also known as maladapted individuals, can be helped by the counsellors. It has been found that improvement in vocational adjustment has brought about improvement in the overall adjustment of such persons. A criterion of the wisdom of working on it is the client's readiness to work on the vocational adjustment problem. Nevertheless, this alone is not enough; the maladjusted client must also be willing to work at least occasionally in his/her related emotional problems in other areas. This may be a prerequisite to a programme in vocational adjustment.

Q29. What is the role of teachers in career planning of students? Discuss.

Ans. Teachers play a crucial role in career planning of students. One of the most difficult tasks is to choosing a course that will qualify for one's chosen career. However, the choice depends on a number of factors such as stream, subject, duration, location and financial expense and aligning two or more of these specifications are not that simple. In today's complicated technology world, the window to success lies in deep thinking. One has to think a lot before one chooses any career. Many new careers are emerging like production director, TV journalist, video editor, sound recorder, web-engineer and so on. It is difficult for students to keep track. In this complicated situation, teachers can play an important role in determining the career patterns of students. Teachers need not have a separate degree in this area, but they will have to take a little interest in this field. Today, most of the leading dailies, both national and state, cater to the career related needs of youth. Each of the leading newspapers has reserved a day of the week to include a supplement on career information; usually it covers all the major aspects of career patterns. It covers articles on a particular career, or an institution. It deals with current career fairs, admission in foreign universities, career information queries, etc. It gives guidelines for the preparation of entrance tests for various courses, interviews with heads/directors of the institutes. Additionally, it deals with happenings in educational circles or university campuses and articles on development of qualities, skills and attitudes for better performance in various professions or jobs. Following are the various roles a teacher play in career planning:

(1) **Facilitating Career Exploration:** Career counselling techniques focus on facilitating exploration of one's own characteristics and exploration of the work environment. One of the major career development tasks is to understand oneself and how one's personal characteristics could be applied in the world of work for a satisfactory outcome for both individuals and the work environment. To do so, it is critical to have as much as possible accurate knowledge of individuals' own interests, values, needs and aspirations as well as of requirements, expectations, and rewards of occupations. Work and life are intertwined, therefore, various roles one plays and how these roles interact with one's career identity needs to be clarified. Clearer understanding of oneself and world of work is essential for career decision-making and other career development tasks.

Career exploration is an important component of models and theories of job search. All the teachers should try to help learners to develop career plans. While organising effective career exploration, s/he should consider learning objectives, learning styles of students, available resources, available staff and compatibility of techniques within the existing programme.

There are two dimensions of career exploration. *Self-exploration* involves exploring one's interests, values, skills, needs, personal goals, and experiences and reflecting on one's career to gain a deeper understanding of oneself (Stumpf *et al.*, 1983; Werbel, 2000). Engaging in self-exploration can facilitate a clearer understanding of one's career ambitions and interest in working in different types of work environments as well as specific work activities (zikic & Klehe, 2006). Self-exploration can also influence the job-search process because it provides greater focus and goal direction (Werbel, 2000)

Environmental exploration involves exploring various career options by collecting information about jobs, organisations, occupations or industries. This can also include learning about organisations and the demands and requirements of different jobs (Werbel, 2000). As a result, environmental exploration enables individuals to learn about different employment opportunities and to identify those that they want to pursue. This is important for job-search readiness and can result in more informed career decisions (Phillips & Blustein, 1994). That is, environmental exploration prepares and guides individuals in their job search by reducing the number of opportunities considered, providing greater focus, and making the job-search process less overwhelming and stressful (Werbel, 2000).

According to **Wanberg *et al.* (2002)**, individuals who do not have clear job-search objectives might need to spend more time in career exploration owing to a lack of self-understanding and of information about the work world and job opportunities. Thus career exploration should help individuals to obtain greater clarity regarding the desired type of work, job, or career. In addition, by exploring various work options and understanding their own capabilities better, job seekers may also develop increased confidence in their ability to search for the find the right job (i.e. job-search self-efficacy).

It accomplishes several goals including the following:

(i)   develop positive work attitudes.

(ii) help them in developing decision-making, problem-solving and planning skills.

(iii) increase the students' knowledge about themselves, their interest, abilities, needs and values.

(iv) develop job-seeking skills.

(v)   increase their knowledge of occupational possibilities, the structure of the world of work, job duties and requirements.

(vi) group setting provides an opportunity to use simulation in career exploration.

(vii) improve skills in seeking, creating, evaluating and communicating vocational information.

(viii) point out the implications of occupational and self-knowledge for educational and vocational choice.

(ix) motivate the students to attend schools regularly.

(2) Providing Career Information: Today, young generation is in dire need for career related updates and information. Besides opening their eyes to the world of work, information motivates them in choosing and preparing for the work also. The dissemination of career information should begin at the elementary school stage. Here, the teacher should integrate career information inputs into teaching of subject matter. S/he can explain the relationship of various subject contents with variety of work as well as the career options in his/her teaching subject. At all stages, the school teacher should promote the development of positive attitudes towards education as preparation to careers and decision-making. The school teachers should also help them to develop values which are appropriate to future careers.

(3) Providing Career Literature: Knowing and then reading about various types of jobs or occupations is highly stimulating. This helps to develop understanding about various occupations, the nature of work, qualifications required, method of entry, salary and other benefits and scope for further advancement. The teacher should look for career books, admission notices, magazines and periodicals on careers and other material and expose their students to the latest career information. S/he can recommend to the library to procure the career literature. The career literature helps a lot in motivating students to plan for a career and make related decisions.

(4) Providing Role Models: Adolescents lack suitable role models to identify with, and to develop work-related identity. They require people as role model who are achievers, career-oriented and successful. The role models should be selected from a variety of careers, traditional as well as non-traditional who are satisfied with their career and life style. The role models can be presented in a number of ways:

(i)   Teacher can talk about successful workers in traditional and non-traditional occupations.

(ii) Pictures of successful alumni with their achievements could be displayed.

  (iii) Ideally, guest speakers selected as role models should be invited to the school to interact with students about their achievements, work and how they achieved and established themselves.

  (iv) Mention may be made about local achievers and achievers from disadvantaged sections of the society.

  (v) The files on achievements of persons in various fields, such as, toppers in academic and co-curricular activities, award recipients, leaders, social workers, writers, eminent researchers, defence and police services, etc. could be maintained and displayed. Even students could be asked to collect and file this type of material.

  (vi) Special achievements of staff member may be highlighted through display or in school assembly.

(5) Providing Individual Assistance: Children with special needs require more strategies. Such students include girls and other disadvantaged and deprived sections of students. Such students need special attention. Teachers through their support and care can help them to enhance their self-esteem. But as the teachers also have limited time to work individually on each student, they should identify such students and refer them to school counsellor. But, as teachers, they should facilitate their social and emotional development and encourage them to continue their education.

Q30. State the role of parents in career development.

Ans. Parents serve as a major influence in their children's career development and career decision-making. Parents want their children to find happiness and success in life and one factor, which influences happiness and success, is career choice. Research also indicates that when students feel supported and loved by their parents, they have more confidence in their own ability to research careers and to choose a career that would be interesting and exciting. This is important because studies show that adolescents, who feel competent regarding career decision-making, tend to make more satisfying career choices later in life. (Keller 2004).

  Parents influence the level of education or training that their children achieve; the knowledge they have about work and different occupations; the beliefs and attitudes they have to working; and the motivation they have to succeed. Most of this is learned unconsciously – children and teenagers absorb their parents attitudes and expectations of them as they grow up.

  The parents can do the following in order to promote career development:

- The parents should understand the importance of education especially In the case of girls.
- They should consider them as individuals who have the right to develop and enjoy in this world.

- They should bring them up in such a way that they are equipped with positive qualities.

Parents must provide opportunities, facilities and environment conducive to career development.

Q31. What are the salient features of career development of girls? Discuss.

Or

Explain various types of career patterns of women.

Ans. Career development means the overall development in the life style of a person. It involves person's experiences that contribute to the formation of his/her identity including life experiences, education, career choice, on the job training, level of professional achievement and degree of satisfaction. It has always been studied with reference to men, ignoring its concern for women, even in the developed countries where participation of women in labour force is significant. One reason may be that it is difficult to study career development in women. Traditional theories of career development have not taken into consideration the important elements in women's life such as marriage, family, spouse's attitude towards wife's work, etc. in their career development. The vocational and career studies have also largely been focussed on male population, ignoring the female population or just assuming that they "fit" the male behaviour patterns. With women opting for higher education and exhibiting varied career ambitions, perhaps more research is required to study what they are, what they want from life as individuals, and as women.

The gender affects career development in numerous ways. Following are some of the types of career patterns of women:

(1) **Homemaker Role for Women:** A homemaker is a person whose main job is to take care of his/her own family, home and children. Traditionally in India, women play the role of a homemaker, and men play the role of a provider; but both men and women can be providers and homemakers. In career planning, women are usually supposed to think of marriage and homemaking along with career, which is not demanded of men. The homemaker roles affect women's interest in joining the labour force, performance at work and even stay in it. Thus, career does not occupy a major position in the lives of women as it is in the case of men. That is why the career development processes in both the sexes differ. There may be differences in career aspirations and goals of individual at gender basis, but there may not be significant gender differences in abilities and interests.

(2) **Work Role Perceptions:** Girls, at the earlier stages (3-6 years), may show preference for masculine role in contrast with the feminine role as the children find masculine role more rewarding and stronger, but later on they adapt to feminine role for which they are rewarded. Thus, a girl's

self-concept is not what she is or she 'should' be, but what the society wants her to be. Importance of work in case of women is hardly visualised. A working mother is not visualised as working for satisfaction, she is perceived as earning for buying comfort for the family. Similarly, a single working woman is not appreciated as the society wants women to be married at the "right" age and have children too at the right age. This also makes girls more inclined towards marriage than towards work-role orientation. Today, some of the women have started exploring beyond the traditional homemaking role. The learning process in role perception in women is undergoing change and influencing the role expectations for women, which are becoming less definite.

According to cognitive development theorists, after the 'sex-assignment', which occurs after birth, the next major event of sex-typed development occurs at the age of two or three years when the child develops self-categorisation as girl or as boy. Not only that children look to other people to try to understand what it means to have the label "girl" or "boy", they strive for competence in being what they think they are supposed to be because of the label. Hence, the "sexual-identity" becomes more and more "sex-role identity". The result is that boys at all ages show strong preference for the male role and identify themselves with work. Thus, a boy develops his identity through work. His academic, vocational and external achievements are expected and rewarded. However, it is absolutely opposite in the case of girls.

Today, women are in conflict with traditional thinking and learning, and with their new interests, aspirations and explorations. The resulting changes further influence to a considerable extent the career patterns of women.

(3) Women's Participation in Work: The Constitution of India guarantees the right of equal opportunity with regard to employment to men and women without distinction. However, a large number of women are still without work. According to census data, the work participation of women has improved during the past. The type of work performed by women workers is one of the most important aspects to be considered from the point of view of their career development. The following could be said about women's work participation:

(i) Participation of rural women in work is more in comparison to urban women.

(ii) Public sector employs more women than private sector.

(iii) Women are behind men in work participation.

(iv) Women are concentrated in community, social and personal services, which is the direct extension of their feminine role at home.

(v) Women are generally engaged in unskilled work as agricultural or other labour. Their percentage is, however, more than men. Some of them are also engaged in home based industries, small business activities and services.

(4) Factors Influencing the Work Participation of Women: The work participation of women have been continuously increasing day by day. However, in Indian societies, men have been bread winners and women have tended to attend to their household duties constituting care of all family members. The small numbers of women who participate in the work do so because of the following reasons:

(i) **To Utilise the Higher Education:** Some of the educated women in the cities, who belong to middle class, do not like to waste their education and, therefore, join the white-collar jobs. Among these women, some become career conscious and continue working. Moreover, rising aspirations towards a higher standard of living and a higher level of education also motivate women to take up some job.

(ii) **Status and Empowerment:** In any society, work is rewarded with money and is recognised as important means of status and empowerment. A housewife may not be economically in need of work but she undermines her status as unpaid person, holds low esteem in household work and, therefore, prefers to work outside home. These women, many a times, begin their careers quite late in life.

(iii) **To Meet Domestic Needs:** Women usually work outside the home to earn money to meet the domestic needs. These women belong to the lower class and lower middle class categories. They are generally employed in unskilled and semi-skilled occupations or traditional occupations like clerical, teaching, nursing, etc.

(iv) **Change in Social Attitudes and Values:** There has been a gradual change in social attitudes and values towards women's development in the country since independence. This evolution has encouraged women to develop their potential in education and career.

(v) **Small Family Size:** In a small family with one or two children, after the children leave school for higher education, women find more leisure time. Some of them engage themselves with some earning activities at home while others look for paid employment. However, employment at this stage is sometimes difficult due to high and ever increasing unemployment rate.

(vi) Increased Job Opportunities for Women: With government's conscious efforts towards women's development, educational and job opportunities for women have expanded rapidly in the recent past. These opportunities exist mainly in clerical, sales and service occupations, where a large segment of educated women get employed.

(vii) To Prove Self-worth: There are a few women who have the desire to achieve and prove their worth. They pursue higher education, excel in performance, have increased occupational aspirations and join the careers not the jobs. Most of these women are found in non-traditional careers. They also work hard to reach the top positions in hierarchy.

(viii)Dissatisfaction with Home Making Role: Most of the middle class and upper middle class women suffer from isolation. It is not possible for most of them to participate in social-recreational or other outside home activities. Husband and children, away at place of work or study, do not provide sufficient emotional satisfaction when they are at home. Emergence of household gadgets has made household chores easy and time saving. Thus, in order to fulfil their needs, these women take up work outside their homes.

(5) Educational Participation of Women: The work participation of women is influenced through formal education; and it continues to facilitate women's development of their potential. Since independence, literacy rate of women has continuously improved, although it is still low in comparison to men. The number of women enrolled in the institutions of higher education has also increased considerably.

In technical and professional stream, the participation of women has shown a marked increase. There has also been an increase in the number of women students in Engineering and Technology streams.

(6) Values and Motivation: Generally, in case of boys, the level of education attained is directly related to occupational opportunity, but it is not in case of girls. Usually, parents do not encourage or motivate girls for higher studies. They go to college but not motivated enough to compete with boys on choice of subject or to develop themselves. Perhaps major importance of college education is marriage than long-term occupational choice and career commitments.

Thus, for girls, meaning of college education is an end to itself, i.e. education promises a better life, greater capacity to meet the challenges of adulthood or eventualities, to find a better match, to be a better mother and not as a preparation for career. This kind of value attached to education leaves hardly any scope for motivation among girls to reach at higher level of education or career.

(7) **Intelligence, Academic Achievements and Occupational Aspirations of Women:** The attitude of women towards career and their career aspirations are likely to be shaped in the early years of development. Occupational aspirations occupy a central role in many career development theories. It is presumed that higher education, intelligence and better achievements stimulate the individual occupationally. However, studies have shown that the women's attitudes towards career could not be linked with their intelligence, academic achievement and history of achievements in other school activities as is the case with the men. Men during their school/college days verbalise about their vocational goals and are found to be concerned with the extrinsic rewards of the work. They are also concerned about the future and prestige in careers while girls pursuing school education or even higher education hardly speak out their concerns for careers. At the most, they talk about non-career type work, which hardly speaks about their interests or aspirations. Even the achievers don't seem to be planning for higher level occupations. The situation is still worse for the girls from lower socio-economic background and other disadvantaged sections of the society. For these girls, the chances of pursuing higher education or career goals are much reduced even if they are highly intelligent or can excel educationally. In short, it is the highest need for self-approval, which is related to social approval in the role of wife and mother, which determines women's concern for marriage and family, and not the career.

(8) **Cultural and Environmental Factors:** Girls' career development is also largely determined by parental attitudes, economic conditions at home and the cultural environment. It has been found in various research studies that girls from the better socio-economic backgrounds and especially having educated parents (at least father) relatively opt for higher education. Working mothers who derive satisfaction from their work and home are also known to be acting as source of inspiration for their daughters. The girls who are exposed to strong role models at home or in their near environment have positive attitude towards their career.

(9) **Career versus Non-career Women:** Women can be broadly classified into career women and non-career women with respect to career development, the latter being either totally devoted to marriage and family life, or holding some

non-career type jobs as and when required. The career women could be further divided into two categories, i.e. one who plans to work but in feminine occupations and the other who aspire to enter traditionally masculine occupations. The first type of career women work outside their homes but in the female dominated occupations or in accepted work settings. They seem to have favourable attitude towards home and family, and integrate home, family and career. This group is generally successful and characterised by feminine personality traits. The women opting for non-traditional role model have personality traits usually identified as masculine and have interests different from non-career or traditional career type women. These women are also known as "pioneer career women". Career development among women who have orientation towards career is a function of their achievement, motivation and satisfaction of mastery in the field of work than only the economic rewards — indicated studies.

Q32. Discuss the theories of career development of women.

Ans. Women are a legitimate focus of career interventions due to the challenges, barriers and societal role prescriptions they presently face; in response to this need, career development theories that seek to explain or apply to women's experiences and behaviour have emerged and proliferated over the last four decades. Many of the accepted career paradigms have been revised to incorporate the changes that the American vocational landscape has undergone in terms of women as workers rather than homemakers. By default, these theories have been criticised as remaining too limited in scope to fully explain the career behaviour and developmental patterns of women.

The theories of career development of women are as follows:

(1) **Self-efficacy Theory:** A major theoretical approach to understanding women's career development was emerged in the 1980s. This theory has been extensively utilised and researched over the last two decades. The self-efficacy approach to women's career development was first proposed by Gail Hackett and Nancy Betz (1981). Based on Bandura's (1977, 1982, 1986, 1995) theory of self-efficacy, which stated that individuals hold expectations about their own ability to effect change or produce a desired result through their own behaviour, career self-efficacy theory postulates that although low self-efficacy expectations may negatively impact the career behaviour of both women and men, women's limitations and disadvantages in the occupational realm may be directly related to gender-differential expectations of self-efficacy (Hackett & Betz, 1981).

The four sources of information that guide the formation of one's expectations of self-efficacy are different for males and females (Hackett & Betz, 1981).

(i)   The first information source, based on Bandura (1977, 1982, 1986, 1995) includes **performance accomplishments**, which women are thought to experience to a lesser degree than men. Because masculine traits are more likely to result in attempting new and different tasks as well as achieving success in those tasks, a subsequent increase in self-efficacy results. Typically, males grow to possess masculine characteristics; therefore, males are more likely to experience higher degrees of self-efficacy by virtue of the socialisation process.

(ii)   Women are postulated to suffer from a lack of **vicarious learning** opportunities, which is the second information source contributing to self-efficacy. In general, females are underrepresented in certain occupational fields, possibly because males are portrayed in a greater number and a wider variety of occupational roles are provided in the media in all its forms. Thus, fewer role models and observable career paths for females are available. Feelings of inadequacy or lack of exposure to non-traditional or unfamiliar situations or activities may perpetuate the perception of low self-efficacy in women and girls.

(iii) The third source of self-efficacy enhancing information is **emotional arousal**, or the opportunity to learn new tasks in a relatively anxiety-free state. Higher levels of anxiety, which have been shown to exist in feminine-typed individuals, are thought to be associated with lower degrees of self-efficacy, leading to the possible conclusion that societal messages towards females and males who perceive themselves as feminine may reduce perceptions of self-efficacy.

(iv) Finally, **verbal persuasion** contributes to an individual's sense of self-efficacy. Traditionally, males have been actively encouraged and rewarded for career motivation and pursuits, whereas women have not, perhaps leading to perceptions of inability and lack of confidence in females.

Hackett and Betz's theory not only takes into account the effects of gender role socialisation, it also attempts to understand the cognitive and societal mechanisms that occur and exert influence on subsequent behaviours in women, such as career-related preferences, expectations, confidence and choices. This has provided a basis for designing and delivering methods of intervening at a variety of levels in order to address women's vocational development and behaviour.

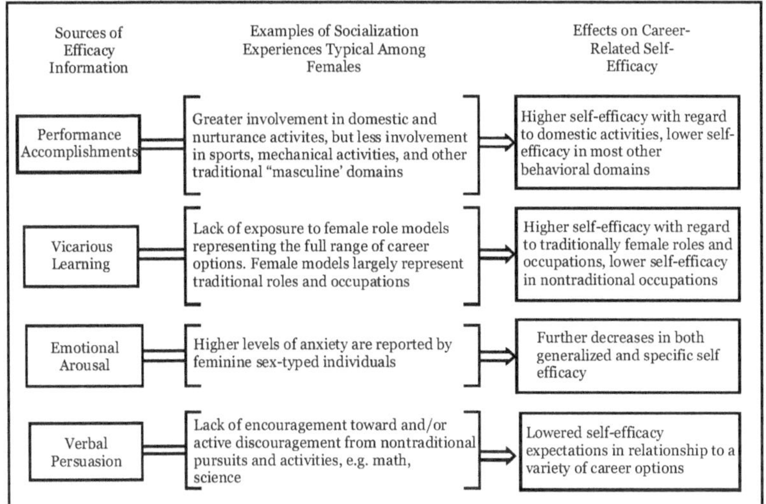

Fig. 3.1: A model depicting the postulated effects of traditional female socialisation on career-related self-efficacy expectations

(2) **Circumscription Theory (Gottfredson 1981):** This theory, developed by Linda Gottfredson in 1981, attempts to describe how career choice develops in young people. Many developmental theories focus on how an individual's self-concept develops with age. Circumscription and Compromise also focuses on the development of an individual's view of the occupational choices available. The theory assumes that we build a cognitive map of occupations by picking up occupational stereotypes from those around us.

According to Linda Gottfredson, self-concept (impacted by factors such as gender, class, intelligence, etc.) is an important determinant in the occupational aspirations and career choices of individuals. She postulates that when individuals (women) are faced with career compromises, they readily forgo their interests rather than being in an occupation that is not gender 'appropriate', which means not matching with their self-conceived notions of gender stereotype. So, women tend to reject occupations that are not matching with their self-concept. Career development of women also depends on their perception about career and training opportunities available to them. The occupational choices for women are usually limited.

(3) **Socio-psychological Model (Astin, 1984):** Astin (1984) cited that the psychological and sociological (culture and environment) factors interact and, thus, influence the choice

of career and work behaviour of individuals. Astin's model has the following four factors, which are interrelated:

(i) **Work Motivation:** Work is important for individuals as it fulfils the basic needs of survival, pleasure (pursuing one's interests through work) and contribution (need to be useful to family and society and the recognition it brings to the individual). Astin found that both men and women shared same basic needs (survival, pleasure and contribution) that motivated them to work.

(ii) **Work Expectations:** This refers to the individual's perception about his/her ability to perform a job, the availability of the job, and the kind of job that fulfils his/her requirements.

(iii) **Sex-role Socialisation:** Astin viewed that work expectations are different for men and women. This is because of the differences in the gender socialisation experiences of girls and boys. Gender stereotypical roles are reinforced in boys and girls through play, family orientations and schooling process. Such internalised gender-appropriate role and behaviour can be expanding (choosing from a wide range of work options) or restricting (choosing from the gender stereotypical work options). In case of women, gender socialisation experiences restrict their work opportunities.

(iv) **Structure of Opportunity:** Men and women, according to Astin, differ in their perception of the structure of opportunity, therefore, have different work expectations. Astin suggests that the structure of opportunity is not static, it changes as society diversify its economic activities in transforming sociopolitical climate. Thus, according to her, the structure of opportunity has to be seen in terms of distribution of jobs, gender stereotyping of jobs, discrimination, job requirements, economy, family structures and emerging reproductive technology. As society changes, men and women confront new environmental challenges (social, cultural, economic and political), and modify their career options and work behaviours.

Q33.Delineate career patterns' categories of women given by Super (1957).

Ans. The career patterns of women are different from men. Many studies have classified women into two major groups, i.e. pioneer women or those engaged seriously in career activities, and the traditional women who participate in full-time home making activities. They are also known as non-traditional or career women versus traditional women or homemakers, respectively.

Although the original sample for Super's theory was White middle-class male adolescents, Super was concerned about the career patterns of women, He proposed the following seven career patterns for women (Super, 1957, pp. 76-78):

- **Stable Homemaking Career Pattern:** Women marry shortly after they finish their education and have no significant work experience afterward.
- **Conventional Career Pattern:** Women enter work after high school or college; how-ever, after marriage, they cease work to enter full-time homemaking.
- **Stable Working Career Pattern:** After high school or college, women work continuously throughout their life span.
- **Double-track Career Pattern:** Women combine career and homemaking roles throughout their life span.
- **Interrupted Career Pattern:** Women enter into work, then marriage and full-time homemaking, and later return to a career, often after children can care for themselves.
- **Unstable Career Pattern:** Women drop out of the workforce, return to it, drop out, and return—repeating the cycle over and over again.
- **Multiple-trial Career Pattern:** Women work but never really establish careers. They may have a number of different unrelated jobs during their lifetime.

In 1990, Super pointed out that the career patterns for women, which he described more than 40 years ago, would be different now. Many changes in society have taken place to allow women to enter a much broader spectrum of careers. In her review of women's career development, Fassinger (2005) examines the career development of women from different theoretical points of view and describes how society's impact on women has affected their career development. Examining Super's life-span theory. Coogan and Chen (2007) make suggestions for counselors in helping women with career issues. They discuss concerns that women have in dealing with multiple roles and the influences of others. In a study of 105 women over a 14-year span, Vincent, Peplau, and Hill (1998) report that women's career behaviour was predicted by their gender-role views and their views of the preferences that their boyfriends and parents had for them 14 years earlier. When considering combining work and being a mother, adolescent girls may have difficulty dealing with pressures they see to be a mother and to give up work to raise children (Marks & Houston, 2002). Research shows that women see themselves in many roles and that there are several reasons for these perceptions.

Q34. Elucidate career problems of women.

Or

Mention major difficulties faced by girls in making vocational choice.

Ans. Despite the major advancements women have made in becoming a significant part of the workforce, they are still facing important career development issues. Some of the serious problems that they have to face are as follows:

(1) **Girl's Access to Education:** Some of the prominent problems in girls' education are:

(i) **Economic Problems:** When there is no one to feed the family and educate the male 'sought after' child, how can the parent afford to enroll the girl child in a school? Who will take care of siblings, perform household chores, earn and contribute to family income? In the families where they can afford education, it is the boys who get this benefit.

(ii) **Social Problems:** Social attitude towards education of girls is generally not positive. Education for the girl is considered as unimportant. Practice of early marriage, parental illiteracy, lack of educational facilities at home, male teachers in the schools and girls' responsibilities at home, etc. are some of the obstacles in girls' access to education.

(iii) **Educational Problems:** The major educational problem is lack of educational institutions especially beyond elementary level areas. The schools lack in physical facilities such as furniture, water, blackboard, toilets, etc. The unattractive textbooks, male teachers, lack of sports and extracurricular activities, unsuitable school timings are discouraging factors for girls to attend schools. The girls who can reach the high school level are very few, and they have no access to further education or training in rural areas. There are some institutions for men but they too are far away from the villages. Moreover, they lack in hostel facilities for girls. The problem is both ways. On the one hand, the girls are not prepared (socially) to join further education or training and, on the other hand, there are no institutions and facilities available to them.

At places where the institution or training facilities for girls are available, the courses offered to girls are traditional which lack in market value. Sometimes the girls have to opt for such courses due to their earlier educational preparation. It has been found that due to the universalisation of elementary education policy, more and more girls are crossing 8th standard and reaching high school. But these girls are weak in science and mathematics, therefore, they go for softer options, which don't require science and mathematics, that is, joining home science courses such as tailoring, cooking, bakery, etc. and not the technical and engineering courses.

As the educational status is directly related to career development, the above mentioned educational problems severely restrict the educational development of girls and, hence, hinder their career development.

(2) Problems in Making Vocational Choice: Unexpected personal events such as death of significant one, divorce or financial crisis may influence a woman's decision to take up work but it is not necessary that she gets the work for which she is qualified or the type of work she desires. Thus, she may not have career involvement.

However, there are other contingency factors and difficulties, which women face in making career choices. These are:

(i) The girls receive very little orientation towards career choice while the question of career choice is emphasised for boys.

(ii) Parents, teachers and significant others are more likely to emphasise salary and status in boy's career choice while for girl's emphasis on career is even missing. Also, the jobs available to them are of poor status and remuneration.

(iii) The options open to girls are considerably more restricted than for men and they are forced to consider their role as a homemaker before making career selection.

(iv) Women are more influenced by what they think about men and society in general will accept as a woman's job and vice-versa.

(v) The girls have fewer opportunities for vocational training and higher education.

(vi) Very often, girls wait for marriage before choosing or joining any job as marriage and husband's home takes priority over career.

(vii) Although, approximately all types of courses and occupations are open to women, they frequently lack awareness of these opportunities and the financial support for their education and training.

(viii) Above all, girls also lack information about their abilities and interests, and awareness of skills in them, which are the motivating factors to make career decisions. Most of the girls, still believe that girls are weak in science and mathematics, and they are better in social sciences and home science subject.

(ix) The girls also lack positive role models to identify with and develop their career potential. The above influences though come from a variety of sources both internal and external but sometimes decidedly create problems in girls' career development.

(3) Poor Self-image or Self-esteem: The girls are treated in many societies with specific behaviours, attitudes and expectations. The discriminatory treatment which a girl receives prior to her birth through her childhood and till her death is the best indicator of formation of self-image in case of girls. Often, a girl is not preferred even prior to her birth, treated as unwanted after birth; neglected in nutrition, health and education; treated as a helping hand at home and outside; suppressed, neglected throughout her life and treated as sex-object. Thus, she develops a poor image of herself. The discrimination against girls is prevalent across all cultures, castes and socio-economic strata. Development of poor self-image or low self-esteem is a strong psychological barrier in individual development.

(4) Gender–biases: Gender-bias is common everywhere whether it is at home, educational institutions, place of work or society, in general. These biases create barriers both structural and attitudinal in women's career development.

    (i) Gender-biases at Home: The feeling of difference between the boy and the girl is introduced first in the family. Here, the gender-bias begins from conception of a child. The uninvited and unwanted girl child who is deprived of proper food, love and care in comparison to the male child; whose education is of secondary importance and who is not allowed to play or participate in any activity except the household chores and sibling care, grows into a female adolescent with expected feminine behaviour and marriage goals. Hence, her physical, personal, social and emotional development is restricted. Her bringing up does not prepare her for higher education or vocational training or employment.

    (ii) Educational Institutions: After home, the place which affects children's behaviour is school. Here, children face gender-bias in almost all the aspects, for example, gender-bias in textbooks, curriculum transaction, allocation of subjects, SUPW activities; participation in some of the co-curricular activities, etc. Once inculcated, these behaviours become part of children's lives. In colleges and universities also, the biases are further propagated. In this way, the quality of girls' education do not match with that of educational, vocational and personal development. Even the teacher training programmes both in-service and pre-service seemed to ignore de-sensitisation of teacher against gender-biased behaviour till recently. The revised curricula of teacher education of different universities have introduced a new course 'Gender School and Society' recently.

    (iii) Place of Work: Employers often don't accept women as workers like men. They even hesitate to employ women. A woman seeking employment is viewed as a future wife and mother who will have primary responsibility towards her home and family, and not work. In comparison to a man, she is less preferred in employment and is paid less. She is also not given required leave for homemaking and child rearing by employers other than public sector. Above all, she may sometimes face sexual harassment at work.

(iv) In-society: Many societies are strongly gender-biased. The expectations of family, neighbours and other social groups from a girl is of 'traditional woman' who has "no sense of *Me*". She is expected to be subservient, committed homemaker, obedient wife and daughter-in-law and a sacrificing mother. She is expected to be submissive, soft spoken, reserved, shy, docile, tolerating and not protesting against atrocities towards her by the husband and his family. If otherwise, then she is labelled as home-breaker and uncultured. All these biases severely hinder the process of career development of girls as the girls prefer to be obedient homemakers rather than decision-makers and career-oriented.

(5) Fear of Success: Usually, women prefer the occupations, which are extension of their household duties such as teaching, nursing, secretary, personal assistant, social worker, etc. This is also the reason that the work that women do, is not held in high esteem as the work that men do. The occupational preference of women for 'typical' women's fields suggests two motives operating behind — Firstly, girls think of marriage and societal approval before they plan for career; and Secondly, the women are highly conditioned to avoid success. They perhaps feel secure if they opt for more traditional occupations than for non-traditional ones. It is generally believed that the more successful a man is in his job, he will make a desirable husband, the more successful a woman is, most people are afraid she may not be a successful wife.

(6) Role Conflict: Most of the working women, especially well educated, suffer from role conflict. Like her family and society, she considers her role of housewife and mother equally important to her career. Neglecting one at the cost of other or feeling of neglecting one at the cost of other, adds strains in women's relationship with her husband and family. The result is that many women feel compelled to leave the job to get rid of this painful situation. This not only stops their career development but sets a bad example for young girls.

(7) Dual Role: When a woman decides to take up a career, she has to do so while performing all the duties of housewife, mother and daughter-in-law, etc. In fact, she is taught from the beginning that her career is of secondary importance and her first priority is to look after her home.

Q35.Discuss some interventions that teachers can take up to promote career development of girls.

Or

What is the role of teachers in promoting career development of girls? Discuss.

Ans. Since schools are looked on as an agency of society for developing the students' potential, suggested below are some interventions, the teachers can take up to promote career development of girls.

(1) **Providing Career Information and Literature:** Girls often do not have access to information. Besides opening their eyes to the world of work, information also motivates them in choosing and preparing for the work. The dissemination of career information should begin at the elementary school stage. Here, the teacher should integrate career information inputs into teaching of subject matter. S/he can recommend to the library to procure the career literature. The career literature helps a lot in motivating the girls to plan for a career and make career related decisions.

(2) **Approach to Girls' Education:** The approach of the teachers to girls' education should be to develop a human resource. They should help girls to develop as individuals through encouragement and assistance in identification and nurturing of their talents. Teachers should examine their own biases and gender-stereotyped behaviours, which cause hindrance in realisation of career potential in girls. They should also discourage segregation of subjects, skills, activities, hobbies and behaviours, etc. by gender, which is a major hurdle in the way of girls' development as individuals and their adoption of new roles.

(3) **Providing Individual Assistance:** Children with special needs, especially girls, who have become strongly gender stereotype due to their traditional development, home and community environment, require some other strategies. They find it difficult to perceive themselves as individuals and improve their self-esteem. They don't feel the necessity of education for them and generally drop-out at early school stages. Such girls need special attention. If the teacher through her interest, support and care can help them to come out of their shells and develop self-respect and useful lifestyle, there is nothing like it. But, as the teachers also have limited time to work individually on each student, they should better identify such girls and refer them to a trained counseller.

(4) **Favourable Environment of Learning:** The teacher should try to create favourable environment or conditions for learning. S/he should not encourage the prevalent stereotyped appropriate or inappropriate behaviours for girls. S/he should not encourage girls to be timid, anxious, fearful, passive, dependent, compliant and incompetent in technical ability,

etc. Rather s/he should help the girls to overcome these pressures and develop positive attitude and respect for their worth. The teacher should also challenge the adult-imposed biases which the girls often face and help the girls to improve their self-image.

(5) **Providing Role Models:** The girls lack suitable role models to identify with and develop work related identity. They need women role models, who are achievers, career-oriented and successful. If a woman works only for economic necessity and not for personal gain, she suffers from role-conflict and lack of self-worth. Therefore, they are not suitable role models. The role models for girls should be selected from a variety of careers, traditional as well as non-traditional, who are satisfied with their career and lifestyle while respecting themselves as women. Only these type of role models can help girls in improving their self-image, instill in them confidence to choose suitable career and experience self-fulfilment in the chosen career path.

The role models can be presented in many ways:

(i)   Teachers can talk about successful women workers in traditional and non-traditional occupations.

(ii)   Pictures of successful alumni with their achievements could be displayed. These women could also be invited to the school to interact with the students.

(iii)   Ideally, women guest speakers selected, as role models should be invited to the school to talk to the girls about their work achievement and how they established themselves. There is no comparison to presentation of live role models with other methods as the girls can interact with them and may clarify their personal doubts and difficulties.

(iv)   Mention may be made about local women achievers and achievers from disadvantaged sections of the society.

(v)   The files on achievements of girls and women in various fields, such as toppers in academic and co-curricular activities, award recipients, leaders, social workers, writers, eminent researchers, defence and police services, etc. could be maintained and displayed. Even the girls could be asked to collect and file such type of material.

(vi)   Special achievements of women staff members may be highlighted through display or in school assembly.

The role models can be presented at all stages of school and college education and are effective in promoting career development among girls.

Q36.What is the role of parents in promoting career development of girls?

Ans. Parents too can do the following to promote career development of girls:

- It is urgently required that the parents should understand the importance of education for their children, especially girls. They should change their attitude of educating girls only for acquiring suitable grooms or procuring employment in case of eventuality. The parents' interest in their girl child's development is very crucial for her career development.

- Rural parents and economically weaker parents are required to understand that their girl child should not be used to subsidise their brother's education through work. Rather both boys and girls can pursue education through distance and other alternative modes while earning for the family.

- They should consider their girl child as individuals who have also the right to develop and enjoy in this world. They should bring up their girl child in such a way that they are equipped with positive qualities of both the gender.

- The parents who favour their girl child's education should go one step further and should allow them to choose the courses and careers for which they are suitable and are interested. They should not perpetuate the traditional gender role based career engagement for their children, especially girls.

- The child rearing in our culture is generally recognised as mother's privilege and responsibility. Mothers who themselves have been socialised in a traditional way with all the gender biases perpetuate the same while rearing their children. It is the mothers, who need to change their attitudes and outlook. They should not treat male and female children differentially to teach them gender appropriate behaviour. Then only a girl child can realise her potential as an individual.

- The government has initiated many schemes for girls and women for their education, vocational training, skill development, self-employment, etc. The government also provides loans to women who want to start their own economic activity. These programmes cover all types of women population, rural/urban, illiterate/literate/highly educated, tribal, scheduled castes and backward classes. The parents should encourage their daughters to get benefit from these schemes.

- Parents should change the traditional belief of great economic value of male children in comparison to female children who are considered as economic burden or *'Parayadhan'*. Instead of early marriage, they should educate their daughters. Now, the girls are given free education, uniform, stipends and other benefits by the government to promote their development. The parents should avail detailed information about these schemes which are also publicised on media and use the assistance for the benefit of their daughters.

✍ ✍ ✍

Guiding Students with Special Needs

INTRODUCTION

Although many of the needs of children in the same developmental stage are common to all, some of them may have special needs due to their special ability. Understanding the varying needs of the learners would help parents and teachers to provide them with appropriate guidance. Disability may lead to problems when the individual accepts it as a condition of inadequacy. Individuals with disability face a number of problems because of their impairment, societal attitude to disability and lack of acceptance by parents and other family members. The social stigma attached to disability forces the PWD often to withdraw into oneself. The difficulties they face in day-to-day life may lead to certain behavioural problems, which further complicate their socialisation and relationship with others. Parents, counselors and teachers have a significant role in facilitating the development of persons with disability.

Q1. Which factors cause learning problems and performance difficulties? Also, enlist home and school environment factors responsible for these causes.

Ans. In a classroom, teachers have to face more than one student, who may have some kind of learning difficulties. The problems are of various types and due to various reasons. The factors that cause learning problems and performance difficulties can be listed as under:

- vision problems;
- damage to limbs – absence, deformation or problems with movement of muscles restricting performance in certain areas;
- lower level of intellectual functioning and development delay (retarded development); and
- problems with psychological processes like perception, attention, memory and problems of visual-motor co-ordination resulting in specific learning difficulties in reading, writing, spelling and arithmetic.

Besides, there are home and environmental factors. These are:

- lack of acceptance by other family members;
- inappropriate child-rearing practices;
- lack of parental love and affection; and
- lack of opportunities for interaction and learning.

There are other factors which cause learning problems and which are related to school environment. These are:

- Non-congenial social and emotional climate of the classroom.
- Absence of quality teaching matching with individual needs.
- Lack of teachers' acceptance of the student and low expectation regarding learning and performance of the student.
- Lack of adjustment and adaptation of physical facilities to special needs of students.
- Lack of acceptance by non-disabled peers and willingness to share feelings, responsibilities, privileges and other facilities.

The learning problems may arise out of one single factor or a number of factors or due to interplay of different sets of factors.

There are millions of people suffering from varying degree of disability in India. Thus, it is very natural that teachers would definitely come across such students in schools. Each student should be a unique person to teachers. Though, human abilities are, to a great extent, inherited, yet quite a substantial part of it is also acquired through environment in the process of socialisation.

Q2. What do you understand by disability? What is the meaning of children with special needs? Discuss.

Or

Explain the meaning of children with special needs.

Ans. Children with special needs may have been born with a syndrome, terminal illness, profound cognitive impairment, or serious psychiatric problems. Other children may have special needs that involve struggling with learning disabilities, food allergies, developmental delays or panic attacks.

The designation 'children with special needs' is for children who may have challenges, which are more severe than the typical child, and could possibly last a lifetime. These children will need extra support and additional services. They will have distinct goals, and will need added guidance and help meeting academic, social, emotional as well as sometimes medical milestones.

The teacher may have to deal with children with special needs in his/her career. Some of these problems are evident, and therefore, the teacher is aware of it and can include their needs in his/her teaching and classroom plan. However, sometimes, the problems are not as evident and manifest themselves as a learning or behavioural problem. The teacher has to be vigilant in his/her observations and learn to identify the real problem, which may be more deeper than just delayed development. A teacher may have to seek help of other professionals like doctors, counselors or special education teachers while so that s/he understands children with special needs better and is able to plan a responsive teaching learning programme for them and work out a truly inclusive programme for them.

Q3. What are the various types of disabilities? Discuss.

Ans. Following are the different types of disabilities:

    (1) Physical Disability

        (i) Locomotor disability means disability of the bones, joints or muscles leading to substantial restriction of the movement of the limbs or any form of cerebral palsy. Following are the various causes of Locomotor disabilities:

            (a) Arthritis: Arthritis affects the joints but sometimes involves other systems of the body, such as vision. Affected joints, mostly the hands and feet become swollen and tender causing pain and restriction in mobility.

            (b) Cerebral Palsy (CP): Cerebral Palsy is a group of non-progressive disorders of posture and movement. This is caused by damage or injury to the developing brain. There are three main types of Cerebral Palsy, depending on the area of the brain damaged.

            (c) Muscular Dystrophy: Children with this disability are characterised by progressive weakness of all muscles where heart and lung muscles are affected by child attains the age of twenty.

            (d) Spine Bifida: When bones of spinal column do not join completely around the spinal cord to form a column. Spinal cord at the site of the defect is exposed and nerves at that level damaged. There will be varying degrees of lower limb and trunk muscle paralysis.

(e) Head Injury (cerebral trauma): The term "head injury" is used to describe a wide array of injuries, including concussion, brain stem injury, closed head injury, cerebral haemorrhage, depressed skull fracture, foreign object (e.g., bullet), anoxia and post-operative infections.

(f) Stroke (cerebral vascular accident; CVA): The three main causes of stroke are thrombosis (blood clot in a blood vessel blocks blood flow past that point), haemorrhage (resulting in bleeding into the brain tissue; associated with high blood pressure or rupture of an aneurysm), and embolism (a large clot breaks off and blocks an artery).

(g) Loss of Limbs or Digits (Amputation or Congenital): This may be due to trauma (e.g., explosions, mangling in a machine, severance, burns) or surgery (due to cancer, peripheral arterial disease diabetes).

(h) Muscular Dystrophy (MD): Muscular dystrophy is a group of hereditary diseases causing progressive muscular weakness, loss of muscular control, contractions and difficulty in walking, breathing, reaching and use of hands involving strength.

(ii) Visual Impairment

(a) Blindness: The term "blindness" is typically used to describe individuals with no usable vision or only the ability to perceive light.

(b) Low Vision: A person with normal vision typically has a visual acuity of 20/20 in both eyes and a visual field of approximately 160 to 180 degrees. An individual with low vision may have a visual acuity of 20/70 or worse and a visual field of 20 to 40 degrees or less.

(iii) Hearing Impairment

(a) 'Deaf' people mostly have profound hearing loss, which implies very little or no hearing. They often use sign language for communication.

(b) 'Hard of hearing' refers to people with hearing loss ranging from mild to severe. People who are hard of hearing usually communicate through spoken language and can benefit from hearing aids, cochlear implants, and other assistive devices as well as captioning.

(iv) Speech Impairment: Speech impairments may range from mild to severe and refer to an impaired ability to produce speech sounds. They include articulation disorders (omissions or distortions of sounds), fluency disorders (a typical flow or rhythm) and voice disorders (abnormal pitch, volume, vocal quality or duration).

(2) Intellectual Disability: The term, 'intellectual disability', refers to a condition in which a person has certain limitations in intellectual functions like communicating, taking care of him/her, and has impaired social skills. Intellectual disability includes:

(i) "Specific learning disability" means a disorder in one or more of the basic psychological processes involved in understanding or in using language, spoken or written, that may manifest itself in an imperfect ability to listen, think, speak, read, write, spell or to do mathematical calculations, including conditions such as perceptual disabilities, brain injury, minimal brain dysfunction, dyslexia and developmental aphasia.

(ii) "Autism spectrum disorder" is a condition related to brain development that impacts how a person perceives and socialises with others, causing problems in social interaction and communication. The disorder also includes limited and repetitive patterns of behaviour. The term "spectrum" in autism spectrum disorder refers to the wide range of symptoms and severity.

(3) Mental Behaviour: A mental illness is a condition that affects a person's thinking, feeling or mood. Such conditions may affect someone's ability to relate to others and function each day. Each person will have different experiences, even people with the same diagnosis. There are more than 200 classified forms of mental illness. Some of the more common disorders are depression, bipolar disorder, dementia, schizophrenia and anxiety disorders. Symptoms may include changes in mood, personality, personal habits and/or social withdrawal.

(4) Disability Caused due to:

(i) chronic neurological conditions, such as –

(a) "multiple sclerosis" means an inflammatory, nervous system disease in which the myelin sheaths around the axons of nerve cells of the brain and spinal cord are damaged, leading to demyelisation and affecting the ability or nerve cells in the brain and spinal cord to communicate with each other;

(b) "Parkinson's disease" means a progressive disease of the nervous system marked by tremor, muscular rigidity, and slow, imprecise movement, chiefly affecting middle-aged and elderly people associated with degeneration of the nerve cells of the brain, which causes deficiency of the neurotransmitter dopamine.

(ii) Blood Disorder

(a) Haemophilia is an inherited bleeding disorder, manifesting predominantly in worldwide male population. However, about 30 per cent of haemophilia patients have no prior family history of bleeding disorder. In these cases, it is caused by mutation in their genes that lead to bleeding disorder. It is a lifelong disease.

(b) Thalassemia is a group of inherited blood disorders. It can affect people of any nationality, but it is particularly common in people with ancestry from the Mediterranean and across a broad region extending through India, the Middle East and Asia. It can occur in both male and female population. It is a lifelong disease.

(c) Sickle cell disease is a term used to describe a group of disorders called hemoglobinopathies. These disorders involve a defect in a substance in the blood. In some people, haemoglobin is abnormal and this causes the red blood cells – which are normally round – to change shape. The resulting sickle (or crescent) shaped red blood cell is where the disease gets its name.

(5) Multiple Disabilities: "Multiple Disabilities" is a broad umbrella term meaning, simply, that the student has more than one disability. The specifics of this diagnosis are almost endlessly variable, and great care needs to be taken to adjust individual educational support to the child's particular needs.

Q4. Explain partial and total disabilities for visual and hearing impairment.

Or

Describe the categories of visual and hearing disabilities given by the Government of India.

Ans. The Government of India (2001) provides the following definitions of mild, moderate, severe and profound categories of visual and hearing disabilities as given below:

Table 4.1: Categorisation of Visual Disability

Category	Better eye	Worse eye	per cent of Impairment
Category 0	6/9-6/18	6/24-6/36	20 per cent
Category I	6/18-6/36	6/60 to nil	40 per cent
Category II	6/40-4/60 or field of vision 10° – 20°	3/60 to nil	75 per cent
Category III	3/60- 1/60 or field	F.C. at 1 ft.	100 per cent

	of vision 10°	to nil	
Category IV	F.C. at 1 ft. to nil or field of vision 10°	F.C. at 1 ft. to nil	100 per cent
One eyed persons	6/6	F.C. at 1 ft. to nil Or field vision of 10°	30 per cent

Note: *F.C. means Finger Count*

The classification for the hearing impairment is as follows:

Table 4.2: Categorisation of Speech and Hearing Disability

Category	Type of Impairment	DB level	Speech discrimination	Percentage of impairment
I	Mild hearing impairment	26-40 db hearing impairment in better ear	80-100 per cent in better ear	less than 40 per cent
II (a)	Moderate hearing impairment	41-60 db hearing Impairment in better ear	50-80 per cent db in better ear	40 per cent-50 per cent
II (b)	Severe hearing impairment	61-70 db hearing impairment in better ear	40-50 per cent db in better ear	51 per cent - 70 per cent
III (a)	Profound hearing impairment	71-90 db hearing impairment in better ear	Less than 40 per cent in better ear	71 per cent-100 per cent
III (b)	Total deafness	91 db and above hearing impairment in better ear	Very poor discrimination	100 per cent

Q5. Which institutions are established for the rehabilitation, education, training and welfare of persons with disabilities by Government of India?

Ans. Following institutions are established by the Government of India for the rehabilitation, education, training and welfare of persons with disabilities:

- Chief Commissioner for Persons with Disabilities
- National Handicapped Finance Development Corporation
- Rehabilitation Council of India
- National Institute for the Visually Handicapped, Dehradun
- National Trust for the Welfare of Persons with Autism, Cerebral Palsy, Mental Retardation and Multiple Disabilities
- National Institute of Rehabilitation Training and Research, Cuttack
- Indian Sign Language Research and Training Centre, New Delhi
- Ali Yavar Jung National Institute for the Hearing Handicapped, Mumbai

- National Institute for Mental Health and Sciences, Bangalore
- Pandit Deendayal Upadhyaya Institute for the Physically Handicapped, New Delhi
- National Institute for Empowerment of Persons with Multiple Disabilities, Chennai
- National Institute for the Mentally Handicapped, Secunderabad
- National Institute for the Orthopaedically handicapped, Kolkata
- Artificial Limbs Manufacturing Corporation

Q6. Delineate the concept and approach to inclusive schooling.

Ans. The right of every child is to get education. The society needs variety of people for the progress of humanity. Inclusive education becomes important to fulfil this. The National Policy of Education-1986 (NPE-1986) advocated the approach of providing integrated education for children with mild disability and of special education for children with severe disability. It says:

The objective should be to integrate the physically and mentally handicapped with the general community as equal partners, to prepare them for normal growth and enable them to face life with courage and confidence.

The following measures were recommended in this regard:

- Special schools with hostels will be provided as far as possible at district headquarters for the severely handicapped children.
- Teachers Training Programme will be reoriented in particular for teachers of primary classes, to deal with special difficulties of the handicapped children.
- Wherever it is feasible, the education of children with motor handicaps and other mild handicaps will be common with that of the others.
- Voluntary efforts for the education of the disabled will be encouraged in every possible manner.
- Adequate arrangements will be made to give vocational training to the disabled.

The Salamanca Conference, in Spain, modified the integrated education into "inclusive schooling" concept wherein it has been reiterated that, instead of providing special teacher in each school to deal with handicapped children (as in integrated education), the existing teacher: be enabled to handle such children by providing special training to regular teachers.

According to the RPWD Act-2016, "inclusive education" means a system of education wherein students with and without disability learn together and the system of teaching and learning is suitably adapted to meet the learning needs of different types of students with disabilities.

Q7. Enlist the provisions of rights of Persons with Disabilities Act, 2016.

Ans. The appropriate Government and the local authorities shall endeavour that all educational institutions funded or recognised by them provide inclusive education to the children with disabilities and towards that end shall:

- ensure that the education to persons who are blind or deaf or both is imparted in the most appropriate languages and modes and means of communication;
- provide transportation facilities to the children with disabilities and also the attendant of the children with disabilities having high support needs;
- admit them without discrimination and provide education and opportunities for sports and recreation activities equally with others;
- provide necessary support individualised or otherwise in environments that maximise academic and social development consistent with the goal of full inclusion;
- detect specific learning disabilities in children at the earliest and take suitable pedagogical and other measures to overcome them;
- make building, campus and various facilities accessible;
- monitor participation, progress in terms of attainment levels and completion of education in respect of every student with disability; and
- provide reasonable accommodation according to the individual's requirements.

The appropriate Government and the local authorities shall take the following measures for the purpose of section 16, namely:

- to conduct survey of school going children in every five years for identifying children with disabilities, ascertaining their special needs and the extent to which these are being met: provided that, the first survey shall be conducted within a period of two years from the date of commencement of this Act;
- to establish adequate number of teacher training institutions;
- to train and employ teachers, including teachers with disability who are qualified in sign language and Braille, and also teachers who are trained in teaching children with intellectual disability;
- to train professionals and staff to support inclusive education at all levels of school education;
- to establish adequate number of resource centres to support educational institutions at all levels of school education;
- to promote the use of appropriate augmentative and alternative modes including means and formats of communication, Braille and sign language to supplement the use of one's own speech to fulfil the daily communication needs of persons with speech, communication or language disabilities and enables them to participate and contribute to their community and society;
- to provide books, other learning materials and appropriate assistive devices to students with benchmark disabilities free of cost up to the age of eighteen years;

- to provide scholarships in appropriate cases to students with benchmark disability;
- to make suitable modifications in the curriculum and examination system to meet the needs of students with disabilities such as extra time for completion of examination paper, facility of scribe or amanuensis, exemption from second and third language courses;
- to promote research to improve learning; and
- any other measures, as may be required.

Skill Development and Employment

The Act, with regard to the skill development and employment of persons with disability, mandates that the appropriate Government should formulate schemes and programmes constituting provision of loans at concessional rates to facilitate and support employment of persons with disabilities especially for their vocational training and self-employment. The schemes and programmes referred to in sub-section shall provide for:

- inclusion of person with disability in all mainstream formal and non-formal vocational and skill training schemes and programmes;
- to ensure that a person with disability has adequate support and facilities to avail specific training;
- exclusive skill training programmes for persons with disabilities with active links with the market, for those with developmental, intellectual, multiple disabilities and autism;
- loans at concessional rates including that of microcredit;
- marketing the products made by persons with disabilities; and
- maintenance of disaggregated data on the progress made in the skill training and self-employment, including persons with disabilities.

Special Provisions for Persons with Benchmark Disabilities

Following are special provisions for persons with benchmark disabilities:

- The appropriate Government and local authorities shall ensure that every child with benchmark disability has access to free education in an appropriate environment till he attains the age of eighteen years.
- The persons with benchmark disabilities shall be given an upper age relaxation of five years for admission in institutions of higher education.
- Notwithstanding anything contained in the Rights of Children to Free and Compulsory Education Act (2009), every child with benchmark disability between the age of six to eighteen years shall have the right to free education in a neighbourhood school, or in a special school, of his choice.
- All Government institutions of higher education and other higher education institutions receiving aid from the Government shall reserve not less than five per cent seats for persons with benchmark disabilities.

Q8. Describe how Sarva Shiksha Abhiyan (SSA) helpful to support children with special needs.

Ans. Sarva Shiksha Abhiyan (SSA) is a programme for Universalisation of Elementary Education covering the entire country, started in 2001. The objective of SSA can be achieved if the education need of every child, whatever nature s/he may be is catered. A good number of children have been found in the category of disabled with various disabilities. CWSN have often been marginalised on account of their disability, lack of awareness on the part of the parents and community about their potential. Apprehensions on the part of the teachers to teach such children also have denied them right to education. A general societal attitude of sympathy towards such children focussing more on what they cannot do rather than on what they can do has also been a barrier. Realising the importance of integrating CWSN in regular schools, SSA framework has made adequate provisions for educating CWSN.

The Sarva Siksha Abhiyan (SSA) aims to provide useful and relevant elementary education to all children including children with disabilities in the age range of 6-14 years by 2010. The person with Disability Act (1995) makes it mandatory on the part of government to provide needed educational facilities for the disabled. SSA programme lays special thrust on making education at the elementary level useful and relevant for children by improving the curricula, child centered activities and effective teaching-learning strategies. It ensures that every child with special needs, irrespective of the kind, category and degree of disability, is provided education in an appropriate environment. It adopts "Zero rejection policy" so that no child is left out of the education system.

CWSN need to be facilitated to acquire certain skills that will enable them to access elementary education as envisaged in the Act. For instance, they may need mobility training, training in Braille, sign language, postural training, etc. Thus, school preparedness of children with special needs must be ensured by providing 'special training' as envisaged in the RTE Act. This training may be residential, non-residential or even home-based, as per their specific requirements. The existing non-formal and alternate schooling (including home-based education) options for children with disabilities can be recast as 'special training'. This means that (1) all children with special needs who are not enrolled in schools or have dropped out, will first be enrolled in a neighbourhood school in an age appropriate grade, (2) they will be entitled to 'special training' through regular teachers or teachers specifically appointed for the purpose. Facilities available to CWSN in the district should be identified. Efforts to get functional and formal assessment of CWSN done should be undertaken. Special transport and other facilities required to enroll out of school CWSN in regular schools should be assessed. Data on the proportion of identified CWSN requiring aids and appliances have been provided these assistive devices through convergence with State Departments, NGOs, ADIP/ALIMCO/IEDC/ other schemes, SSA funds or need to be collected other sources.

SSA has made provision for expenditure up to ₹3000/- per disabled child which could be incurred in a financial year to meet the special learning needs of such children.

Q9. Discuss Inclusive Education for Disabled at Secondary Stage (IEDSS).

Ans. The IEDSS scheme was launched in 2009-10 replacing the earlier Integrated Education for Disabled Children (IEDC) scheme. While inclusive education for disabled children at elementary level is being provided under the SSA, this scheme provides 100 per cent central assistance for inclusive education of disabled children studying in Classes IX-XII in mainstream government, local body and government-aided schools. The aim of the scheme is to facilitate continuation of education of children with special needs up to higher secondary level.

The objectives of the scheme will be to ensure that:

- Every child with disability will be identified at the secondary level and his educational need assessed.
- Every student in need of aids and appliances, assistive devices, will be provided the same.
- All architectural barriers in schools are removed so that students with disability have access to classrooms, laboratories, libraries and toilets in the school.
- Each student with disability will be supplied learning material as per his/her requirement.
- All general school teachers at the secondary level will be provided basic training to teach students with disabilities within a period of three to five years.
- Students with disabilities will have access to support services like the appointment of special educators, and establishment of resource rooms in every block.
- Model schools are set up in every state to develop good replicable practices in inclusive education.

Components: Assistance is admissible for two major components:

- Student-oriented components such as medical and educational assessment, books and stationery, uniforms, transport allowance, reader allowance, stipend for girls, support services, assistive devices, boarding and lodging facilities, therapeutic services, teaching learning materials, etc.
- Other components include appointment of special education teachers, allowances for general teachers teaching such children, teacher training, orientation of school administrators, establishment of resource room, providing barrier-free environment, etc.

The scheme, for the first group of components, provides Rs. 3000/- per disabled child per annum for assistance. The State Government provides a top up of `600/- per child per annum towards scholarship for

each child. The amount of `3000/- per disabled child per annum can be spent on the following components:
- Identification and assessment of children with disabilities;
- Aids and appliances;
- Learning materials like Braille textbooks, audiotapes, talking books, textbooks in large print, etc.;
- Transport facilities, hostel facilities, scholarships, books, uniforms, assistive devices, support staff (readers, amanuensis);
- Stipend for girl students with disabilities (Rs.200/- per month);
- Access to ICT;
- Development of teaching learning material; and
- Support service from educational psychologists, speech and occupational therapists, physiotherapists, mobility instructors and medical experts.

For the second group of non-beneficiary oriented components, separate fund is provided. These components are:
- Removal of architectural barriers;
- Training of special/general school teachers;
- Orientation of principals and educational administrators;
- Strengthening of teacher training institutions;
- Resource rooms and equipments for the resource rooms;
- Appointment of special educators;
- Development of model inclusive schools;
- Research and monitoring; and
- Awareness programmes.

The IEDSS scheme mandates the Boards of Examinations to make provision for adaptation of examination procedures and alternative modes of examination wherever required by children with disability according to their special needs. All concerned implementing agencies are mandated to make provisions for relaxation of rules relating to admissions, minimum or maximum age limit for admission, promotion, and examination procedures so as to facilitate access of CWSN to education. At the secondary level, CWSN beyond 18 years will be supported for a period up to 4 years to help them complete secondary schooling.

Q10. Write short notes on the following:

(i) Counselling students with single or multiple disabilities

Ans. Counselling students with single or multiple disabilities is a weak area. Counselling of parents and children is of great importance. No specific or long-term courses are conducted in this particular area, though the primary teachers are exposed to some training through the SSA. The secondary school teachers are expected to receive training through the IEDSS. The teachers have a positive role in the education of the disabled students. Normally, one sympathises with such students, which have adverse effect on the psyche of the child. They are reminded time and again that they are deficient. This is not a correct approach for the development of these children. What is, therefore, important is that the teacher makes conscious efforts to understand the special needs of such students and help them overcome their learning difficulties. Teachers should also recognise the social and emotional needs of these children and help them to develop positive self-esteem. Simultaneously, in the inclusive school settings, the teachers should help the peer group to develop children with disability. Perhaps this is the most important aspect of the teacher's role in the education of such children.

(ii) Seating arrangements and special attention

Ans. In classrooms, teachers may have children with poor eye sight or hearing problems. Teachers are required to identify them and make them sit nearer and see the blackboard clearly. When presenting the teaching content, teachers should make use of audio and visual aids. Teachers should never speak with their back towards a child with hearing problem. Teachers should face the child and speak slowly. For the benefit of children with poor eyesight, the teacher can increase the size of the letters when writing on the board or presenting a chart or map. Teachers will also need to learn how to identify these children.

Q11. Describe the importance of the socio-emotional needs of the persons with disability.

Ans. A disabled child also requires emotional and social security, and ironically, such children are left behind when it comes to socialise them, and families having hesitation, grief, anger and insecurities tend to keep the disabled child behind the walls. Many of the disabled children have been found to be emotionally and socially insecure and it is also a responsibility of the family to understand their emotional and social needs besides looking after their physical needs as well.

Each and every child is born with certain basic needs that must be satisfied before s/he can develop physically, socially or intellectually. Growth in any one of these areas is necessarily related to and influenced by growth in the others. One method of viewing social and emotional needs within this context has been formulated by Maslow (1954) who conceived of individual needs leading to psychological health as forming a hierarchy. According to his model, higher order needs such as belonging, love, self-esteem and self-actualisation can only be achieved once more potent physiological and safety needs have been met. Even in the higher order needs, achievement of each level leading towards self-actualisation depends upon the satisfaction of the previous level's needs.

The emotional and social growth are also important for the overall development of the child, whereas the satisfaction of physical and health needs are essential to survival. The child's psychological growth is fostered by feeling loved or accepted by the significant people in his/her life as well as by being active and stimulated.

Emotional and physical security give a basis for the development of trust, allowing the child to explore and examine aspects of environment and to strive towards developing a sense of self.

People with disabilities have to face problems due to societal handicap, lack of attention to their social and emotional needs may compound their problems. It is, therefore, necessary to understand their socio-emotional problems so that they can develop their potentials to the maximum.

Q12. Discuss the emergence of socio-emotional problems of the persons with disability.

Ans. Pupils with social, emotional and behavioural difficulties (SEBD) are an obvious cause of concern for many teachers as well as for themselves. Compared with other special needs groups, they are more likely to have problems in completing their education successfully and to obtain lower reading and math scores (Groom and Rose 2004). They are twice as likely to drop out of the education system prematurely than pupils without SEBD (Landrum, Tankersley, and Kaufmann 2003). Moreover, those with severe conduct problems run a serious risk of developing lifelong patterns of social maladjustment (Kauffman 2005).

Individuals with disability cannot do certain things that are normally expected in the ordinary time available. They cannot keep up with the standards of performance and ways of behaving that are presented by the surrounding society. This inability to do things at par with other normal individuals may cause discomfort and feeling of 'looked down upon' and results in a low self-esteem. This low self-esteem leads to a feeling of inferiority.

However, if individuals with special needs have been regarded and treated with respect by their family and other people in close contact with them, especially, during their early years, it will positively influence their 'self image' – their own conscious and sub-conscious view of themselves.

A series of successful activities in any child tend to build up morale and confidence, whilst a series of unsuccessful attempts leading to no recognition or reward tend to lower his/her confidence which may further affect his/her chance of success in future activities. For example, a child with physical disabilities is likely to find some of his/her sensory motor experiences such as learning to control his/her hands accurately, eye and hand co-ordination quite frustrating, especially, if his/her parents become impatient or critical of his/her efforts at using a spoon or building the blocks, etc.

The standard of performance expected of a child at a certain age is set largely from parental expectations. The child with special needs is as likely a normal child to make comparisons between his/her performance and that of children of similar age, assuming, of course, that s/he is not leading a very isolated existence. Resultantly, in addition to sensing parental dismay at his/her clumsiness, s/he is becoming aware that his/her performance is not matching up to that of other children.

Therefore, a child experiences that s/he is not keeping up to the expectations of his/her parents and it results in a poor self-image with low morale and confidence. Thus, socio-emotional problems are related to what an individual with disability feels about him/herself. Attitudes of 'normal' individuals also contribute to the socio-emotional problems of persons with disability.

There is a tendency among 'normal' people to dwell on the problems and frustrations associated with disability to such an extent that the person with disability ceases to be regarded as an individual with his/her own personal abilities and contributions to make to the society.

People tend to generalise from the disability and attribute it to the whole individual. As one spastic child puts it, "Just because my legs are wobbly, people think my mind is wobbly too." Such a generalisation is one of the primary aspects of faulty attitude towards individuals with disability.

Therefore, the feelings of persons with disability about themselves and the feelings of others towards them lead to a number of socio-emotional problems.

Q13. What are the various socio-emotional problems of the individuals with disability? Discuss.

Ans. Following are the various socio-emotional problems of the individuals with disability:

(1) Behavioural Problems of the Persons with Disability: Sometimes, individuals with intellectual or other developmental disabilities display challenging behaviour, like aggression and self-injury, which may be a symptom of a health-related disorder, physical or emotional pain or other circumstances (e.g., insufficient supports).

There is no one method that should be prescribed for any one problem. The first essential is to study the individual concerned, i.e. his/her likes and dislikes, circumstances, idiosyncratic behaviour patterns, history, family set-up and so on. Only following that study will a treatment programme, tailored to the characteristics of the individual and to his/her environment, be arrived at. There are, however, certain procedures that will normally be considered. These are changing the surroundings, positive reinforcement, differential reinforcement of other behaviours, extinction, time out from positive reinforcement, functional communication training, stimulus control, the least restrictive alternative, and fading programmes. Parents and teachers should try to create a more favourable attitude, i.e. an attitude of acceptance and non-segregations of the children with disability. Without an appropriate attitude on the part of the society, it is difficult for the parents to bring up children with disability and more difficult to allow adults to live in the society, enjoy as much independence as possible and work according to their actual capacities.

Parents usually overprotect their children. They do not let the individual grow up into an independent person. Adults who have been overprotected during their childhood days might be immature, insecure and mostly depend upon others for taking decision for them.

It is parent's over expectation that brings lack of confidence and insecurity in the individual. The individual may have many abilities but s/he will experience severe inferiority feelings due to critical attitudes of his/her parents. Majority of the persons with disability could be helped to lead socially useful and independent lives if they were able to obtain proper encouragement, early stimulation and guidance.

(2) **Problems in Employment:** Persons with physical disability and other chronic health problems can enter occupations commensurate with their abilities. When adequate measures are taken to protect them, and those with whom they work from possible hazards arising from their disability, they can contribute productively.

The disabled persons are discriminated against in getting the employment. Most employers do not want to recruit persons with disability in their workforce. This attitude blocks their entry in the employment markets. This also leads to lot of emotional problems.

(3) **Stigmatisation and Withdrawal:** Disabled people are often considered weak, worthless and, in some cases, sub-human by their societies. Myths such as disabled children can't learn. This stigma generates profound social barriers. Disabled people often live in isolation and are excluded from their communities, from the education system, from healthcare and other vital services. Degrees of stigma vary from place to place. In India, social stigma is more as compared to developed countries. This attitude acts as a barrier in their integration into the society.

As in the case of physical and visual impairment, the visibility of disability leads to rejection by others. The presence of a visible impairment appears to negatively affect the self-concept of individuals with such disability, even though other factors are also involved. These individuals may perceive themselves as different and not fitting in, and as a result, they may withdraw from their peer contacts. The ignorance of the society towards disability may result in the non-acceptance of disabled individuals who may then withdraw and remain segregated. For example, the individuals with visual impairment do not suffer because they yearn for sight but because of the negative social altitude towards them.

In individuals with intellectual disability, the withdrawal problem is caused by the pathetic or mostly hostile attitude of society towards them, which magnifies their problem and even threatens their freedom and existence.

(4) Problems in Interpersonal Relations and Social Adjustment: Interpersonal adjustment problems frequently are assumed to be a major social-emotional manifestation of learning disabilities. The hypothesis that learning disabled individuals are at high risk for developing interpersonal relationship and adjustment problems has been studied extensively. As a heterogeneous group, for example, learning disabled individuals typically are not well liked by non-learning disabled peers (Bryan, 1974b, 1976; Garrett & Crump, 1980; Scranton & Ryckman, 1979; Sheare, 1978; Siperstein, Bopp & Bak, 1978). Despite this research, conclusions about the prevalence and severity of such problems, as well as the relationship between a diminished capacity to perceive relevant social cues and academic competence (i.e. the social cognition hypothesis), are equivocal.

Satisfactory adult relationship is largely dependent upon a satisfactory first relationship (mother and child). In the care of a blind infant mutual attraction fails to develop, which leads to adjustment problems later. Because of the deprivation and maltreatment from others, the individuals with disability may exhibit characteristics like, irritability, temper outburst, aggressiveness along with moodiness and emotional instability. The teasing and criticism of others leads to low self-esteem in the individuals with disability.

(i) Individuals with visual impairment have problems with mobility, because of which their opportunities for social-interaction are affected. The acquisition of movement skills should be encouraged through games which involve activities like climbing, balancing, bouncing and soon. These activities promote sense of confidence and self-control, which serve as a base for healthy social interaction.

(ii) Individuals with intellectual disability may be slower to incorporate values of right and wrong and to develop internal controls. As a result, they may frequently exhibit inappropriate or socially unacceptable behaviour.

(iii) Individuals with hearing and speech impairment have a lot of communication problems which lead to social-interaction problems.

(5) Emotional Problems of the Individuals with Disability: People with physical or visual impairment have to face physical hazards that may lead to insecurity and emotional disturbances to them as compared with normal persons. The effect of this is more if as a child, they encounter negative experiences in the community as well as at school and home.

People try to hide their disability because the visibility of the disability attracts contemptuous attention. It is for this reason people often resist the use of walking stick, crutches, eye glasses and hearing aids even if it leads to functional impairment. Attempts to hide the disability are sometimes made by parents who do not wish their children to be exposed to such behaviour of others or are ashamed of their deformed offspring. This leads to embarrassment for the disabled individuals, which often leads to emotional trauma. Some of the psychosomatic complaints include emotional instability, insecurity, reduced appetite, negative attitude towards self and family, anxiety, insomnia and gradual loss of interest in life.

Emotional problems are not caused by the presence of hearing impairment itself. If deafness is present from early childhood, it may create considerable stress and adversely affect personality development. Because of the hearing impairment in their children, parents either do everything for them, thereby creating delay in self-dependence or neglecting their children which leads to anxiety in them. Sometimes, because of the discriminatory treatment from parents, children with disability may develop feeling of jealousy towards their brothers and sisters who, they think, are better treated by their parents.

Among people with visual impairment, fear of being watched may create an emotional strain, and this fear may persist well into later life. Since individuals with intellectual disability have fewer coping skills, stresses of daily living are greater for them. It is found that there is high incidence of emotional disturbances among persons with mild intellectual disability than in general population. They are subjected to greater stresses, frustrations and conflicts, and consequently, more likely to develop behavioural disorders.

The conditions of multiple disability can increase an individual's social and emotional problems. Potential for effective social functioning decreases as the number of impairment increases. In studies of individuals with intellectual disability associated with hearing and visual impairment, poor social relationships and, generally, maladaptive interpersonal behaviour such as aggressiveness has been reported.

(6) **Negative Self-concept:** The concept of self denotes the evaluation of an individual of his/her worth and limitations in all those aspects of which s/he is aware of. To feel that life is worth living the individual should have a positive concept about his/her self. People around us play a significant role in the formation of our self-concept. Individuals with impairment are likely to receive cues of negative evaluation. It is reported that the persons with disability often feel that their conditions prevent others in recognising their positive attributes. If the teachers and parents focus only on his/her impairment by making comments such as "you can't do this", "it is not possible for you to achieve", etc., s/he will lack in confidence and develop a negative self-concept.

(7) **Communication Problems of the Individuals with Disability:** Communication difficulties may include problems with expression-intelligibility, fluency and rate of speech and the ability to use language to clarify, negotiate and express needs, choices and decisions; as well as reception-hearing, recalling and comprehending spoken and/or written language (Byng *et al.* 2003; Van der Gaag 1998). These difficulties can occur to varying degrees depending upon the type and extent of intellectual disability and depending upon the presence of any associated physical disabilities such as cleft palate, cerebral palsy or hearing impairment (Van der Gaag 1998).

Learners with hearing impairment are more likely to experience frustrations due to not understanding or not being understood, due to which they often show temper tantrums in their early years.

However, recently, there have been positive developments in increasing opportunities for individuals with hearing impairment. Access to computer and specially designed portable devices helps in establishing effective personal contacts.

Individuals with hearing impairment tend to have difficulties in articulation. Speech problems not only impede children's social relationship but may also make it particularly difficult for them to make their needs known effectively. They are likely to be less flexible in acquiring social skills and in dealing with their social environment as compared to other individuals who can express discomfort, pinpoint dissatisfaction and ask questions about something they do not understand.

Q14. What are the roles of parents and teachers for persons with disability?

Ans. Following are the roles of parents and teachers for persons with disability:

- Parents and teachers should encourage play, talk and free imagination. Play is one of the most powerful means of socialisation.
- The PWD do possess potentials for development as fully independent individual. Parents and teachers should create and

provide conditions for creative development of the PWD and foster their creativity.

- Parents and teachers tend to make wide generalisation about the capabilities of the PWD, which are unwanted and unrealistic. Perception of the discrepancy between his/her ability and social expectations contribute to tension and discomfort to the child, and consequently, his/her behaviour undergoes some changes.
- Social activities should be arranged to foster socialisation in them.
- Considerate and unprejudiced attitudes towards the persons with disability can help them in attaining self-sufficiency and self-actualisation.
- Handicapped children are either not understood or misunderstood as far as their social needs are concerned. Teachers and parents should be aware of their characteristic needs of given stages of social development, which may help them to intervene more effectively.
- As far as possible, parents and teachers should try to provide as normal a life as possible to them.
- The persons with disability (PWD) should be encouraged to accept their limitations without succumbing to them.
- The emotional relationship between parents, their social behaviour with the child as well as with other family members forms models for the child's social behaviour. Quarrelsome and hostile parents, for example, inculcate aggressiveness and hostile behaviour in children. Emotionally unstable parents cause insecurity to children that leads to poor adjustment.
- Parents should accept the child's special needs. Parents unconsciously tend to reject or punish their children with disability or develop over protective attitudes. Both rejection and over protection have negative effects on the integrated personality of the individual.
- Emotionally well-balanced and stable family surroundings need to be provided to children with disability. This lays a foundation for the healthy social and emotional development of the child.
- Parents and teachers should try to make the home and school environment accessible to the PWD. For example, provisions like stairs as well as ramps, doors wide enough for wheel chairs, etc.
- Emotional problems should not be tackled by force or punishment. They should allow healthy and constructive expression of sexual interest and provide appropriate information to help them to understand what is helping to their body.

Q15. Interpret the role of guidance counsellor for persons with disability.

Or

How can a guidance counsellor help students with disability and their families? [June-2018, Q.No.-3 (a)]

Ans. Counsellors that work with individuals with disabilities and/or their families should be aware of the impact of historical and societal perceptions towards disability and how that affects societal beliefs (Rubin & Roessler, 2008). In addition, counsellors have a professional responsibility to be cognizant of their own word-choice and use of terms when referring to persons with disabilities and its potential impact. More specifically, they need to be mindful of whether they view the person as an individual who has the same rights, needs and desires as anyone else or if they perceive him/her as incapable, weak, less than, suffering, pitiful, handicapped, or physically/mentally challenged and so forth (Smart, 2009; Titchkosky, 2001).

Counsellors are encouraged to learn more about appropriate terminology including the use of "person-first" language. Although this is not a perfect system, it represents where the profession is at the moment. In most instances, persons with disabilities may be referred to as just that or as "individuals with disabilities" (Falvo, 2009). Perhaps, a more suitable and appropriate way to refer to persons with disabilities is simply by their "first name"; however, this is often not what takes place. In all of these instances, the focus rests on recognising and valuing the fact that each individual is a person first and foremost with many endearing qualities and of which disability comprises only one feature. Complicating these guidelines is the fact that some people living with a disability have other preferences and ways for identifying and describing themselves. In these instances, counsellors should be sensitive to the terms used by the person served, yet not assume that this "chosen term" is how they can refer to her. When unsure of how to proceed, counsellors should ask the person with a disability about his/her personal preference.

When parents learn about the disability of their child, they go through a chain of reactions. There can be a feeling of shock and disbelief, denial, anger, guilt, frustration, depression, recognition and adaptation. A counsellor should be supportive in these stages.

Parents and children, both should be involved in the process of counselling and training. The diagnostic evaluation should emphasise what the child will be able to do. The family members should be counselled in order to assist them in rising above the stigma of disability and its accompanying problems. The counsellor should help the PWD in planning their future.

Q16. Discuss the nature of behavioural problems.

Or

What are the physical, psychological and educational needs of children?

Or

What are the behavioural problems of children and adolescents?

Ans. Behaviour problems of students can be as serious a handicap to their development and learning as the mentally retarded children's slowness to learn. Behaviour problems arise from external influences whose effects are not often noticed or understood by others. Often, emotional and psychological factors in apparently normal children are neither readily seen nor understood but are often labelled as depression, hostility, withdrawal or day dreaming to combat the stress. They may be battered and abused sexually, emotionally or physically. Most of these children are often in regular classrooms trying to cope with their problems (themselves) without being understood.

Teachers and parents are faced with the difficulty of dealing with the behavour problems of their children. Behaviour problems of children often interfere with the learning process and are incompatible with their educational programme.

As a result of their behaviour problems such children are seldom liked by their peers, teachers, brothers or sisters, or even parents. Even sadder, they often don't even like themselves.

It is important for a teacher to understand the factors which could be responsible for the observable behaviour problem of their student's behaviour or else she might deal with such students in a way which might aggravate the result. Students with behaviour problems often offer the most frustrating problems or the most rewarding challenges for teachers.

The behaviour reflecting behaviour problems range from extreme withdrawal to intense hostile aggression. These students, if not identified and helped during their school days would continue to have difficulties dealing with society and their problems may become progressively more serious later in life.

Students have a number of physical, psychological and educational needs which are basic to their growth and development. Student needs are:

- **Physical Needs:** Proper food, clothing, protection from pain, sickness, time to play.
- **Psychological Needs:** To be accepted as a unique individual, emotional satisfaction constant reassurance, affection, help in regulating emotional responses, help in accepting his or her own sex, help in learning how to behave with other people.
- **Educational Needs:** Education that does not arouse fear, help in studies, warm and understanding atmosphere at school, sense of achievement, education to meet life's challenges, encouragement for new learning.

The above described all needs are inter-related to each other. They interact with one another and leave their imprint on the growing child.

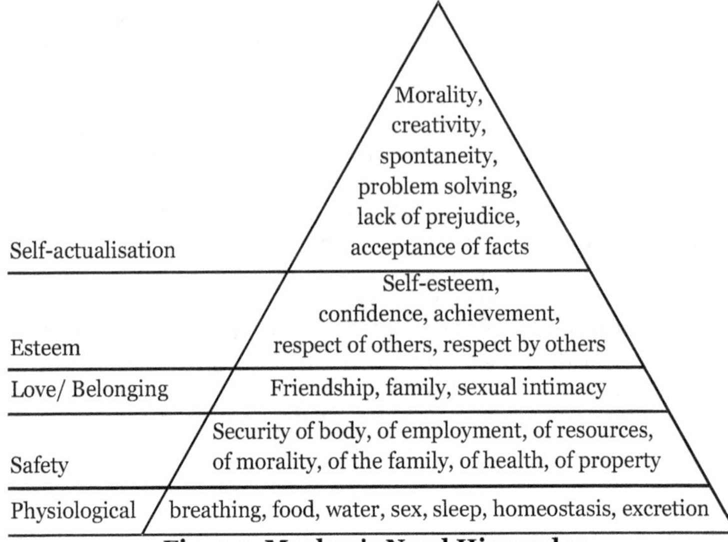

Fig. 4.1: Maslow's Need Hierarchy

In 1970, Abraham Maslow saw human motivation as a hierarchy of needs, with the most basic being physiological needs and the highest being self-actualisation. Only after basic needs are satisfied we can work on achieving higher needs.

Problems of Children

Some problems faced by children are extreme shyness, fearfulness, aggression, attention getting, hyperactive, excessively dependent, day dreaming, lying and cheating, stealing, etc.

Most of these problems of children can be handled by the teacher/parent by using rewards such as adult praise, treats and trinkets and parents/teachers can be trained to engage children with such problems in appropriate behaviour in order to earn these rewards. However, their understanding of social situations that lead to such behaviour problems severely limited, and they may have difficulty in comprehending how their behaviour affects children or why children behave as they do.

Problems of Adolescents

Oftenly, adolescence is marked by intense striving for independence and by rebellion directed at adult authority. Problems with parental and school supervision, drugs and alcohol misuse, truancy, theft and sexual experimentation are common at this age. Therefore, it is not surprising that adolescents with such problems are generally reported to be suspicious of adults (including the therapist), rebellious, defiant and resistant to treatment attempts. Such unwilling adolescents may blame others for their own problems and lack motivation to change their own behaviour. Group treatment methods are often used with adolescents in order to create a less threatening and more inviting atmosphere and to attempt to enlist peers support for behaviour change. Teenagers who are primarily fearful, withdrawn, depressed or mentally confused are often given individual therapy.

Q17. What are the various types of behaviour problems? Explain.

Ans. Generally behavioural problems seen in children in schools can be categorised into emotional problems, conduct problems and specific problems. Among emotional problems, anxiety, excessive fear, phobia, extreme sensitivity, shyness and timidity, difficulty in maintaing friends, social withdrawal, moodiness, depression, day dreaming, nail biting, thumb sucking, compulsion, jealousy, school refused, soiling, emotional factors and physical illness. But coming to high school students all these emotional problems may not be seen and in some case unusual emotional problems are seen.

Conduct problems are common among school going children and more seen in high school students. They are lying, stealing, demanding and stubborn, temper tantrums, aggression, truancy, gang activities. These problems are not only troublesome to the individual but also distressing to those around the field.

Coming to the specific problems seen in high school students, the prominent ones are those relating to sex. These are masturbation, homosexual activities, abnormal heterosexual interest and other related sexual problems. To better understand the behavioural problems of high school students a brief description of each problem is presented here.

- **Truancy:** Truancy means fleeing or absconding from school or roaming outside the school without obtaining necessary permission from the authorities concerned. This sort of delinquent behaviour is prompted mainly by improper handling of such children by their teachers in school and parents at home. In the class these children are subjected to harsh criticism and punishment by the teachers for their lack of interest in studies, inattentiveness in class activities, poor performance and failure to cope with the level of education. The children running away from school mostly idle away their time in some nearby park, street-corner or in cinema halls. One of the major causes of increasing truancy may be that children do not find this school curriculum interesting. The world outside school is full of exciting stimuli which lrue them.

- **Lying:** The dictionary meaning of lying is telling an untruth, i.e. an incorrect or a false fact. It is a deliberate attempt of willful telling, falsifying, distorting or misrepresenting a fact. A child may resort to lying or cheating because of trouble with parents or at school.

- **Stealing:** By stealing we mean to take away some object from a person without his consent or knowledge. No matter whether stealing implies a petty objects, it is considered to be not only undesirable but in some cases unlawful also.

- **Juvenile Delinquency:** Juvenile Delinquency means youthful offence. To be more precise it means any law-breaking behaviour in a youth presumably below 18 and above 10 years of age. Truancy and stealing also come under Juvenile Delinquency if they are committed by a youth below 18 years of age. Such behaviour is common though it is not acceptable to society and is generally regarded liable to some kind of admonition, penalty, punishment or corrective action. Thus, delinquent behaviour may range from truancy, stealing free trips (travelling without ticket), eve teasing and use of illegal drugs to commit murder, rape or any other serious criminal act.

- **Gang Activities:** The child associates with a group of children whose actives are not desirable, and as part of the group the child may steal, drink, beat up others, and so on. A child is influenced greatly by the environmental s/he lives in.

- **Anxiety and Achievement Anxiety:** Anxiety means fear like reaction without the presence of adequate stimuli. A child who is anxious is uncomfortable and frightened. Anxiety may be connected with something specific, like taking an exam or talking to teacher. In children, anxiety may be chronic condition. The extent, to which the child gets upset about tests, scores and is sensitive to criticism or correction.

- **Aggression and Violence:** The child resorts to violence in which s/he harms others property, or even her/his self, perhaps as a reaction to stress. A hostile or angry behaviour directed to harm or injure a person or property.

- **Shyness and Timidity:** The child may not answer questions even when s/he knows the answers, and may not participate in classroom or extracurricular activities, withdrawing rather than making the effort to communicate. In this case the child is basically fearful but hides her/his fears behind withdrawn and timid behaviour.

- **Day Dreaming:** Day dreaming, to combat boredom during adolescence, is normal. If a child day dreams excessively throughout the day, it shows, that s/he is distressed in her/his daily life.

- **Nail Biting and Odd Facial Movements:** The highest incidence of nail biting is around adolescence. These symptoms are generally indicative of nervousness and tension in the child, and are manifested when the child feels insecure.

- **Sexual Problems (Homosexual Activity):** Interest in a partner of same sex can also be viewed as a passing phase. This may be less common than masturbation and may be present both in boys and girls, particularly among those who stay in hostels and boarding schools. This again is a developmental phase, very few will continue to indulge in it when they grow up.

Some more categories of behavioural problems are also identified. They are:

- **Classroom Disturbance:** The extent to which the child teases and torments classmates, interferes with other's work and is quickly drawn into noise making and must be controlled;
- **Impatience:** The extent to which the child starts work too quickly, is sloppy in work, is unwilling to go back over work and rushed through work. Physically more active and restless;
- **Disrespect-Defiance:** The extent to which the child speaks disrespectfully to teachers, resists doing what is asked of belittles the work being done and breaks classroom rules;
- **External Reliance:** The extent to which the child looks to others for direction, requires precise direction and has difficulty making one's own decisions;
- **Inattentive-withdrawn:** The extent to which the child loses attention, seems to be oblivious to what transpires in the classroom and seems difficult to reach, or is preoccupied;
- **Irrelevant-Responsiveness:** The extent to which the child tells exaggerated stories, gives irrelevant answers, interrupts when the teacher is talking and makes irrelevant comments during classroom discussion;
- **Need for Closeness to Teacher:** The extent to which the child seeks out the teacher before or after class, offers to do things for the teachers, is friendly towards the teacher and likes to be physically close to the teacher;
- **Anxiety-Depression:** The child seems to be tense with face drawn and rigid, cries easily at the smallest pretext, does not talk to anyone, doesn't take interest in things. The child gets upset about test and test scores, sensitive to criticism or correction;
- **Quiet and Withdrawn:** The child is withdrawn and quite in the class, doesn't have friends and is mostly isolated. Tends to be self-centered, preoccupied with own thoughts and problems and disinterested in or unenthusiastic about anything else;
- **Attention Deficit:** The child has difficulty in attending to tasks and instructions for any length of time. Easily distracted, a fidget excessively, has difficult in sitting still. The child who is frequently absent in school for vague reasons or minor ailments;
- **Physical Injury:** Recurrent and multiple injuries are observed for which no adequate evidences is given for delay medication, spots like strap marks, bites and burns.

Q18. Elucidate the causes of behaviour problems.

Ans. The object of study is to examine the behavioural problems of high school students, viewing that the brief idea of the causal factors of behavioural problems may provide and understanding about the causes and impetus of the study. The causal factors can be classified as factors related to home and family environment and school.

The cause of a particular child's behaviour problem is, in all probability a peculiar combination of some of the contributing factors, discussed as follows:

(1) **Personal and Social Needs:** A child's need for attention, recognition, approval and belonging are just as real and compelling as the need for food and drink. A child deprived of attention might resort to any activity which promises being into the limelight.

A child or adolescent often does not know to get social satisfaction properly. For example, the bully, the liar, the off, the joker, the habitual interrupter—is probably trying to satisfy social needs.

Besides social needs, the need for self-respect, the need to feel that one is free and independent and important as an individual might be expressed by an individual in the form of disobedient, disorderly, uncooperative, truant, or talks when s/he should be listening, or pushes when s/he should be waiting for his/her turn.

Children who are notably above or below average in mental ability are apt to misbelieve in order to help satisfy their social and personal needs because their desires are not otherwise being met.

(2) **Effects of Maturation:** Regardless of what an individual's chronological or even mental age may be, s/he may be no more mature in self-control or human relations than an average individual who is some years his/her junior. Behaviour problems such as temper tantrums, negativism and attention-seeking are indicative of immaturity.

Other contributing factors are the individual's physical development. The small boy for example, may adopt defiant, aggressive mannerism in order to demonstrate to himself/herself as well as to others that s/he is a force to be reckoned with despite his/her shortness of stature. The fat child may try to live up to the reputation s/he has acquired as the class clown. The big child may feel that his/her in the group is to act as ring leader whenever any mischief is contemplated, for s/he too has a reputation to uphold. His/her peers expect a certain among of unruly behaviour from his/her and s/he cannot afford to let them down.

(3) **Rejection:** Rejection is one of the most important causes of problem behaviour in a child. Many a time's rejection is due to overprotection. Many parents do not like the child to think independently or act independently. As a result the child suffers in so many ways. Shyness, timidity and dependency are due to these reasons.

Behavioural problems are caused by physical or psychological defects of a child, certain physiological dysfunction of the child and health factors, for example, at times children have behavioural problems because nobody cares for them after a certain disease. As a result, they become very restless and aggressive.

(4) Lack of Parental Concern: Some children become hyperactive too. Consciously or unconsciously they always keep themselves busy with some activity or the other. This hyperactiveness is generally developed in the children, whose parents do not pay proper attention to them.

(5) Broken Homes and Marital Discords: Quarrels between husband and wife and their disagreement contribute to a great extent in creating behavioural problems in a child. Every child visualises its home to be a place where it has understanding, loving, kind and generous parents but the marital discord between the parents leaves a very horrid impression in the child mind.

(6) Lack of Freedom: Every child needs a certain extent of independence in whatever it does. As the child grows, it is desirable to allow it to have independence. However, many parents do not really support this view as they generally think that their child is not capable of handling affairs independently.

Wherever possible and necessary a child should be allowed to do things for itself, think for himself and decide for himself, otherwise it would create behavioural problems.

(7) Size of the Family and Child's Status: Behavioural problems may develop in a child who is staying in a big family or rather who has got many brothers and sisters. In such cases the eldest of all is expected to be much more tolerant, perfect and so on as it should be according to its age. If the child fails to keep upto this expectation of the parents, it leads to many behavioural problems.

(8) Lack of Education in Emotional Aspects: Lack of Education in emotional aspect creates many problems in the child, e.g. at school he does not listen to the teachers. He either does not mix with his fellow students and remains shy or he becomes aggressive and starts fighting with his friends. At home he develops bad habits like stealing money, fighting with the brothers and sisters. These would be avoided if a child has good emotional education.

(9) Educational Abuse of the Child: We often make the mistake of comparing the child performance at school or home with others or cite our own examples or nag the child frequently by saying you cannot do this or that. This develops a sense of inferiority complex and becomes a barrier in achieving self confidence in a child. This kind of emotional abuse of the child, This kind of emotional abuse of the child has serious repercussions.

(10) Neighbourhood: The child's family may not be like others in the neighbourhood and the child may not suitable companions approved by his/her parents.

(11) Teasing and Bullying by Other Children: A child may get into trouble with other children. Teasing, bullying and fighting are commons, problems seen in classrooms. A child with physical handicaps or emotional problems, or one who is intellectually slow, or is suffering from epilepsy, stammering etc., is often ridiculed by other children.

(12) Teacher's Behaviour: Some behavioural problems may be attributed to the teacher. It is improbable that any teacher consciously invites misconduct, but many do so inadvertently. Teachers who are sarcastic or who humiliate their students and those who are down right unfair to them earn the animosity of the students, and they become intent on seeking means of gaining revenge.

The vacillating teacher with no set policy also contributes to students' misbehaviour, since they try out to see what and how much they can do before the teacher demonstrates displeasure. The teacher who is easy going, who tries to be a 'pal' to the students, is another who practically extends the class an invitation to do as they jolly well please.

Teachers, like parents, may behave in a manner that distresses the child. They may punish children excessively, make criticisms and comparisons, expect too much from them or even pick on one child constantly.

The teacher's methodology as well as personality can contribute to the incidence of behavioural problems. If the work of the class is boring, if the interest and attention of the students cannot be held, if there is little for them to do but sit and listen or read, if the lessons are not well planned and if the ordinary matters of class routine are not well organised, if every student is not given some worthwhile task to perform, if the teacher allows discussions to get out of hand and degenerate into a number of private conversations, the teachers is helping to set up the kind of environment in which discipline problems are likely to breed and flourish.

(13) Classroom Situations:

    (i)   The child may manifest certain behavioural problems through limitation of his peers in the class, e.g. delinquent behaviour, truancy, stealing, etc.

    (ii)   The child develops submissiveness, aggressiveness and assault behaviour because of others showing similar undesirable behaviour towards him.

    (iii)   The child dress, food and cultural background may make him feel inferior and uncomfortable, leading to depression withdrawal and aloofness.

(iv) Teachers casual remarks about the child family background, appearance, and habits may lead to problem behaviour. For example giving nicknames to the children like Donkey, Lambu, etc., not only makes him feel odd or fight with others but forces him to even drop out of school.

(v) Classroom atmosphere, when it possesses a threat for the child, may cause anxiety, fears phobias, and other emotional disturbances.

(vi) Defective interaction between teacher and students as well as amongst the peers may lead to various types of behavioural problems.

(14) Social and Cultural Conditions: Among the socio-cultural factors which have been found to contribute to the misbehaviour of children and youth are certain television shows, movies, comics and magazines in which they encounter violence, horror, sadism, disregard of principles of decency and morality. The behaviour problem of adolescents is often explained in terms of the unfavourable world conditions in which they live. Discrimination, persecution and inequality of opportunity on the basis of race, religion or nationality, may also contribute to the misbehaviour in young people (Masten and Reed, 2002).

(15) Home Conditions: Inadequate maternal reactions and family trauma were strongly associated with behaviour problems. A good relationship between mother and adolescent plays an important role in preventing these problems, whereas inadequate maternal reactions and maternal psychiatric morbidity, such as depression, were identified as risk factors for behaviour problems in adolescents. Family traumas, problematic families, stressful events such as death of relatives have also been shown to be positively associated with behaviour problems by Nix, Pinderhughes, Dodge, Bates, Pettit and McFadyen (2000).

Some adolescents have never had their share of attention and recognition, some have had too much in that, all their wishes have been catered to. Such adolescents become accustomed to the belief that the rest of the world exists to serve them. When such adolescents find themselves in a situation where they are not expected to perform tasks, which are not immediately enjoyable or to conform to needed regulations for the good of the group, they do not know how to act. Aggressive adolescents and adolescents with behaviour problems often come from homes in which their parents are inconsistent disciplinarians who use harsh and excessive punishment and who show little love or affection for their good behaviour (Olsson, Band, Burns, Brodrick and Sawyer, 2003).

(16) Occasional Lapses: In some instances, none of the factors that have been mentioned above might be applicable. The explanation of the misbehaviour might be the simple fact that adolescents were unaware of certain regulation or that they had forgotten it or that they did not think it would be enforced or that they were carried away in the excitement of a moment and did something that they know they should not have done (Ann, 2001).

(i) Truancy: Truancy from school can mean one of the two things: either the student is escaping from an intolerable situation in which the school programme brings nothing but failure, shame, disgrace and ridicule from peers or the student is suffering from serious emotional conflicts. In either case, truancy is a symptom demanding immediate attention from a *psychologist* or a responsible adult.

(ii) Withdraw: Sneha was in the sixth grade. The teacher noted that she was unusually quiet, she did not speak to the other students; she did not play with them. The students ignored her because she so successfully pulled within herself. In an endeavour to help Sneha, the teacher tried giving her special tasks or 'privileges' making another quiet child or friendly student sit with her. Sneha did her work quietly but began showing interest very slowly. The teacher decided that it was not helping her so called for her mother. The teacher talked to the mother about Sneha's withdrawing silent behaviour. They realised that Sneha's younger sibling was getting much more attention from the parents and she was burdened at a young age.

The teacher and mother planned ways to help Sneha to be more carefree and childlike by reducing her responsibility and giving her an opportunity to have more 'fun'. The teacher got Sneha to work with other girls in creative and fun activities such as making puppets. By the end of the year, Sneha was still 'shy' but no longer the silent/solitary child she had been in the beginning of the academic year.

(iii) Stealing: It is a common symptom noted in certain disturbed children. For example, the teacher found ₹500/- missing from the students' welfare fund. However, a few days before the teacher had heard some students talking about Kapil spending money on treating his friends to Pepsi and snacks for two evenings in a row.

The teacher was alert and put two and two together. The teacher privately confronted Kapil. After a few attempts to lie out of it, he admitted to the mistake. On inquiring into the details of Kapil's background, the teacher realised that he belonged to an average economic background but had friends from higher socio-economic standards. In order to spend like others in the group he stole the money so that he too could show off and treat his friends. The teacher decided to make Kapil pay back the stolen money on installment plan. In three weeks, Kapil paid up the debt. The teacher congratulated Kapil for the way he had stuck by his promise to make things right.

This example illustrates better the 'making it right' aspect of restitution than punitive measures as expulsion from school, staying after school for being bad or being sent to a juvenile detention hour. Restitution, if followed by appropriate rewards, is very effective restraining device and should not to be confused with punishment.

(iv) **Anxiety and Fear:** Anxiety can play a major role in interfering with adolescent's academic performances. It can hamper their abilities to perform well in tests, to speak in public and to ask questions when they do not understand something. Some children are so concerned about the way others view them that they cannot attend to their academic tasks. For some adolescents, conflicts about success and fears of the consequences imagined to accompany the attainment of success can hamper academic success. Freud described persons with such conflicts as 'those wrecked by success' (Gould, Greenberg, Velting and Shaffer, 2003).

Q19. What are the various measures or suggestions for dealing with behavioural problems? Discuss.

Or

Provide suggestions for dealing with behaviour problems of students.

Or

Describe the techniques of behaviour management of students. **[June-2018, Q.No.-3 (e)]**

Ans. Measures or suggestions for dealing with behavioural problems are as follows:

(1) **Punishment does not Improve Behaviour:** In schools, it has been continuously observed that a teacher, sometimes, punishes a student whenever s/he consciously inflicts physical or mental pain or discomfort upon other student. There is a substantial qualitative difference between withholding gratification and inflicting punishment. A student may be

denied the privilege of going out during recess because he has disobeyed safety rules and endangered the health of his classmates and himself. This will cause the learner some discomfort. However, it differs substantially from being whipped, embarrassed in front of his peers or forced to hold heavy books at arm's length until exhaustion sets in.

The fear of re-experiencing unpleasantness in child becomes the major reason for stopping the undesirable behaviour. This is a positive technique. Research shows that the punishment may suppose deviant behaviour for a time, but it does not weaken the bad habit. The only time when punishment is effective for eliminating a deviant behaviour is when a correct alternative behaviour is performed and reinforced. Teachers usually make generous use of punitive control techniques often defend their actions by saying, "It works". What the teacher usually means is that the deviancy doesn't occur or spread. Research corroborates the principle that the longer the duration of a punishment, the longer the punished response will be suppressed.

(2) Management of Behavioural Problems: Some control techniques that have proved effective in managing behavioural problems in the classroom are:

(i)   *Signals* such as finger on the lips or a 'frown' shaking of the teacher's head might be all that is required to get the students quietly back to their work;

(ii) *Moving nearer* the noisy pair could remind them of the proper classroom decorum;

(iii) The girls *interest might be boosted* if the teacher says "That's a pretty important report you are writing. May I see how it's coming along?

(iv) *Ignoring the noise* for a moment might be Mr. Sood's choice of technique if he believes that the noise will soon subside by itself;

(v)   *Power with reason* is one technique that Mr. Kapoor could use in a laboratory situation. Saying, "you have to treat those acids with respect. You could very easily burn someone badly", might reduce mishandling or chemicals markedly;

(vi) *Verbal clarity* of a command produces results. For example, 'John, stop drumming or your desk and get busy on those arithmetic problem;

(vii) *A firm control technique* conveying 'I mean it'. A serious, business like tone of voice, walking closer to the deviant, or continuing to look at the deviant until he desists: all these contributes firmness to a teacher's at control;

(viii) *A task-focussed technique* dealing with noise in the 'I hear noise in the back of this room. We will never finish learning how to do square root if that continues';

(ix) *Increase your repertory of techniques.* Part of misbehaviour control is using the right technique at the right time since students are individuals and react in different ways;

(x) *Know your class leaders well.* Discipline problem should decrease by knowing every student well, since it is important to know what things are reinforcing to a student before you can reward him for his good behaviour;

(xi) *The more interesting a subject* can be made, the more effective a teacher's control efforts become;

(xii) *Encourage* the students by pointing out their good points to him/her and peers, point out his/her successes;

(xiii) *Comment positively* when the attention deficit student is attending appropriately to a task. Let him know he is working constructively. Praise him;

(xiv) *Stop misbehaviour in time.* Do not wait until the situation is totally out of hand before stopping it. Stop the act before you become angry and lose control or before the whole class gets into the act;

(xv) Establish limits and maintain consistent, clear ground rules. He knows what is appropriate in inappropriate.

He needs to know what the consequences of his behaviour will be. Be consistent in following through with legitimate consequences. Threats and bribes will not work.

These are certain actions which we should avoid dealing with students. These actions have been found inappropriate. Thus, for helping a behaviour problem student do not include the followings:

(i) Using brute force: 'you hit me, I'll hit you back!

(ii) Accusing the student of misbehaving. 'You are, in a sense, forcing the student to lie to save force';

(iii) Comparing the student's behaviour with that of his/her peers or siblings;

(iv) Arguing—you cannot win an argument with a student. Usually, you both lose;

(v) Embarrassing the student in front of his/her peers or others elders;

(vi)   Removing the student from activities she does well and enjoy doing;

(vii) Ridiculing the student for his/her mistakes or misbehaviour;

(viii) Not to label the student—until sure.

Most of the preceding suggestions and guidelines are simple and applied common sense.

Thinking through problems and alternatives in advance, as suggested here, may help to save the day for the parent/teacher and for the behaviour problem student.

(3) Behaviour Modification Techniques: This technique is helpful for parents and teachers who wish to relate more effectively with children and to assist them to grow in the most healthiest way, both physically and mentally. Major terms used in this context are:

(i)   Reinforcement: Reinforcement relates to the consequences of a behaviour, which will affect its frequency. Positive reinforcement such as a reward tends to increase the frequency of the behaviour with which it is associated. In negative reinforcement, an unpleasant stimulus is removed when a desired behaviour occurs so that the learner modifies behaviour to avoid the unpleasant stimulus.

(ii) Punishment: Punishment involves linking an unpleasant stimulus with an unacceptable behaviour.

(iii) Extinction: In extinction, the reinforcers of unacceptable behaviour are eliminated. For example, screaming may be reinforced by adult attention. Denying this at the same time as ensuring the learner's safety would tend to reduce the incidence of screaming.

(iv) Shaping: Shaping involves developing existing behaviour. If the behaviour required is for a pupil to greet others politely, reinforcement would be given for slight, early efforts to do so. Gradually closer approximation of the target behaviour would next be required until the target behaviour was achieved.

(v)   Consistency: Consistency is following through with a selected approach. For example, each time a child gets out of bed after being put to bed, the parents need to immediately return the child to bed.

(vi) Observation: Observation is watching a behaviour for a specific period of time in order to determine the frequency of the behaviour's occurrence. For example, a child who is hyperactive and distracting to her peers, the teacher records the number of times the child having a temper tantrum.

(vii) Recording: Recording is the systematic record keeping of the number of times a behaviour occurs.

<table>
<tr><td colspan="2">Students Name: ....
Date: ....</td></tr>
<tr><td>1 minute

....
....</td><td>2 minutes

....
....</td></tr>
<tr><td>3 minutes

....
....</td><td>4 minutes

....
....</td></tr>
<tr><td>5 minutes

....
....</td><td>6 minutes

....
....</td></tr>
<tr><td>7 minutes

....
....</td><td>8 minutes

....
....</td></tr>
</table>

Fig. 4.2: Sample of chart by systematic record keeping of number of times a behaviour occurs

(viii)Consequence: Consequence is the event that follows the occurrence of a behaviour. For example, a child finished his homework and is allowed to watch the TV programme of his interest as a reward (consequence).

(ix) Baseline: Baseline is the frequency of occurrence of a behaviour prior to intervention. For example, an observer records the frequency of whining (inappropriate) behaviour before attempts are made to change that behaviour.

(x) Manipulation: Manipulation is the intervention technique in order to change a behaviour. For example, a child throws his books. In order to decrease the occurrence of this behaviour the child is placed in a chair each time he throws the book (timeout).

Q20. What remedial measures do counsellors, parents and teachers take to manage behaviour problems among children? Discuss.

Or

Discuss the role of teachers, parents and counsellors/psychologist to manage behaviour problems among children.

Ans. Some of the measures that counselors, parents and teachers may take to manage behaviour problems among children are as follows:

- **Role of Counsellors/Psychologists:** Counsellors provide guidance to the learners. They have two primary responsibilities to fulfil. The very first is to make sure that s/he does no further damage to the child and second, to manipulate the child's present environment in order to cause more appropriate behaviour to develop in spite of past and present circumstances that cannot be changed. The emphasis is on the present and future, not the past and on improving the school and home environment or using community resources for the benefits of the children.

A counsellor would usually talk with the teacher/parent to get a first hand report and assessment of the problem of the child when s/he receives a request for assistance. Following a detailed picture and understanding of the child's problem from the source of referral, a counsellor would then decide whether the parent or teacher or himself/herself handled the particular problem of the child.

The counsellor, if in case, feels that the problem is severe, s/he makes use of a number of diagnostic techniques in making her/his study, such as psychological tests, interviews, observations of the child, etc. The child's physical health in some cases may also be ascertained through a physical examination or consultation with the parents.

The findings will be discussed with the child's parents and recommendations will be made to help him/her after the completion of the detailed study. The recommendation may be therapy for the child, together with counselling for one or both parents. Just as the child needs help, so do the parents in knowing how to work with the child at home. The counsellor would also discuss helpful procedures with the child's teacher. S/he maintains a contact with the parent and teacher to check on the child's progress after a plan of assistance has been established, determine whether the planned strategy is working with the child or it needs to be changed and further determine whether assistance is required.

- **Role of Parents:** Adolescents with pervasive conduct problems typically come from multi-problems families in which parents have limited resources for coping with high levels of stress and low levels of social support. Often these parents find it difficult to follow through on plans to implement rules, roles and routines worked out in therapy sessions. The parents' own psychological difficulties, marital problems and life stresses prevent them from sticking to their plans to provide consistent rewards or sanctions for rule-following or rule-breaking behaviour, particularly during the early stages of therapy. As a result of this, the youngster's conduct problems persist.

  There are two main types of effective solution to this problem: parent counselling and treatment foster care. With treatment foster care, the child may be placed with a foster family trained in social learning theory-based methods for socialising children with conduct problems (Smith & Chamberlain, 2010). As the conduct problems abate and as the natural parents are concurrently trained to negotiate with their youngster and implement consistent rewards or sanctions for rule-following or rule-breaking behaviour, the youngster spends increasingly longer visits with the natural parents. Thus, the burden of socialising the child is shared by the natural parents and the foster parents.

With parent counselling, the parents are provided with individual or marital counselling to help them better manage their personal and marital difficulties so that these factors will not compromise their capacity to follow through on implementing consistent rewards or sanctions for rule-following or rule-breaking behaviour.

The art of effective family works with multi-problem families where children present with conduct problems is to keep a substantial portion of the therapy focussed on resolving the conduct problem by altering the pattern of interaction between the child and the parents that maintains the conduct difficulties, and only to deviate from this focus into wider family issues when it is clear that the parents will be unable to maintain focus without these wider issues being addressed. Where parents have personal or marital difficulties and require individual or marital counselling or therapy, ideally separate sessions should be allocated to these problems; other members of the involved professional network may be designated to manage them or a referral to another agency may be made. Common problems include maternal depression, social isolation, financial difficulties, paternal alcohol and substance abuse and marital crises. A danger to be avoided in working with multi-problem families is losing focus and becoming embroiled in a series of crisis intervention sessions, which address a range of family problems in a haphazard way.

- **Role of Teachers:** Teachers too play a vital role to manage behaviour problems among children. Teachers should be concerned with the total development of the students and not just the academic achievement. The teacher is in a position to make significant contributions towards the formation of healthy personalities and have opportunities and responsibilities in this regard. The teacher with a training in human behaviour and has opportunity to observe children in a classroom is in a better position to identify students with problem behaviours. Most behaviour problems of students are mild to moderate problems that can be treated effectively in the regular classroom and at home. However, a psychologist should handle severe behaviour problems of students.

  Teachers who are dealing with these types of students must be effective and creative, and able to adapt curriculum materials and activities to the individual needs of the students. The teacher can help a student who has an inadequate self-image by creating psychologically safe environment in which the student can express herself/himself freely without fear of rejection. Teachers can encourage individual students to explore her/his own positive and negative feelings freely by showing unconditional positive regard for the students.

Most behaviour problems would be eliminated if teachers create school and home environment in which students receive continuous love and regard. People value the good will and positive regard of others and will try to obtain it.

While dealing with behaviour problems of students, the primary task of a teacher is to teach them improve their social skills – helping students replace their maladaptive behaviours with more socially appropriate responses. This is often a difficult and demanding task, particularly when the teacher seldom, if ever, knows all of the factors that affect the students' behaviour. On top of this, there are sometimes a lot of contributing factors over which the teacher can exert little or no control (for instance, the delinquent friends with whom the student associates after school). Inspite of these limitations, it does little good to bemoan the student's past (which no one can alter) or to use all of the things in the student's environment that cannot be changed as an excuse for failing to help the student in the classroom.

Teachers can establish realistic, natural and logical consequences instead of threaten and make it (hopefully) more comfortable for the students to choose the more responsible activity. Consequences need to fit in the situation and be such that can be followed through.

Q21. Define mental health. Enlist different theoretical models of mental health.

Or

State the difference between the biomedical and biopsychosocial models of mental health.

Ans. Mental health is a state of well-being in which the individual realises his/her own abilities, can cope with the normal stresses of life, can work productively and fruitfully and is able to make a contribution to his/her own community. (World Health Organisation)

The definition of 'mental ill health' or 'mental health problems' covers a very wide spectrum, from the worries and grief we all experience as part of everyday life to the most bleak, suicidal depression or complete loss of touch with everyday reality.

The positive dimension of mental health is stressed in WHO's definition of health as contained in its constitution: "Health is a state of complete physical, mental and social well-being and not merely the absence of disease or infirmity."

The importance of good mental health to individual functioning and well-being can be amply demonstrated by reference to values that are fundamental to the human condition. The following values are particularly important:

(1) **Independent thought and Action:** The capacity of individuals to manage their thoughts, feelings and behaviour, as well as their interactions with others, is a pivotal element of the human condition. Unsurprisingly, health states or conditions that rob individuals of independent thought and action – such as acute psychosis, advanced stages of dementia or profound intellectual disability – are regarded as among the most disabling.

(2) **Pleasure, Happiness and Life Satisfaction:** There is a longstanding and recently re-emphasised argument that happiness represents the ultimate goal in life and is the truest measure of well-being. Again, it is difficult, if possible, for a person to flourish and feel fulfilled in life when s/he is beset, whether temporarily or permanently, by health problems such as depression and anxiety.

(3) **Family Relations, Friendship and Social Interaction:** Individuals' self-identity and capacity to flourish is deeply influenced by their social surroundings, including the opportunity to form relationships and engage with those around them (family members, friends, colleagues). Loneliness, social isolation and difficulties with communication all heighten the risk of developing or prolonging mental illness.

Models of Mental Health

Mental health of an individual can be understood through the following types of models:

(1) **Normative Model:** According to this model, mental health is something above normal. Normality is perceived as being on a continuum, encompassing the major portion of the adults on the continuum, while abnormality is the remainder. Thus, the normal refers to the reasonable, rather than optimum level of functioning. However, mental health would be considered as above average. For example, in the military, a jet pilot must be required to be above average in mental health for his occupational demands.

To understand this concept, it is important to trace the historical changes, which have occurred in this concept in the past century. What is normal in relation to mental health has been a matter of debate for a long time.

According to one prevalent concept, it is the absence of psychosomatic symptoms. This concept was practiced from 1940s to 1970s. This definition of mental health was initially used in the United States by John Clausen and his co-workers in 1941 to assess the young men enlisted into the United

States army. Thus, the absence of psychopathology was considered as synonymous with normal.

Changes in the procedure of assessment of mental health were seen after the World War II. Normal adaptive behaviour of those who served in the army was studied and the observations were published in scientific literature. There was a focus on the adaptation of the army veterans into civilian life.

(2) Social Model: The social model of mental health refers to the social causation approach to mental health. Here, the focus is on the social factors, which mean the external life experiences (as opposed to the internal life experiences in the psychological model) as the trigger leading to mental ill-health or disorder. Research evidence suggests that a range of social factors such as poverty, educational backwardness, social discrimination (for example gender, caste) or life altering experiences such as sexual abuse, being bullied/ragged in school/college increase the likelihood of people experiencing mental disorder in some form or the other.

(3) Bio-psychosocial Model: This model views mental ill-health as resulting from the psychological and social factors interacting with the biochemical factors of the person. Thus, in this model, medical diagnosis not rejected but the personal context is emphasised over the medical categorisation. So, we can say, this model takes an inclusive approach to mental health in both scientific and humanistic terms.

(4) Biomedical Model: Mental health, according to this model, is usually determined by an individual's genetic disposition. This model considers mental ill-health as bodily malfunctioning and a disease of the brain. Each mental disorder is associated with a different pathology of the brain and has a different cause and origin. Thus, mental-illness is a disease and must be treated medically. The medical model movement led to the classification of mental disorders that described characteristic features of each disorder.

(5) Psychological Model: The biomedical disease model was criticised as a form of social control by use of medicine. In the psychological model, mental ill-health is "...defined in terms of dysfunctional responses to current circumstances-perhaps misperceiving or misinterpreting current reality through depressive or delusional thinking patterns, or experiencing disturbances in feeling due to echoes of unresolved past experiences intruding into the present"(Glasby & Tew p8, 2015). This model locates mental difficulties in specific emotional, cognitive and behavioural processes and takes a developmental perspective.

(6) Resilience Model: More recent understanding on mental health suggests that genetic predisposition and psychosocial stressors acting together always do not lead to mental disorder. This is because people learn to develop coping skills or resilience skills to deal with psychosocial stressors. The supportive psychosocial environment (family and community) around the vulnerable persons help them to develop resilient skills and, thus, avoiding the possibility of developing mental disorder.

(7) Psychosocial Model: Mental health is explained by this model from the perspectives of cognitive and emotional development, family environment, cultural influence, and social and economic support available to the individual. This theory takes the position that:

(i)   Mental ill-health involves dysfunctional emotional, cognitive and behavioural processes and their interaction;

(ii) Dysfunctional behaviour may be responses to problematic life circumstances;

(iii) Mental ill-health may reflect beliefs, attitudes and coping mechanisms that are not compatible with the present life experiences;

(iv) Stressful personal relationship, social and economic discrimination may increase the likelihood of mental ill-health (Glasby & Tew, p9, 2015).

(8) Stress-vulnerability Model: It has been argued by Zubin and Spring (1977) that vulnerability together with stress can affect mental health. Here, vulnerability means the genetic predisposition as well as life altering experiences such as childhood trauma and stress is the psychosocial factors in the life of the person. Studies have shown that genetic disposition as a lone factor had small while psychosocial stressors had more effect on mental disorder. However, the combination of genetic/biological and psychosocial factors tends to increase the possibility of mental disorder.

From the above models, it can be concluded that mental health is a complex issue and one particular model alone cannot explain the complexity involved. The biological, social and psychological factors and their interactions are important in understanding mental ill-health.

Q22. Explain the provisions of Mental Healthcare Act 2017.

Ans. The Mental Healthcare Act, 2017 — was passed by the Rajya Sabha in August 2016 and the Lok Sabha in March 2017 — is a landmark law for many reasons. For the first time in our country, the Act creates a justiciable right to mental healthcare. The right to mental healthcare is the core of the Act and represents the government's attempt to address the neglect of this aspect of healthcare for decades.

The Act provides persons with mental illness protection from cruel, inhuman and degrading treatment, right to information about their illness and treatment, right to confidentiality of their medical condition and right to access their medical records, to list just a few rights. The government is explicitly made responsible for setting up programmes for the promotion of mental health, prevention of mental illness and suicide prevention programmes. Given the huge shortage of trained mental health professionals in the country, the Act requires the government to meet internationally accepted norms for the number of mental health professionals within 10 years of passing this law. It has also effectively de-criminalised suicide attempts by 'reading down' the power of section 309 of the Indian Penal Code.

Mental illness of a person shall not be determined on the basis of:

- Non-conformity with moral, social, cultural, work or political values or religious beliefs prevailing in a person's community; and
- Political, economic or social status or membership of a cultural, racial or religious group, or for any other reason not directly relevant to mental health status of the person.

Q23.What is the impact of mental illness? Discuss briefly.

Ans. The Report of World Health Organisation (2013) shows that more than 25 per cent of all years of population lived with disability and more than 10 per cent of the total burden of disease is attributable to mental, neurological and substance use disorders. Mental disorder can be handicapping to the individual as well as to the nation in that it affects the economic activities and production. Individuals with mental disorder may be unable to work or remain absent from work for longer period, thus, reducing economic productivity. If the person cannot work, s/he becomes dependent on other family members or if s/he is the sole breadwinner of the family, then the entire family suffers with serious consequences to the emotional, educational and economic well-being of the children. In such situations, the cycle of misery continues to the future generations without facilities for education and employment. The impact of mental disorder is adversely far reaching not only to the affected persons but also to the family members and the nation.

Q24.What are the characteristics of mentally healthy persons?

Ans. The characteristics of mentally healthy persons are as follows:

- Mentally healthy persons have an ability to make adjustments.
- They have a positive self-concept.
- Mentally healthy persons have a sense of personal worth, feels worthwhile and important.
- They feel good about themselves.
- Mentally healthy persons solve their problems largely by their own efforts and make their own decisions.
- They are not overwhelmed by emotions.

- They have a sense of personal security and feels secure in a group, show understanding of other people's problems and motives.
- They feel secure and comfortable in a group.
- They have lasting and satisfying personal relationship.
- Mentally healthy persons have a sense of responsibility.
- They approach and handle their problems with equanimity.
- They can give and accept love.
- They don't blame others when things go wrong in their life.
- They can shape their environment and make adjustments when necessary.
- They can balance their personal, professional and recreational life.
- They know their strengths and weaknesses.
- They are self-directed.
- Mentally healthy persons live in a world of reality rather than fantasy.
- They have respect for others even if there are differences.
- They show emotional maturity in their behaviour, and develop a capacity to tolerate frustration and disappointments in their daily activities.
- They can balance their personal, professional and recreational life.
- They can laugh at themselves and with others.
- They have a sense of responsibility towards themselves and others.
- They don't blame others when things go wrong in their life.
- Mentally healthy persons have a variety of interests and generally live a well-balanced life of work, rest and recreation.

Q25. Develop and implement strategies for the promotion of mental health of your learners.

Or

Interpret the role of teachers in mental health promotion.

Ans. Mental health promotion is about creating environments that promote and sustain positive mental health for everyone. Activities and interventions are designed to enhance protective factors and minimise risk factors (individual, family related, environmental and economic in nature). Schools are an ideal setting in which to promote mental health for children and youth, providing an opportunity to reach large groups of children during their formative years of cognitive, emotional and behavioural development.

The most effective school-based programmes for promoting mental health are comprehensive and target multiple health outcomes, involve the whole school, focus on personal skill development, include parents and the wider community and are implemented over a period of time.

The WHO (2013, p.12) advocates for undertaking the following actions by the Governments and other stakeholders:

- provide better social and financial protection for persons with mental disorders, particularly those in socially disadvantaged groups;
- provide better information, awareness and education about mental health and illness;
- provide better legislative protection and social support for persons, families and communities adversely affected by mental disorders; and
- provide better (and more) health and social care services for currently underserved populations with unmet needs.

WHO has developed a comprehensive Mental Health Action Plan 2013-2020 with an emphasis on promotion, prevention, treatment, rehabilitation, care and recovery to take the advanced cause of mental health. With respect to children, the action plan places emphasis on the developmental aspects, for instance, having a positive sense of identity, the ability to manage thoughts, emotions as well as to build social relationships, and the aptitude to learn and to acquire an education, ultimately enabling their full participation in society. The action plan recognises that the determinants of mental health and mental disorder include both individual attributes such as the ability to manage one's thoughts, emotions, behaviours and interactions with others as well as social, cultural, economic, political and environmental factors such as national policies, social protection, living standards, working conditions and community social supports.

Teachers and Mental Health Promotion

WHO action plan has envisaged important role for schools in its multi-sector approach to promotion and prevention of mental health. WHO places the position of teachers as powerful and assumes that teaching profession has a positive role to play in the promotion of mental health. Children and adolescents spend a lot of their active time in schools. They may experience mental health violations in home and community environment or in school. Schools and teachers can do the following to promote mental health and prevent mental disorder among children and adolescents:

- provide training to counter bullying;
- pay attention to children subjected to domestic violence and take measures to prevent domestic violence against children in partnership with community leaders;
- address the needs of children with parents who have mental disorders;
- help parents to establish healthy child – parent relationship;
- create awareness about mental health and reduce stigma attached to mental illness;
- develop and implement life skills programme;

- encourage children to report about mental health violations and seek help;
- provide support services to children who have experienced adverse life events and help them recover from the trauma;
- organise psychosocial support from the community for children who live with parents with mental disorder; and
- create awareness about and reduce exposure to harmful substance (alcohol, drugs etc) around schools.

Q26. Delineate the teacher behaviours that cause harm to the mental wellness of the learners. Also, suggest what can teachers do to promote mental health and prevent mental illness.

Ans. Some of the teacher behaviours that cause harm to the mental wellness of the learners are given below:

- Always praising one or two learners and ignoring others.
- Neglecting and refusing to provide additional academic input to learners who come from less resourceful background.
- Labeling or branding the learners. For example, some teachers give labels such as slow learner, dull, etc. to their learners.
- Not reaching out to learners who have been through traumatic situation in life.
- Discounting or denigrating the identity of the learners. For example, adverse remarks about the caste, colour, family background, disability, etc. of the learner.
- Humiliating and punishing certain learners in front of others while letting others go scot free for the same behaviour.
- Passing derogatory remarks about learners or their family members who have come in conflict with law.
- Using curricular content that may hurt the sentiments of some learners.
- Inability to recognise the psychosocial needs of learners belonging to different strata of the society. For example, the RTE Act, 2009 has reserved 25 per cent of seats for learners from economically weaker sections in a school that otherwise cater to learners from economically forward sections of the society. When teachers ignore the psychosocial needs (for example, sense of belonging) of learners belonging to EWS and do not create an inclusive environment it affects the mental wellness of these learners.
- Blaming it on and not reaching out to learners who are isolated by others.
- Using teaching methodology that doesn't accommodate the needs of all learners.
- Ignoring the unacceptable behaviours by peers towards certain learners. For example, some teachers ignore even if a learner is bullied regularly by the other.

- Ostracising certain learners because of their illness, disability or for the deeds of their family members.
- Humiliating or discounting learners whose family members are affected by mental health problems.

Teachers can promote mental health and prevent mental illness and disorder among their learners by following points:

- Teachers should help those children who have been subjected to such violations to develop coping skills.
- Teachers need to demonstrate to their learners that they care for their well-being and want to help them achieve it.
- Teachers should identify children at risk of life altering experiences such as physical/sexual/substance abuse and train them to counter such situations.
- Teachers should desist from those behaviours which are harmful to the mental well-being of their learners.

Q27. Define stress. What are the sources of stress in a life of students?

Or

What are the sources of stress for students?

[June-2018, Q.No.-3 (b)]

Ans. Stress is defined as "a state of psychological and physiological imbalance resulting from the disparity between situational demand and the individual's ability and motivation to meet those needs."

Dr. Hans Selye, one of the leading authorities on the concept of stress, described stress as, "the rate of all wear and tear caused by life."

It is also worth noting that stress is an inevitable part of student-life; as it takes a toll on most students' physical health, emotional well-being and academic performance. The rise of this pandemic in students is on account of factors such as the somewhat sudden change in lifestyle, increased study load, new responsibilities among others.

According to Bernstein (2012, p.519), stress is defined as the internal processes that occur as people try to adjust to events and situations. Stress is not a specific event but an ever-changing process in which the nature and intensity of our responses depend not only on what stressors occur but also on how we think about them and how much confidence we have in our coping skills and stress coping resources at a given time.

Sources of Stress

In general, substantive changes in life (these are expected changes in life nevertheless eventful, for example, 12th board examination and end of school and beginning of University life), catastrophic events (these are sudden and unexpected events such as death of a parent or accident), daily struggles managing between home and work place, daily commuting between home and work place, serious/chronic illness, strained relationship with family members/friends or such other events and situations in life are stressors. Following are some of the sources of stress in the life of school students:

- Managing between coaching classes for entrance exam and school schedules.
- Difficulty in understanding a teacher.
- Examinations in general, especially board examination.
- Not having friends in school.
- Peer competition and performance anxiety.
- Separation of parents.
- Change of school.
- Catastrophic events such as sexual abuse, accidents, physical assault, earthquake, disastrous cyclone, terrorist attacks, etc.
- Parental pressure to join a stream of higher education, which is not the choice of the student.
- Unfriendly neighbourhood where anti-social elements roam around.
- Strained relationship with the peer group.
- Family member seriously/chronically ill.
- Unfriendly teachers.
- Difficulty in understanding a subject.
- Death of a parent or loved one.
- Difficulty in commuting between home and school.
- Engaging in household chores and less study time at home.
- Less material and academic resource at home.
- Peer pressure to engage in unlawful activities.
- Strained relationship between parents.

Q28. What are the effects of stress in a learner's life? Discuss.

Or

How do you help learners to develop coping skills for managing stress?

Ans. Stress adversely affects the life of the learners, especially those learners who have board exams. Even learners who are preparing for joint entrance examination seek their admission to engineering or medical colleges committing suicide or going through mental break down. The effects of stress may be manifested as physical, psychological or behavioural responses.

People or individuals react differently when confronted with stressors. Some of the students enduring examination stress may respond physically, for instance, with migraine, nausea or diarrhea. This is psychosomatic consequences of stress.

Individual's psychological responses to stress may appear as emotional changes, for instance, when we feel the earth tremor, which is a warning sign of impending earthquake, we experience fear along with the physical response. Sometimes, the emotional changes to stress situation may be anger, frustration or anxiety. Usually, emotional stress responses reduce after the stressors disappear. Preparing for board and entrance examinations is an expected event but with a long-term build up to it. Hence, examination related stressors persist for longer duration and many students respond psychologically with increased anxiety, changes in eating and sleeping habits, poor concentration, etc. Those who do not recover emotional balance may start feeling tense, anxious, sad or irritable. The extreme effects of stress may lead to mental disorder or depression. Read GPH books and score excellent marks.

Another form of psychological response to stress is cognitive changes. Cognitive stress reactions affect many students when they prepare and appear for examination.

Most students are too anxious about the consequences of the examination. Anxious students are likely to think, "Will I remember the answers?" or "Will I get marks that get me admission in my preferred branch of study?" or "Will I fall behind my friends and score low?" or "Can I perform up to the expectations of my parents?" Such thinking impairs cognitive functioning and hinders performance in examinations.

Other behavioural responses to stress are lack of sleep, over sleeping, eating less or over eating. Under stress, some people easily pick fight with others over insignificant issues. For some students, schooling or preparing for examination can create long lasting stress. In the face of such severe stress, they may drop out of school or examination or even commit suicide. Trying to avoid and escape from stressors, people may turn to smoking, alcohol or other unhealthy substances which may give them temporary relief from stress. But such tactics deprive them from developing healthy coping skills. Aggression towards others is another common behavioural response to stressors.

Coping Strategies

Coping is the process of spending conscious effort and energy to solve personal and interpersonal problems. In the case of stress, coping mechanisms seek to master, minimise, or tolerate stress and stressors that occur in everyday life. These mechanisms are commonly called coping skills or coping strategies. All coping strategies have the adaptive goal of reducing or dealing with stress, but some strategies can actually be maladaptive (unhealthy) or merely ineffective. Maladaptive behaviours are those that inhibit a person's ability to adjust to particular situations. This type of behaviour is often used to reduce one's anxiety, but the result is dysfunctional and non-productive. The term "coping" usually refers to dealing with the stress that comes after a stressor is presented, but many people also use proactive coping strategies to eliminate or avoid stressors before they occur. Personal choice in coping strategies is determined by personality traits and type, social context, and the nature of the stressor involved. To be a top scorer — Read only GPH Books.

✍ ✍ ✍

Question
Papers

Guidance and Counselling: BESE-132
June, 2018

Note: *All questions are compulsory. All questions carry equal weightage.*

Q1. **Answer the following question in about 600 words:**
Discuss the need and purpose of guidance in schools.

Ans. Refer to Chapter-1, Q.No.-1 and Q.No.-2 (Pg. No.-2 and 3)

Or

Explain the meaning and process of group counselling.

Ans. Refer to Chapter-1, Q.No.-34 and Q.No.-36 (Pg. No.-47 and 49)

Q2. Answer the following question in about 600 words:
Explain the concept of career patterns. Discuss the relationship of career patterns with life stages.

Ans. Refer to Chapter-3, Q.No.-23 and Q.No.-24 (Pg. No.-171 and 173)

Or

Describe the factors influencing the work participation of women and discuss the self-efficacy theory of career development of women.

Ans. Refer to Chapter-3, Q.No.-31 and Q.No.-32 (Pg. No.-184 and 189)

Q3. **Answer any four of the following questions in about 150 words each:**

(a) **How can a guidance counsellor help students with disability and their families?**

Ans. Refer to Chapter-4, Q.No.-15 (Pg. No.-221)

(b) **What are the sources of stress for students?**

Ans. Refer to Chapter-4, Q.No.-27 (Pg. No.-248)

(c) **Explain sociometry as a technique of guidance.**

Ans. Refer to Chapter-2, Q.No.-3 (Pg. No.-65)

(d) **What are the advantages of group guidance in schools?**

Ans. Refer to Chapter-2, Q.No.-35 (Pg. No.-94)

(e) **Describe the techniques of behaviour management of students.**

Ans. Chapter-4, Q.No.-19 (Pg. No.-233)

(f) **What are the steps involved in organising guidance activities in schools?**

Ans. Refer to Chapter-1, Q.No.-32 (Pg. No.-44)

Q4. Answer the following question in about 600 words:

Explain the concept of transactional analysis (TA). Identify any one of your dominant ego state behaviours and illustrate how that behaviour affects your life as well as others around you.

Ans. Refer to Chapter-2, Q.No.-52 (Pg. No.-124)

I am a man with Nurturing Parent ego state behaviour. The Nurturing Parent ego state is about providing love, care, support and protection. It is concerned with the feelings and emotions of the people. It is founded in understanding and comforting others. In this ego state, we are accepting of others for what they are, which means in the Nurturing Parent ego state we are non- judgmental of the other person. We appreciate people for their achievements and positive behaviours. We don't criticize them. The Nurturing Parent in you would tell your student, "I know you are working hard for the exam and I am there for you whenever you need me". The negative Nurturing Parent in you would say, "You are intelligent and need not take the exam so seriously because you will be the topper anyway". Such over indulging (negative) nurturing behavior sends a negative message to the student that he/she doesn't need to regulate himself/herself and behave responsibly.

☙ ☙ ☙

Note: All questions are compulsory. All questions carry equal weightage.

Q1. Answer the following question in about 600 words:
Discuss the various counselling skills. Give appropriate examples for each counselling skill.

Or

Discuss the social cognitive theory of career development.

Q2. Answer the following question in about 600 words:
Explain the concept of inclusive schooling. Discuss the various educational facilities provided by the government for persons with disability.

Or

Explain the concept of mental health and discuss the different theoretical models of mental health.

Q3. Answer any four of the following in about 150 words each:

(a) Describe the commonly observed behaviour problems in students.

(b) What is the purpose of providing occupational information service to students?

(c) Explain the use of anecdotal record in school guidance programme.

(d) Explain the concept of group guidance.

(e) Explain Cyber bullying and the ethics to be followed while interacting in the virtual world.

(f) Explain eclectic approach to counselling.

Q4. Answer the following question in about 600 words:
Describe the various guidance services offered in schools. How will you organise guidance programme in your school?

Guidance and Counselling: BESE-132
June, 2019

Note: All questions are compulsory. All questions carry equal weightage

Q1. Answer the following question in about 600 words:
Explain the concept and process of group counselling.

Or

Describe any two standardized techniques of guidance.

Q2. Answer the following question in about 600 words:
Describe the different motives for which people work. How does work affect the life style of people?

Or

What are the commonly observed behaviour problems of school children? Describe the causes of behaviour problems among adolescent children.

Q3. Answer any four of the following questions in about 150 words each:

(a) Define counselling and state how is it different from psychotherapy?

(b) What is cyber bullying and why should teachers be aware of it?

(c) Describe the provisions for inclusive education for children with disabilities at the secondary stage.

(d) What are the factors influencing the work participation of women?

(e) What are the uses of occupational classifications?

(f) Explain the biomedical and normative models of mental health.

Q4. Answer the following question in about 600 words:
What is the Rational Emotive Behavioural Therapy (REBT)? Illustrate, how you will use the ABCDE model of REBT to help a learner.

✍ ✍ ✍

Note: All questions are compulsory. All questions carry equal weightage.

Q1. Answer the following question in about 600 words.
State the common fallacious and ineffective thought patterns people engage in and discuss the various cognitive behavioural therapy techniques to deal with them.

Ans. Refer to Chapter-2, Q.No.-51

Or

Explain Holland's major and secondary assumptions regarding work environment and discuss vocational choice as an integration between the two.

Ans. Refer to Chapter-3, Q.No.-6

Q2. Answer the following questions in about 600 words.
Discuss the theories of career development of Women.

Ans. Refer to Chapter-3, Q.No.-32

Or

Explain the role of guidance service in fostering school discipline.

Ans. Refer to Chapter-2, Q.No.-23, 24 and Q.No.-25

Q3. Answer any four of the following questions in about 150 words each.

(a) Explain the role of career master in schools.

Ans. Refer to Chapter-1, Q.No.-30

(b) What are the benefits of individual counselling?

Ans. Refer to Chapter-1, Q.No.-33

(c) What is follow-up service in the school guidance programme?

Ans. Refer to Chapter-2, Q.No.-27 and Q.No.-31

(d) Describe socio-psychodrama as a group guidance activity.

Ans. Refer to Chapter-2, Q.No.-44

(e) How does the societal system handicap persons with disabilities?

Ans. Refer to Chapter-4, Q.No.-13

(f) What are the commonly observed behaviour problems of school children?

Ans. Refer to Chapter-4, Q.No.-18

Q4. **Answer the following question in about 600 words.**
Discuss the characteristics of mentally healthy persons.
What can teachers do to promote mental health and
prevent mental disorders among adolescents?

Ans. Refer to Chapter-4, Q.No.-24 and Q.No.-25

Guidance and Counselling: BESE-132
June, 2020

Note : (i) *All questions are compulsory.* (ii) *All questions carry equal weightage.*

Q1. Answer the following question in about 600 words:
Explain Holland's theory of career development.

Or

Describe the different determinants and types of career patterns.

Q2. Answer the following question in about 600 words:
Define stress. Describe the effects of stress on our life with suitable examples.

Or

Discuss the nature and need of guidance in schools. Illustrate your answer with suitable examples.

Q3. Answer any four of the following questions in about 150 words each:

(a) Why is it important for a teacher to have knowledge of different types of behavioural problems in children?

(b) What are the provisions in the Rights of Persons with Disabilities Act, 2016 for the education of children with disabilities?

(c) Discuss the difficulties in organising group guidance activities in schools.

(d) Explain the concept of orientation service in school guidance programme.

(e) What do you understand by cyber ethics? How would you help children develop cyber ethics?

(f) Explain the concept of multicultural counselling.

Q4. Answer the following question in about 600 words:
Describe the behavioural model of ego states. Using this model, illustrate your effective and ineffective behaviours as a teacher and as a colleague.

✍ ✍ ✍

Q1. Answer the following question in about 600 words:
Discuss the role of guidance in fostering school discipline, giving relevant examples.

OR

Describe the various services offered in school guidance programme.

Q2. Answer the following question in about 600 words:
Explain Roe's theory of personality development and career choice.

OR

Describe the salient features of career development of women in India.

Q3. Answer any four of the following questions in about 150 words each:

(a) Describe the provisions in the Rights of Persons with Disabilities Act, 2016 for the skill development and vocational training of persons with disabilities.

(b) Explain the concept of career maturity.

(c) State the difference between 'flooding' and 'implosion' techniques of behavioural counselling.

(d) What are the advantages and limitations of using interest inventories in guidance programmes?

(e) What are the functions of peer counselling?

(f) Describe the steps involved in organizing guidance activities.

Q4. Answer the following question in about 600 words:
Describe the teacher behaviours that cause harm to the mental wellness of the learners. How would you promote mental health and prevent mental disorders among your learners?

✍ ✍ ✍